DATE DUE

DEC 2 1 2002		
GAYLORD		PRINTED IN U.S.A.

THE FRONTIER AGAINST SLAVERY

Western Anti-
Negro Prejudice
and the Slavery
Extension
Controversy

EUGENE H. BERWANGER

UNIVERSITY OF ILLINOIS PRESS, 1967   URBANA · CHICAGO · LONDON

Second Printing

Publication of this work has been supported by a grant from the Oliver M. Dickerson Fund. The Fund has been established by Mr. Dickerson (Ph.D., Illinois, 1906) to enable the University of Illinois Press to publish selected works in American history, designated by the executive committee of the Department of History.

77302

To My Father and to the Memory of My Mother

Acknowledgments

For their aid and assistance in research, I wish to thank the library staffs of the following universities and historical societies: the University of Illinois, the Illinois Historical Survey, the Illinois State Historical Society, the University of Chicago, the Chicago Historical Society, the Newberry Library, the Indiana State Historical Society, the Indiana State Library, the Wisconsin State Historical Society, the University of Kansas, the Kansas State Historical Society, the University of Oregon, the Oregon Historical Society, the Bancroft Library, the California Historical Society, and the Manuscript Division of the Library of Congress. Three people from the above repositories merit special mention. James deT. Abajian, director of the California Historical Society, generously offered materials from his private files. Caroline Dunn's constant effort and success in locating additional information at the Indiana State Historical Society lured me back to Indianapolis numerous times. On the Urbana campus of the University of Illinois, the aid of Frank Rodgers secured materials through interlibrary loan and saved me the expense of additional time and travel.

Thanks are due to Robert McColley, Norman A. Graebner, Chester G. Starr, and Paul Schroeder, all of whom read this book in its original form as a doctoral dissertation and offered critical comments. Criticisms and suggestions made by Robert W. Johannsen, my thesis sponsor, proved invaluable. August Meier of Roosevelt University offered suggestions which improved the organization of the first two chapters. The Department of History at the University of Illinois also provided a grant for travel to the more distant repositories. John T. Hubbell, editor of *Civil War History,* permitted me to paraphrase or quote portions of an article previously published in that journal. The encouragement of Ernest G. Hildner, Jr., Alvin W. Lynn, and Elizabeth Zeigler, colleagues at Illinois College, and of Rosemary Masek of Nevada Southern University is much appreciated.

Abbreviations used in the footnotes and in the bibliography:

AHAAR Annual Report of the American Historical Association
AHR American Historical Review
AI Annals of Iowa
CHSQ California Historical Society Quarterly
CM Colorado Magazine
CWH Civil War History
HHLB Henry E. Huntington Library Bulletin
IHC Indiana Historical Collections
IHSP Indiana Historical Society Publications
IJH Iowa Journal of History
IJHP Iowa Journal of History and Politics
IMH Indiana Magazine of History
ISHLC Collections of the Illinois State Historical Library
ISHSC Collections of the State Historical Society of Iowa
ISHSJ Journal of the Illinois State Historical Society
ISHST Transactions of the Illinois State Historical Society
JNH Journal of Negro History
KHQ Kansas Historical Quarterly
KSHSC Collections of the Kansas State Historical Society
KSHSP Publications of the Kansas State Historical Society
KSHST Transactions of the Kansas State Historical Society
MHM Michigan History Magazine
MVHR Mississippi Valley Historical Review
MVHAP Proceedings of the Mississippi Valley Historical Association
NMHR New Mexico Historical Review
OAHP Ohio Archeological and Historical Publications
OHQ Oregon Historical Quarterly
OPAT Transactions of the Oregon Pioneer Association

OSAHQ Ohio State Archeological and Historical Quarterly
PHR Pacific Historical Review
PNQ Pacific Northwest Quarterly
QPHPSO Quarterly Publications of the Historical and Philosophical Society of Ohio
SCHSAP Annual Publications of the Historical Society of Southern California
UHQ Utah Historical Quarterly
WMH Wisconsin Magazine of History
WSHSP Proceedings of the Wisconsin State Historical Society
WSHSPubs Publications of the Wisconsin State Historical Society

Contents

Introduction

This book reveals that prejudice against Negroes was a factor in the development of antislavery feeling in the ante-bellum United States. The study is limited to the slavery expansion phase of the antislavery movement and concentrates on the ever-shifting frontier regions which became free states or territories by 1860, but which, at some time, were threatened with the possible legalization of chattel servitude. These regions include primarily the Old Northwest, Iowa, California, Oregon, and Kansas. The emphasis on the West is deliberate because the people from the Middle West, for the most part, populated the advancing frontier. Except for California, the early settlement of the West, especially the Great Plains and the Pacific Northwest, was undertaken by people from the Old Northwest, Iowa, and Missouri. Their migration was, moreover, a gradual advance over a period of years. Thus, many easterners lived in Ohio, Indiana, or Illinois for several years before finally establishing themselves in Oregon, Kansas, or the other territories. These years of residence in the Old Northwest occurred at a time when the state legislatures, overwhelmed by the fear of being inundated by manumitted slaves or free Negroes from the South, were enacting laws to deprive the Negro immigrants of any semblance of citizenship, to exclude them from the states, and to encourage them to colonize in Africa. Social and political thought in the Ohio Valley shaped the ideas which the pioneers took from that section into the advancing frontier. Depending upon the utility of the particular concept, it was rejected or accepted by them when they settled the virgin lands. Prejudice against the free Negro found special acceptance.

Opposition to the expansion of slavery, rather than abolition, is stressed because in the 1850's slavery in the territories was the dominant issue in the West. Many westerners felt that if slavery were limited it might eventually disappear, but they were unwilling to interfere with

1

the system where it existed. Their major concern was not slavery, per se, but the expansion of the institution. Abolition sentiment did not necessarily decline in the 1850's nor were all abolitionists satisfied merely to limit slavery. However, they took advantage of the anti-extension attitude and encouraged it. Yet even as late as 1860, the more vehement abolitionists found little solace in the Republican doctrine of nonextension but accepted the party hoping that they might partly achieve their aim.

The major sources used to determine the extent of race prejudice were state constitutional debates, legislative laws and reports, and newspaper correspondence and editorials concerning those activities. Manuscript collections, especially for the 1860 election, were also employed. Since many political leaders were delegates to constitutional conventions or members of the national or state legislatures at the same time, they did not correspond with each other about the anti-Negro measures under discussion; therefore, letters between politicians about the racial problems were not abundant. Letters written by other individuals to political leaders, however, revealed the importance of the Negro question and the attitudes of average citizens.

Jacksonville, Illinois
August, 1966

Prologue

"This government was made for the benefit of the white race . . . and not [for] negroes," wrote a Michigan editor in 1861, and he further declared that Negroes were and always had been a distinct group in the United States.[1] The majority of them were held in a system of bondage, while those fortunate enough to escape such a fate lived as unwelcome guests in a white society. Except in several free states along the Atlantic seaboard, free Negroes in 1860 were denied the right to vote, to give evidence in court cases involving white men, to request poor relief, to attend public schools with white children, to serve in the state militias, and to marry outside their race. In addition, the Negro, whether free or slave, became the subject of the most tumultuous discussions and debates which occurred throughout the country as Americans became increasingly concerned about and agitated over the expansion of slavery into the western territories during the 1840's and 1850's. After the passage of the Kansas-Nebraska Act in 1854, the slavery extension question took precedence over every other problem in American political life. During the same two decades, state legislatures or constitutional conventions in the western free states and territories engaged in intense, and often rambling, disputes about the rights of free Negroes within their borders. Indeed, by the mid-1850's one editor wrote that the Negro, bond or free, caused the most "eloquent sounding speeches of modern times."[2]

Although most ante-bellum Americans considered the slavery extension and civil rights questions separate and distinct issues, they were in reality aspects of the same problem, namely the future of the Negro in American life. The inability to distinguish the connection stemmed

---

[1] *Niles* (Michigan) *Republican*, Mar. 30, 1861, in Howard C. Perkins (ed.), *Northern Editorials on Secession* (2 vols., New York, 1942), I, 499.
[2] *Alton* (Illinois) *Daily Morning Courier*, Feb. 4, 1853.

from the fact that the average citizen regarded the granting of political privileges to be the sole prerogative of the state but he presumed that the extension of slavery concerned the entire nation. In those portions of the United States which were settled after 1800 but which became free states or territories by 1860, the two aspects of the Negro question, as it was called, were too intertwined to be treated as different issues.

From the beginnings of their settlement the western free states and territories enacted stringent restrictions against free Negroes. Whereas North Carolina and Tennessee had permitted free Negroes to vote until the mid-1830's, this right was not granted in the Middle and Far West until after the Civil War. In fact, the illiberal racial attitudes in the Old Northwest caused Alexis de Tocqueville to comment in the 1830's that prejudice against Negroes was more extreme in "those states where slavery has never been known."[3] Had de Tocqueville revisited the United States during the decade preceding the Civil War, he undoubtedly would have noticed that prejudice and discriminatory statutes in the western free states and territories had become more widespread.

Discrimination against Negroes in the Middle West reached its height between 1846 and 1860, the same years in which the slavery extension controversy became most acute. Perhaps the arguments over the expansion of slavery made midwesterners more aware of the presence of free Negroes, increased their racial antipathy, and produced additional legal measures to restrict the race.

Throughout the Middle West, especially in Indiana, the movement to colonize Negroes in Africa became increasingly popular in the late 1840's. Colonization supporters, agents of the American Colonization Society, and state authorities eagerly grasped the initial enthusiasm and attempted to keep it alive during the 1850's. Although their propaganda seemed humanitarian in that it always stressed the advantages the scheme offered to the Negro, it also emphasized that the success of the movement would reduce the Negro population. Moreover, future antislavery leaders, such as Abraham Lincoln, Lyman Trumbull of Illinois, and Oliver P. Morton of Indiana, did not overtly oppose the discriminatory legislation or the colonization effort. On the contrary, Lincoln in 1857 urged the Illinois legislature to appropriate money for

---

[3] Because slavery had been recognized during the colonial period in the other free states, the statement was a direct reference to the Old Northwest. Alexis de Tocqueville, *Democracy in America,* ed. Phillips Bradley (2 vols., New York, 1945), I, 359-360.

colonization in order to remove free Negroes from the state and prevent miscegenation.[4] The originator of the 1853 measure prohibiting Negro immigration into Illinois, John A. Logan, was a radical Republican in post-war years.

Both pro- and antislavery factions vigorously advocated the exclusion of free Negroes from the trans-Mississippi West during the 1850's. Slaveholders and their sympathizers endorsed exclusion because they considered free Negroes the natural allies of slaves and feared their possible leadership in promoting servile insurrection. Furthermore, the presence of thrifty, industrious, and honest free Negroes was tangible evidence and a constant reminder to slaveholders that Negroes could be successful without masters. But a study of the legislative records and constitutional debates of the free states and territories west of the Mississippi River reveals that free Negro exclusion was not urged solely by proslavery sympathizers. In California, Oregon, Kansas, and Nebraska legislators or delegates to constitutional conventions simultaneously demanded the prohibition of slavery and the exclusion of free Negroes. To the settlers on the plains and in the Far West it was not inconsistent for antislavery leaders to insist that the territories be limited "to the use of the white man, and exclude the negro."[5] Indeed, too many people agreed with such sentiment, thereby indicating that the presence of the Negro, free or slave, was also objectionable to them.

Although racial enmity was widespread, not all people in the western states and territories were prejudiced against Negroes or opposed to the extension of slavery because of racial antipathy. To make such an assertion distorts the fact that a segment of the population considered slavery morally repulsive. The pernicious effects of the institution on both the Negro and the white man were justification enough to advocate its termination. Certainly the activities of the students at Lane Seminary indicated that a benevolent attitude toward Negroes existed in the West.[6]

In the complex make-up of the western population, moreover, some individuals favored the extension of slavery in order to help develop the wilderness and to ease the labor shortage so prevalent on the fron-

[4] Roy P. Basler (ed.), *The Collected Works of Abraham Lincoln* (9 vols., New Brunswick, New Jersey, 1953), II, 298-300, 409.
[5] Charles Henry Carey (ed.), *The Oregon Constitution and Proceedings and Debates of the Constitutional Convention of 1857* (Salem, 1926), 362.
[6] See Gilbert Hobbs Barnes, *The Antislavery Impulses, 1830-1844* (New York, 1933), 68-73.

tier. And where the pro- and antislavery elements existed and where each group attempted to achieve its aim, conflict erupted. Indiana, Illinois, California, Oregon, and Kansas all underwent a slavery extension struggle. The extent of each controversy varied. The most violent struggle occurred in Kansas; in Oregon and California the slavery question was debated publicly and in the state constitutional conventions. If George Flower, an Englishman who settled at Albion, Illinois, is correct, the slavery battle in that state involved political conniving by the proslavery forces.[7] But no matter how the struggles were carried on, they produced an exchange of opinions regarding the institution of slavery and the Negro which revealed that not everyone was opposed to slavery for moral, economic, or social reasons and that racial enmity played a part. The attempts to establish a bondage system in Illinois and Indiana in the early 1820's further indicated that the slavery extension controversy was not limited solely to Missouri before it became a raging question in American political life. The struggle to prevent the extension of slavery ominously began in the Old Northwest before it erupted on the Pacific slopes and the western plains.

---

[7] George Flower, *History of the English Settlement in Edwards County, Illinois, Founded in 1817 and 1818 by Morris Birkbeck and George Flower* (Chicago, 1882), 200.

1 Northwest of the Ohio, 1787-1824

The Northwest Ordinance did not abolish slavery in the Northwest Territory. Instead, the generally accepted interpretation of Article 6, the slavery prohibition clause of the ordinance, only forbade its further introduction. This interpretation was formulated by the slaveholders in the territory, particularly the French inhabitants in the Illinois Country who had held slaves under the French and English colonial governments and retained them, after 1776, under the laws of Virginia. In order to prevent the emancipation of their chattels, which they presumed was intended by the wording of Article 6, slaveholders in the Old Northwest insisted that the Virginia cession agreement voided Article 6 insofar as it might affect them, and they spent almost a decade seeking a guarantee of their human property. Several members of Congress privately assured the slaveholders' special agent, Bartholomew Tardiveau, that the slavery provision "was not meant to affect the rights of the ancient inhabitants," but no official statement was made.[1] Therefore, slaveholders sought the opinion of the territorial governor, Arthur St. Clair, when he arrived in the territory to assume his duties. Undoubtedly St. Clair's decision that Article 6 did not emancipate Negroes held in bondage before 1787 and his subsequent action to enforce the decision pleased the slaveholders.[2]

---

[1] "Memorials to Congress," July 8, Sept. 17, 1788, and John Hamtramck to Joseph Harmer, Aug. 14, 1789, in Clarence W. Alvord (ed.), *Kaskaskia Records* (Vol. V, *ISHLC*, Springfield, 1909), 485-488, 493, 508-509; Jacob P. Dunn, *Indiana: A Redemption from Slavery* (Boston, 1888), 244.

[2] When two slaves owned by Henry Vanderburgh, an early settler in the Illinois Country, sued for their freedom on the basis of Article 6 in 1794, St. Clair informed the presiding judge that the slaves were not entitled to their freedom.

The climate and the soil of the Ohio Valley made the region attractive to slaveholders. The southern sections of Indiana and Illinois are geographically similar to Virginia and Kentucky, and they lie directly west of the greater portions of the two southern states, in the path of a westward movement. As a matter of fact, Cairo, Illinois, is further south than Richmond, Virginia, or Lexington, Kentucky. The wheat, corn, tobacco, and hemp with which many southerners were familiar could easily be raised in the region. In addition, the salt mines near Shawneetown, Illinois, and the lead-producing region, which ran northward from Galena, Illinois, into southwestern Wisconsin, might have lured a considerable number of slaveholders into the Old Northwest. Slave labor was utilized in mining endeavors in the South and slaves were used in the Shawneetown salines. Despite the prohibition of slavery by the Illinois Constitution in 1818, slaves worked the lead mines after extensive mining operations began in 1822.[3] After the lead mines became exhausted, a number of slaves were taken to Wisconsin and Iowa as farm laborers or house servants. Thus, slaveholders with imagination could have utilized their chattels in many areas of the Northwest Territory.

The agricultural potential of southern Indiana and Illinois lured a few slaveholders north of the Ohio River after 1787, but the majority were reluctant to follow because of Article 6. Nevertheless, their interest made land speculators, such as John Edgar and William and Robert Morrison in the Illinois Country, aware that land could be sold more quickly if slavery were permitted. Edgar and the Morrisons had purchased thousands of acres in southwestern Illinois, and they found themselves unable to dispose of the land because nonslaveholders were then moving westward more slowly.[4] Their only recourse, they thought, was to secure the legalization of slavery. Accordingly, in 1796 Edgar, William Morrison, and two other speculators from St. Clair and Randolph counties petitioned Congress, requesting the repeal of Article 6. The petition emphasized the importance of labor in developing the wilderness and predicted that without slavery Illinois would re-

---

St. Clair to Luke Decker, Oct. 11, 1793, and to Judge Turner, Dec. 14, 1794, in William Henry Smith (ed.), *The Life and Public Services of Arthur St. Clair, with His Correspondence and Other Papers* (2 vols., Cincinnati, 1882), II, 318-319, 331; Dunn, *Indiana*, 223-224.

[3] John Nelson Davidson, "Negro Slavery in Wisconsin," *WSHSP*, XL (1892), 82-86.

[4] Solon Justus Buck, *Illinois in 1818* (Springfield, 1917), 52.

main stagnant. The signers also claimed that the petition represented the wishes of the majority of the people in the Illinois Country. Four signatures were hardly a majority of the people; therefore, the House of Representatives rejected the petition, stating that evidence to substantiate the claim had not been presented. In 1800 Edgar and the Morrisons, attempting to overcome the previous objection, obtained 277 signatures on a second petition which they sent to the Senate. This time the petitioners took the humanitarian approach, suggesting a limited form of slavery: male children of slaves would serve until the age of thirty-one and females until twenty-eight. Such a plan, they declared, would "rescue from the vilest state of bondage a number . . . of souls yet unborn." Unimpressed by this newly acquired, benevolent attitude, the Senate tabled the petition.[5]

Undaunted by their lack of success, the proslavery men in the Illinois Country, joined by the slavery zealots east of the Wabash River after the entire region was organized as the Indiana Territory in 1800, sent five repeal petitions to Congress in seven years.[6] The first four petitions presented numerous arguments in favor of slavery, ranging from the need for laborers to the theory that the diffusion of slaves would relieve them from the strenuous labor required of them in the South and would lessen the possibility of servile insurrection. Limited types of servitude, including an age limit or a trial period of ten years, were also suggested. Finally by 1807, the proslavery men desperately insisted that Article 6 was discriminatory: "Slavery is tolerated in the Territories of Orleans, Mississippi and Louisiana; why should this territory be excepted?" Despite the wide range of programs and the urgent pleas presented, Congress steadfastly refused to repeal or revise the article.[7]

---

[5] Robert Morrison and others, *Report of the Committee on the Petition of Sundry Inhabitants of the Counties of St. Clair and Randolph in the Territory Northwest of the River Ohio* (n.p., 1796), 1-11; *Annals of Congress,* 6 Cong., 2 Sess., 735; Jacob P. Dunn (ed.), *Slavery Petitions and Papers* (Vol. II, *IHSP,* Indianapolis, 1895), 456; Robert McColley, *Slavery and Jeffersonian Virginia* (Urbana, Illinois, 1964), 177-178.

[6] The more prominent proslavery leaders in Indiana were John Rice Jones, Francis Vigo, Luke Decker, Benjamin Chambers, and Jesse B. Thomas; in Illinois, Edgar, the Morrisons, Pierre Menard, Robert Reynolds, and Shadrach Bond, Jr. Later John Jones and Thomas moved to Illinois. Dunn, *Indiana, passim;* Clarence W. Alvord, *The Illinois Country, 1673-1818* (Vol. I, *Centennial History of Illinois,* Springfield, 1920), 420-421.

[7] *Annals of Congress,* 7 Cong., 2 Sess., 473-474; 9 Cong., 1 Sess., 293; 10 Cong., 1 Sess., 25-26; Dunn, *Indiana,* 297-302, 368-370.

In addition to the ingenuity of the frontier mind, the anxiety of recently arrived slaveholders to guarantee the retention of their chattels and of speculators to entice other slaveholders into the territory produced three laws between 1803 and 1807 in the Indiana Territory, which at that time included the Illinois Country, establishing an elaborate indenture system. Briefly, the laws permitted any person who owned slaves over fifteen years of age in another state to bring them into the territory and place them under lifetime indenture. However, one of the laws relieved children of indentured servants from further obligation after the age of thirty if male, twenty-eight if female. Besides providing for a code of relationship between the master and the servant, the laws placed restrictions on servants similar to those placed on slaves in the southern states: an indentured servant was not allowed to travel without a pass, to visit other "plantations," or to attend public gatherings unattended. Slaves refusing to sign papers of indenture were to be removed immediately from the territory.[8]

These indenture laws were adopted in the Illinois Territory, created in 1809. Moreover, the craving of some Illinois political leaders for slave labor led to a law permitting its use in the salt mines at Shawneetown. The solons justified the act by arguing that Negroes were better suited to withstand the arduous labor of the salines than white men. Any slave, with the consent of his master, could "hire himself out" to work in the mines for one year; after that time he had to return to his master.[9]

The indenture system was chiefly the work of former southerners, and no objection against it was raised by the federal government under the control of southern presidents.[10] Yet, the system was not highly

---

[8] Francis S. Philbrick (ed.), *The Laws of Indiana Territory, 1801-1809* (Vol. XXI, *ISHLC,* Springfield, 1930), cxxxv-cxliii, 42-46, 136-139, 463-467.

[9] Just before Illinois became a state, the territorial representative in Congress, Shadrach Bond, Jr., attempted to secure congressional sanction of the law but failed. Evidence of opposition to his action was seen in Bond's statement to Governor Ninian Edwards that the request for federal approval "will make a fuss with some." Francis Philbrick (ed.), *Pope's Digest, 1815* (Vol. XXX, *ISHLC,* Springfield, 1940), 190-191; Lulu Merle Johnson, "The Problem of Slavery in the Old Northwest, 1787-1858" (unpublished Ph.D. dissertation, State University of Iowa, 1941), 85.

[10] Ephraim Cutler, an Ohio politician, asserted that Jefferson favored partial slavery in the Old Northwest. The President assumed that the diffusion of Negroes would improve their condition and achieve emancipation more quickly. The best explanation of this is found in William T. Utter, *The Frontier State, 1803-1825* (Vol. II, *The History of the State of Ohio,* Columbus, 1942), 18-21.

successful in luring slaveholders into Indiana and Illinois. The number of Negroes in these two territories held as slaves or indentures grew from 405 in 1810 to 1,107 in 1820 — 917 of whom were in Illinois. During the same decade the slave population of Missouri and Arkansas increased by 8,828.[11] Slaveholders did not bypass Illinois and Indiana because the region lacked agricultural potential or other economic endeavors adaptable to slave labor. Besides economic opportunity slaveholders wanted an unqualified guarantee that their slaves would not be freed at some future date. As long as Article 6 remained in force, such a guarantee did not exist. Thus, the indenture system failed because "the cunning slave-holder [felt] too flimsy a security to bring his horde to a country where the term of holding them [was] so precarious."[12]

Whereas slaveholders were reluctant to move into the Old Northwest, nonslaveholders pushed into the region at a slow but steady pace, bringing with them a firm opposition to slavery. Even in the earliest years of settlement, the majority of the people in the eastern portion of the Indiana Territory consisted of nonslaveholders. They were not politically influential, however, because slaveholders and proslavery advocates held the important governmental positions and dominated the territorial legislature. As a result, antislavery sentiment was virtually ignored by political leaders. Ill-feeling over the situation became intense enough for a group of settlers in Dearborn County, Indiana, to petition Congress for annexation to the state of Ohio.[13] A group of antislavery people in Clark County, Indiana, along the Ohio River, realizing the futility of protesting to the territorial legislature against its proslavery activities, adopted the policy of sending counter-petitions to Congress. One in 1807 revealed that proslavery sentiment in the territory was not unanimous despite the predominance of a southern population. As Kentuckians, the signers assured the federal legislature that many of their fellow Kentuckians were opposed to forced labor and were "preparing [to immigrate, or had] actually immigrated to the territory, to get free from a government which does tolerate slavery." Finally the petitioners stated the nucleus of the popular sovereignty

---

[11] In 1810 there were 3,011 slaves in the Louisiana Territory, which consisted of Arkansas and Missouri. By 1820 Arkansas and Missouri, now each separate territories, contained 11,839 slaves. U.S. Bureau of the Census, *Seventh Census of the United States: 1850, Statistics* (Washington, D.C., 1853), ix.

[12] *Liberty Hall and Cincinnati Gazette,* n.d., in Dunn, *Indiana,* 33.

[13] *Annals of Congress,* 10 Cong., 1 Sess., 1331.

doctrine by suggesting that Congress ignore the slavery question in the territory and let the people decide the matter when statehood was granted.[14]

The influx of more nonslaveholders strengthened the political position of the antislavery element and it began to gain control of the Indiana territorial legislature. Upon assembling in 1808, the antislavery lawmakers demanded the repeal of the indenture system. The likelihood of success panicked the proslavery men in the Illinois Country; they immediately petitioned Congress and undertook other steps which resulted in a division of the Indiana Territory in 1809.[15] With the absence of the Illinoisans from the Indiana assembly, the antislavery group succeeded in placing limits on the indenture system in 1810. Future contracts of indenture made by Indianians were valid but contracts made by persons from outside the territory were void.[16]

The antislavery element also pushed into Illinois and gained the ascendancy by 1817. In that year the territorial legislature passed a measure repealing the Illinois indenture system, but the governor, Ninian Edwards, vetoed the bill and prorogued the legislature to prevent further discussion of the subject.[17] The governor's action, although adroit, did not end the slavery question in the Old Northwest.

Proslavery advocates suggested the legalization of slavery when the first constitutions were framed in Ohio, Indiana, and Illinois. The Ohio story occurred in 1802, and the slavery issue in the Buckeye State was not a matter of public discussion. Benjamin Van Cleve, a delegate

---

[14] *Ibid.*, 26-27.

[15] The slavery issue lay behind demands for a division of the territory during the entire decade. In 1803 Edgar and the Morrisons condemned the policy of petitioning Congress as ineffective and asked the national legislature to place the western half of the Indiana Territory under the administration of the trans-Mississippi region where slavery was allowed. In 1803 Congress temporarily placed the territory west of the river under the administration of the governor of the Indiana Territory. After the Louisiana Territory was created in 1805, the Illinois proslavery faction raised the separation issue at every session of the Indiana territorial legislature until the Illinois Territory was created. *Ibid.*, 8 Cong., 1 Sess., 489, 555, 623; 8 Cong., 2 Sess., 1684; Alvord, *Illinois Country*, 423-427; Buck, *Illinois*, 192-194.

[16] Louis B. Ewbank and Dorothy L. Riker (eds.), *The Laws of Indiana Territory, 1809-1816* (Vol. XX, *IHC*, Indianapolis, 1934), 138-139. The Indiana Supreme Court in 1821 declared that contracts made under the old indenture laws could no longer be enforced. *State* v. *Lasalle*, 1 *Blackf*. 60 (1821).

[17] (Kaskaskia, Illinois) *Western Intelligencer*, Jan. 1, 13, 1818; Buck, *Illinois*, 215-218.

at the constitutional convention, wrote that strong proslavery sentiment existed within the delegation. In fact, several delegates supported a resolution to permit slavery which was referred to the bill of rights committee in order to prevent extensive discussion of the topic on the convention floor. By a majority of one vote, the committee rejected the resolution because most of the members presumed that Congress would not consent to Negro servitude.[18]

Efforts were stronger in Indiana and Illinois even though there was little likelihood of establishing slavery. It is true that at first the antislavery forces appeared to have little opposition. The formal petition requesting statehood adopted by the Indiana territorial legislature expressed devotion to the antislavery principle of Article 6. Two years later, when the Illinois petition did not, Congress stipulated in the enabling act that the Illinois Constitution should not violate the ordinance. Therefore, antislavery leaders in both states claimed the slavery matter was closed.[19]

The wording of the statehood petition in Indiana and the congressional stipulation for Illinois, however, did not subdue proslavery sympathizers. They agitated for some form of involuntary servitude and were partly successful.[20] Although the constitutions of both states prohibited slavery, other provisions permitted forced labor. The Indiana document of 1816 invalidated all contracts of indenture made by persons from outside the state, but contracts of indenture which became

---

[18] Beverley W. Bond, Jr. (ed.), "Memoirs of Benjamin Van Cleve," *QPHPSO,* XVII (Jan.-June, 1922), 70-71; Julia Perkins Cutler (ed.), *The Life and Times of Ephraim Cutler, Prepared from His Journals and Correspondence* (Cincinnati, 1890), 65-67.

[19] (Vincennes, Indiana) *Western Sun,* Jan. 27, 1816; Charles Kettleborough, *Constitution Making in Indiana* (2 vols., Indianapolis, 1916), I, 17; Buck, *Illinois,* 233.

[20] In the main, proslavery argument maintained that slavery would increase immigration from the South, promote the speedy settlement of the country, lessen the probability of insurrection because slaves would be distributed throughout the nation, and provide the Negro with a partial escape from the more difficult servitude of the South. The antislavery faction answered that slavery would impede settlement and denied the diffusion theory. In Indiana one staunch antislavery writer attempted to introduce the moral issue into the argument but he was severely criticized. To this writer's knowledge and except for that one instance, the moral issue was ignored because the majority of the people were unconcerned about the moral correctness of the institution. *Western Sun,* Mar. 2, 30, May 3, 1816; *Western Intelligencer,* Apr. 1, 15, 1818; (Kaskaskia) *Illinois Intelligencer,* June 17, July 1, 22, 1818; Norman Dwight Harris, *History of Negro Servitude in Illinois, and of the Slavery Agitation in That State, 1719-1864* (Chicago, 1906), 19.

effective before 1816 ·remained in force. The Illinois Constitution of 1818 allowed the French to retain their slaves and recognized as legally binding all contracts of indenture entered into before the constitution went into effect. This latter provision gave Illinoisans a five-month period, from August to December, 1818, to indenture servants. Moreover, a rush to indenture Negroes and a brisk trading of slaves with the French occurred in White and Gallatin counties during those months. The Illinois document also extended until 1825 the territorial statute providing for the use of slave labor in the salt works at Shawneetown.[21]

Possibly the constitution makers in Illinois established the rather vague system of involuntary servitude instead of prohibiting it in all forms only to secure admission into the Union. A revealing letter, written by "Candor" three months before the constitutional convention assembled, predicted that the proslavery delegates, whom "Candor" thought were in the majority, planned, for the present, to submit to the wishes of Congress and then to legalize slavery at a later date. This was possible, he claimed, because "the Ordinance of Congress . . . could only govern us whilst a territory; [thereafter it] would no longer be binding, but merely a dead letter." This theory was substantiated by the proslavery agitation following Illinois' admission, which reanimated the slavery issue in Indiana as well as in Illinois in the early 1820's.[22]

The poor economic conditions created by the Panic of 1819 provoked the renewed demands for slavery.[23] Land speculation had been

---

[21] *Constitution of the State of Indiana, 1816,* Art. XI, Sec. 7; *Constitution of the State of Illinois, 1818,* Art. VI, Secs. 1, 2; Theodore Calvin Pease, *The Frontier State, 1818-1848* (Vol. II, *The Centennial History of Illinois,* Springfield, 1918), 49-50.

[22] *Western Intelligencer,* May 6, 1818.

[23] Norman Harris and William H. Brown explained the revival of the slavery struggle in Illinois in terms of the "devil theory" used to place the blame of the Civil War on the opposing side. Harris claimed that the proslavery element of Missouri, irritated by the antislavery attitude of some Illinoisans during its admission struggle in 1819 and 1820, united with the proslavery faction in Illinois to establish slavery in the state. Brown blamed the "poor whites" in Illinois whom he considered "ignorant and uncouth." Before 1822 Brown was co-editor of the *Illinois Intelligencer.* After he printed antislavery editorials, the proslavery members of the legislature demanded that he terminate his connection with the newspaper or official printing would be withdrawn. See

responsible for the prosperity in the Old Northwest after 1812, but by 1818 overspeculation and bad banking practices brought about the panic. Many speculators presumed that prosperity would return if they could sell their land to slaveholders passing through Indiana and Illinois to Missouri. These emigrants from the slave states admitted that they found the region attractive but would not remain because of the constitutional slavery restrictions. Therefore, speculators, many of them leading politicians, openly declared that the legalization of slavery was necessary to insure the return of economic prosperity.[24]

The controversy began in Indiana when the legislature submitted a proposal for a constitutional convention to popular referendum in 1823. The legislators did not mention slavery but simply declared that a constitutional revision was necessary to enact certain economic reforms, which the present constitution did not permit, in order to curb the panic. Nevertheless, proslavery Kentucky newspapers suggested that a revised constitution in Indiana should sanction slavery, and they printed articles explaining the economic advantages of the institution. The editor of the *Indiana Gazette* retaliated, hinting that the articles were written by proslavery Indianians, and he criticized the Kentucky editors for printing them, insisting that Indiana could manage its own economic problems without interference from her sister states. After a short time, however, the editor of the *Gazette* asked his readers to vote against the proposal because he suspected "that slavery [was] the *summum bonum* of the prime movers of the convention."[25]

The Illinois legislature, also in 1823, recommended a referendum for a constitutional convention to enact economic changes. Because the majority of the legislators openly favored slavery and had carefully placed their supporters in influential positions throughout the state, the antislavery element presumed that the legalization of slavery was behind the recommendation. The recently elected antislavery governor, Edward Coles, was so sure of this fact that he organized the oppo-

---

Harris, *Negro Servitude in Illinois,* 28-29; William H. Brown, *An Historical Sketch of the Early Movement in Illinois for the Legalization of Slavery* (Vol. IV, *Fergus Historical Series,* Chicago, 1876), 8; Robert W. Patterson, "Hon. William H. Brown," *Biographical Sketches of Some of the Early Settlers of the City of Chicago* (Vol. VI, *Fergus Historical Series,* Chicago, 1876), 3-10.
[24] George Dangerfield, *The Era of Good Feelings* (New York, 1952), 185-188.
[25] (Corydon) *Indiana Gazette,* Mar. 19, Apr. 9, 1823; Kettleborough, *Constitution Making in Indiana,* I, xlvii.

sition to a convention and, although successful, ruined his political career in the state.[26]

Prior to the holding of the referenda, debates for and against slavery were carried on in newspapers and privately published tracts. On the whole, the convention proposal created little interest among the newspapers in Indiana except for the *Gazette,* whose editor continued to blame Kentucky editors. Late*r,* referring to Kentucky slaveholders, he asked why Indiana should be made a "market for their negroes." An "Indiana Farmer" expressed anxiety about the adoption of slavery in the Hoosier State but was confident that the convention would fail. He presumed that Illinois was more likely to adopt slavery, and he feared that, as a result, Indiana would become a haven for fugitive Negroes from the West as well as from the South.[27]

Newspapers in Illinois concerned themselves with little else but the slavery issue in the eighteen months between the passage of the legislature's recommendation and the referendum. Proslavery arguments stressed that slavery would relieve economic distress and increase the price of land. The antislavery people vigorously refuted such arguments, claiming that slaveholders would become powerful enough to reduce current land prices. Furthermore, they asked why slaveholders would purchase privately owned property when there were millions of acres of public land available at $1.25 an acre.[28] Roberts Vaux, a Philadelphia Quaker, persuaded by Coles to write an antislavery pamphlet, insisted that even if slaveholders settled in Illinois their farming methods would soon lay waste the land and they would then move across the Mississippi River. The consequences of temporary prosperity, Vaux concluded, would, in the long run, place greater economic hardship on the state.[29]

---

[26] Coles to Morris Birkbeck, Jan. 29, 1824, in E. B. Washburne, *Sketch of Edward Coles, Second Governor of Illinois, and of the Slavery Struggle of 1823-4* (Chicago, 1882), 183 *Edwardsville Spectator,* Mar. 1, 1823; *Illinois Intelligencer,* Nov. 22, 1823; *Kaskaskia* (Illinois) *Republican,* Mar. 30, 1824; Pease, *Frontier State,* 76-77; Thomas H. Ford, *A History of Illinois from Its Commencement in 1818 to 1847,* ed. Milo M. Quaife (2 vols., Chicago, 1945), I, 58-59; Flower, *English Settlement,* 200.

[27] *Indiana Gazette,* Mar. 19, Apr. 9, 16, June 11, 1823.

[28] *Illinois Intelligencer,* Jan. 24, 1823; *Edwardsville* (Illinois) *Spectator,* Sept. 6, 1823.

[29] [Roberts Vaux], *An Impartial Appeal to the Reason, Interest and Patriotism of the People of Illinois on the Injurious Effects of Slave Labour* (n.p., 1824), 7-10.

A pamphlet entitled "An Appeal on the Question of a Convention" and a series of letters written under the name of Jonathan Freeman served as outlets for the antislavery propaganda of Morris Birkbeck, an Englishman who had established a community at Albion, Illinois.[30] He began by refuting the idea that slaveholders would purchase land in Illinois because their capital was already frozen in Negro slaves. Continuing, Birkbeck wrote that the remedy for depression was not slavery because even in the South it was not a specific safeguard against the effects of periodic depression. Instead of the creation of a permanent agricultural economy, which was the ultimate result of the slave system, Birkbeck favored the encouragement of manufacturing.[31]

Indianians rejected their legislature's proposal in August, 1823, by a majority of 9,390 votes.[32] In August, 1824, the Illinois electorate cast 4,950 votes for a convention and 6,822 against it.[33] Following this narrow victory by the anticonventionists, the subject of slavery disappeared. Moreover, no contemporary ventured to suggest why the referenda failed. Perhaps the improvement of economic conditions explains it. By 1823 and 1824 prices were slowly returning to their pre-1819 level and steamboats were causing a sharp rise in trade.[34] Solely on the

---

[30] "I am continually plying the Slave party, through the Illinois Gazette, with popular discussions and sometimes with legal arguments under the signature of Jonathan Freeman, and some others." Birkbeck to Coles, Feb. 19, 1824, in Washburne, *Sketch of Coles*, 186.

[31] Morris Birkbeck, "An Appeal on the Question of a Convention," *ISHST* (1905), 152, 160-161; (Shawneetown) *Illinois Gazette*, June 21, July 26, Aug. 30, 1823; Merton L. Dillon, "The Anti-Slavery Movement in Illinois, 1809-1844" (unpublished Ph.D. dissertation, University of Michigan, 1951), 96-97.

[32] The vote cast in favor of a convention was 2,601; opposed, 11,991. State of Indiana, *House Journal, 1823* (Corydon, 1823), 52. The election returns were reported to the legislature by the secretary of state.

[33] Theodore Calvin Pease (ed.), *Illinois Election Returns, 1818-1848* (Vol. XVIII, *ISHLC*, Springfield, 1923), 27-29. Despite the failure of the proslavery forces to secure a constitutional convention, no attempt was made to abolish the indenture system. In 1830 there were still 746 Negro indentures in Illinois. Three court decisions upheld the system, one of them as late as 1843. However, in 1845 the state supreme court declared that descendants of slaves held by the French settlers were free. U.S. Bureau of the Census, *Fifth Census of the United States: 1830, Enumeration of Inhabitants* (Washington, D.C., 1832), 147-148; *Boon* v. *Juliet* and *Chiosse* v. *Hargraves*, 1 *Ill.* (1 *Scam.*) 258, 317 (1836); *Sarah* v. *Border*, 5 *Ill.* (4 *Scam.*) 341 (1843); *Jarott* v. *Jarrot*, 7 *Ill.* (2 *Gilm.*) 1 (1845).

[34] See Gershom Flagg to Artemas Flagg, Jan. 25, 1824, July 20, 1825, in Solon J. Buck (ed.), "Pioneer Letters of Gershom Flagg," *ISHST* (1910),

basis of contemporary economic data it could be argued that an upward trend in the economy defeated the convention proposals and, simultaneously, terminated the slavery issue. But such a contention would necessitate ignoring other factors.

Southern, nonslaveholding yeomen and, to a lesser extent, people from the middle states, migrating through Virginia and Kentucky, were the principal settlers of the early Old Northwest. Except for the Western Reserve and eastern Ohio, southern culture predominated in Ohio, Indiana, and Illinois until the 1830's.[35] The majority of these early southerners fled across the Ohio River in order to escape the consequences of the slave system as it was extended westward from the tidewater. As extreme individualists, they had a strong sense of democracy and they considered the "haughtiness and pride" of the slaveholder toward those "who possess[ed] no negroes . . . inimical to [democratic] institutions." Moreover, they feared political domination by the slaveholding class. If the earlier nonslaveholding settlers forgot their lack of political influence in the Indiana Territory before 1808, they were soon reminded by the newer arrivals that "the lord of three or four hundred negroes does not easily forgive" the man who "ventures to vote contrary to the will of such an influential being."[36] Many settlers from the South seeking broader economic opportunities migrated to the Old Northwest because slavery was not permitted there. Assuming that the land had been reserved for free labor, they had no intention of legalizing slavery and again establishing "a kind of monopoly of the United States land for slaveholders."[37]

174-176; Robert W. Patterson, *Early Society in Southern Illinois* (Vol. XIV, *Fergus Historical Series,* Chicago, 1881), 104-105, 113-114; O. H. Wallace to David Ports, Nov. 23, 1846, in "Letters from Ogle and Carrol Counties, 1838-1857," *ISHST* (1907), 259.

[35] Detailed analyses of the population movement into the Old Northwest are found in John D. Barnhart, "Sources of Southern Immigration into the Old Northwest," *MVHR,* XXII (June, 1935), 49-62; Barnhart, "The Southern Influence in the Formation of Illinois," *ISHSJ,* XXXII (Sept., 1939), 358-379; Barnhart, "The Southern Influence in the Formation of Indiana," *IMH,* XXXIII (Sept., 1937), 261-276.

[36] "Report of the Indiana Territorial Legislative Committee on the Indenture Laws, 1809," in Jacob P. Dunn, *Indiana and Indianans: A History of Aboriginal and Territorial Indiana and the Century of Statehood* (5 vols., Chicago, 1919), I, 258.

[37] Gayle Thornbrough and Dorothy Riker (eds.), *Journals of the General Assembly of Indiana Territory* (Vol. XXXII, *IHC,* Indianapolis, 1950), 236-237.

Although many of the southern yeomen resisted the extension of slavery into the Old Northwest, they did not object to the institution as it existed in the slave states. Because of their unfriendliness toward the Negro, they were not concerned about the moral correctness of the bondage system. Moreover, this unfriendliness motivated their desire to keep both slavery and free Negroes out of the Old Northwest. Even though southern yeomen did not stress this fact, it came to the surface early. In 1799 and 1800 the legislature of the Northwest Territory, dominated by politicians from the Ohio area, rejected petitions from Virginia Revolutionary War veterans requesting permission to settle with their slaves in the Virginia Military District, between the Little Miami and Scioto rivers.[38] As reasons for rejecting the petitions, the lawmakers cited the sentiments of their constituents that slavery discouraged the growth of manufacturing and the settlement of non-slaveholders. After studying the pioneers' racial attitudes, however, Charles Wilson concluded that anti-Negro prejudice was influential in causing the rejection of the petitions. Wilson stated that the former southerners in Ohio and many settlers from Pennsylvania simply were "not in favor of having blacks in the area."[39]

A petition sent to Congress by the pioneers of the Driftwood Settlement on the White River in Indiana more poignantly indicated the influence of racial antipathy. Requesting that the federal government curtail Indian activities in the area by opening the Indian lands to settlement, the petitioners specifically asked that "People of Colour and Slaveholders . . . be debared from the Priveladges of Setling on the Lands so apropiated."[40] In Illinois, William Bradsby, the antislavery leader who guided the indenture repeal bill through the territorial leg-

---

[38] Seven of the twenty-two members of the lower house represented the people outside of the future Buckeye State, and only one man in the territorial council was from outside of the Ohio area. B. A. Hinsdale, *The Old Northwest* (Boston, 1888), 305-306.

[39] Smith (ed.), *St. Clair Papers,* II, 447, 451; Jacob Burnet, *Notes on the Early Settlement of the North-Western Territory* (Cincinnati, 1847), 306-307, 332; Charles Jay Wilson, "The Negro in Early Ohio," *OSAHQ,* XXXIX (Oct., 1930), 722. Thomas Posey, a signer of the second petition, later regretted his action. The antislavery faction opposed his appointment as governor of the Indiana Territory even though he had come out against slavery since signing the petition. Posey to John Gibson, Mar. 13, 1813, William H. English Collection (Indiana State Historical Society Library).

[40] Clarence Edwin Carter (ed.), *The Territory of Indiana, 1810-1816.* Vol. VIII, *The Territorial Papers of the United States* (Washington, D.C., 1939), 235 (spelling as in the original).

islature in 1817, revealed his prejudice by criticizing the provision of the laws which dismissed children of indentured servants from further obligation after a certain age. The only result of such "cob-web legislation," as he called it, would be an accumulation of free Negroes who might agitate for political and social equality. While he favored the equal rights of man, Bradsby did not think they should be spread too far.[41]

Nonslaveholders in the Old Northwest were hostile to slavery because they presumed that it created a large free Negro population, and their dread of free Negroes was aggravated by Negro migration into the region. In 1800 there were 500 free Negroes in the territory. By 1810 this number rose to slightly over 2,000, and by 1820 the three Ohio River states contained a total free Negro population of 6,459. In the same year the white population in the three states totaled 779,211.[42] Like the white man, many free Negroes migrated to the frontier in search of a brighter future or to escape the dire consequences of remaining in the slave states where laws threatened recently manumitted slaves with re-enslavement if they did not leave. The great majority of the Negroes in the Old Northwest, however, were settled by philanthropic masters who had freed them. Regardless of the reasons, the arrival of free Negroes caused resentment.

In Indiana as early as 1813 the residents of Gibson County, in the southern part of the state, petitioned the territorial legislature to prevent the settlement of free Negroes or former slaves. The citizens of Harrison County took identical action after William Vincett of Kentucky liberated and settled 47 slaves in the county. Certain that the Negroes would rob them of their possessions, the petitioners also suspected that their "wives and daughters may and no doubt will be insulted and abused by those Africans." These southern Indianians had no wish to be "Saddled with" Vincett's former bondsmen and presumed that if action were not taken, more manumitted slaves would be brought into the county. They requested the legislature to prevent by law or proclamation the further settlement of former slaves and free Negroes in the state because, as they wrote, "We are opposed to the introduction of Slaves or free negroes in any shape."[43] Nor were the

[41] *Western Intelligencer,* Dec. 18, 1817.
[42] *1850 Census, Statistics,* 719, 781, 853.
[43] Thornbrough and Riker (eds.), *Journals of the General Assembly of Indiana Territory,* 601; "Memorial of the Citizens of Harrison County," MS (English

legislators of the state more receptive to the settling of former slaves. A special committee of the first state legislature refused such a request on the ground that deep-rooted prejudice among the white people forced their decision. Moreover, the committee presumed that their consent would encourage other slaveholders to send freed Negroes into the state, and the accumulation of a Negro population would result in "a holocast."[44]

Even in Ohio, where antislavery sentiment developed early, protests were voiced about the arrival of manumitted slaves. When a group of former Virginia slaves were settled in Brown County in 1819, one editor wrote a violent protest, demanding that the state government prevent the people from being overrun "by such a wretched population." He became more incensed when informed that the Virginians in the area where the slaves had been held were delighted to see them leave because they were "as depraved and ignorant a set of people as any of their kind."[45]

The policy of settling former slaves did not go unchallenged for long. The Harrison County petition and the editorial comments in Ohio indicated that the white people believed Negroes untrustworthy, lacking in moral restraint, and ignorant. Both this distrust of what were considered innate characteristics of the Negro race and the assumption that the Ohio River states were becoming a dumping ground for penniless former slaves brought demands to curb free Negro immigration. And the demands to place limits upon free Negroes became stronger as antislavery sentiment crystallized.

Restrictions against free Negroes in the Old Northwest did not exist until 1802. Political disputes between the Northwest territorial legislature and the governor generally prevented legislation, or perhaps the lawmakers considered the small number of free Negroes scattered throughout the region insufficient cause for legislation on the subject. More likely, the legislature of the Northwest Territory feared that Congress, with its power to review territorial legislation, would disapprove of discriminatory measures. During the constitutional convention of

Collection, n.d.). Indiana Historical Society officials believe the "Memorial" was written between 1813 and 1815.
[44] State of Indiana, *House Journal, 1816-1817* (Corydon, 1817), 33-34, 43.
[45] *Philanthropist,* Vol. IV, No. 5 (May 27, 1820), 76; (Chillicothe, Ohio) *Supporter,* June 16, 1819.

Ohio in 1802, at any rate, many of the delegates, arguing that Congress might reject a constitution containing extreme restrictions against free Negroes, were reluctant to enact severe limitations. On the whole, the delegation maintained that admission to the Union was of greater importance than anti-Negro laws. The convention debarred Negroes from voting but refused to consider other restrictions despite numerous petitions requesting them. [46]

The Indiana territorial legislature passed its first discriminatory measure in 1803, thereby testing the attitude of the federal government regarding territorial legislation against free Negroes. The lawmakers forbade Negroes from testifying in court cases involving a white person. The silence of Congress about this "black law," a term applied to any legislative measure passed by a free state restricting the civil rights or immigration of free Negroes, soon led to further acts in the territory. Free Negroes were excluded from militia duty in 1807. A year after the Indiana territorial legislature amended the indenture system in 1810, it debarred free Negroes from voting.[47]

These actions weakened the argument of Ohio legislators who had previously feared federal disapproval. Although instrumental in defeating proposals to exclude all Negroes, these Ohio politicians failed to prevent the passage of a bill in 1804 demanding that Negroes and mulattoes furnish proof of their freedom upon entering the state. Still wary of federal disapproval, the legislature hastened to clarify the law, explaining that it did not exclude all Negroes but only prevented fugitive slaves from escaping into Indian territory within the state and creating trouble with the Indians.[48] In the sense that the 1804 act did not set up a barrier completely excluding free Negroes, it cannot be classified as a black law. Although its enforcement was lax, until its repeal in 1849 the measure remained a constant threat to the unhindered migration of the Negro race.

The 1804 law did not achieve its objective. In spite of it, the Negro

[46] Burnet, *Notes,* 356; Wilson, "Negro in Early Ohio," 739; *Journal of the Constitutional Convention of Ohio, 1802* (Chillicothe, 1802), 32, 37, 39-40.
[47] Philbrick (ed.), *Laws of Indiana Territory, 1801-1809,* 40, 400; Ewbank and Riker (eds.), *Laws of Indiana Territory, 1809-1816,* 225-226; Emma Lou Thornbrough, *The Negro in Indiana: A Study of a Minority* (Indianapolis, 1957), 21-22.
[48] (Chillicothe) *Scioto Gazette,* Jan. 9, 1804; Salmon P. Chase (ed.), *The Statutes of Ohio and of the Northwest Territory* (3 vols., Cincinnati, 1833), I, 393-394.

population of Ohio increased by 1,562 between 1800 and 1810, from 337 to 1,899 Negroes. This rapid growth added further tension, and by 1807 the Ohio lawmakers prohibited free Negroes and mulattoes from establishing residence in the state unless they posted a $500 bond to guarantee their good behavior and self-support.[49]

As might be expected by the passage of the 1807 bill, exclusion of the free Negro rather than restriction of his civil rights became the prime concern in the more western regions. The lower house of the Indiana territorial legislature passed exclusion measures on three occasions between 1813 and 1815, only to have them blocked each time by the council or the governor. Finally a compromise bill was approved imposing a yearly $3.00 poll tax on all adult Negro and mulatto males.[50]

The Illinois territorial legislature was more successful. Besides adopting the anti-Negro restrictions of the Indiana territorial code, the lawmakers in 1813 passed a bill requiring justices of the peace to order every incoming free Negro or mulatto to leave the territory. Failure to comply with the order subjected the offender to a whipping of 39 lashes, repeated every fifteen days until he left. Free Negroes already living in the territory were protected from punishment if they registered with the clerk of common pleas and paid fifty cents for their free papers.[51] These laws made it apparent that the growing opposition to involuntary servitude in the Old Northwest was, in part, based on anti-Negro prejudice.

When the Indiana and Illinois constitutions were framed in 1816 and 1818, antislavery propaganda assumed a strong anti-Negro bias in order to counteract proslavery arguments. Although it alluded to the housebreakings, burning of farm buildings, and thefts committed by slaves, the propaganda emphasized that the reputed moral laxity of

---

[49] *1850 Census, Statistics,* 853; Chase (ed.), *Statutes,* I, 555-556.

[50] Thornbrough and Riker (eds.), *Journals of the General Assembly of Indiana Territory,* 634, 644, 711, 765, 809, 811; Ewbank and Riker (eds.), *Laws of Indiana Territory, 1809-1816,* 484-488; Thornbrough, *Negro in Indiana,* 21. Local authorities also discriminated against Negroes. A Vincennes law of 1815 forbade any slave or servant from entering the town without his master. Unescorted Negroes were to be whipped and fined. Those unable to pay the fine were subjected to a period of labor on public projects. *Western Sun,* June 3, 19, 1815.

[51] Francis S. Philbrick (ed.), *The Laws of Illinois Territory, 1809-1818* (Vol. XXV, *ISHLC,* Springfield, 1950), 91-92; Philbrick (ed.), *Pope's Digest,* 192-195.

Negroes would result in miscegenation if slavery were permitted or if free Negro immigration remained unchecked. Moses Wiley, an antislavery Indianian, warned that the loose morals of slaves would "cause a compound of the human species." Alexander Mitchell, an Ohioan firmly committed to the miscegenation theory, candidly wrote: "Suppose a youth should feel an inclination toward a negro, but be restrained from matrimony by his father until of age; and then should immediately join hands with the sable woman." Intermarriage would occur in Indiana if slavery were introduced, Mitchell predicted, and he insisted that Indiana would be better off without Negroes, slave or free, because of "deep-rooted prejudices entertained by the whites." Furthermore, the presence of Negroes would divide the state into parties and produce convulsions among the pro- and anti-Negro groups.[52]

Edward Coles, the antislavery governor of Illinois in 1823, writing under the pseudonym "Agis" in 1818, freely admitted his belief that slavery led to a corruption of public morals. The slave had few inducements to act virtuously because he could never attain distinction, and the more useful he proved to his master the less likely he was to obtain his freedom. "Hence," Coles concluded, "the shameful, the disgraceful, the degrading commerce between white persons of one sex and colored persons of the other sex. These abominable practices . . . are *fashionable* in every country where slavery is admitted." Coles insisted that happiness came only with virtue and that virtue and slavery were incompatible.[53]

Illinois antislavery propaganda in 1818 also stressed that slavery would result in a large free Negro population because of manumissions and because free Negroes moved into areas where slavery existed. "Prudence" noted that the increase of free Negroes had long been a grievance in the Atlantic seaboard states. The sole purpose of the newly founded colonization society, he thought, was to rid those states of free Negroes. If Illinoisans adopted slavery and these slaves eventually became free, "transporting this class from the . . . interior of the country . . . would be almost impossible. Then, in the name of reason," he asked, "why should we bring among us this class of men . . . whom the prejudices of our educations will always render distinct?" Espe-

---

[52] *Western Sun,* Mar. 30, 1816; *Western Intelligencer,* Apr. 1, 1818; Moses Wiley, "Circular Address to the Citizens of Indiana," in *Western Sun,* Feb. 3, 1816; [Alexander Mitchell], *An Address to the Inhabitants of Indiana Territory, on the Subject of Slavery, by a Citizen of Ohio* (Hamilton, Ohio, 1816), 7-10.
[53] *Illinois Intelligencer,* June 17, 1818.

cially did "Prudence" lash out at the advocates of partial slavery for suggesting that slavery might be abolished after ten years. To admit "these dusky Sons of Africa [as slaves] to where the citizens do not want them" he declared was inexpedient, but to establish a system which would eventually create "among us a host of free Negroes" was inexcusable.[54]

The anti-Negro arguments and the continuation of anti-Negro prejudice produced discriminatory legislation soon after Indiana and Illinois became states. In order to obtain a prompt acceptance of their constitutions by Congress, the delegations of both states purposely omitted the more stringent territorial restrictions against free Negroes. The first legislatures quickly re-enacted them, however, and then adopted other measures attempting to prevent the evils raised in the antislavery propaganda. The emphasis on miscegenation in Indiana produced a law forbidding intermarriage and establishing punishment provisions for sexual relationships between members of the two races. An Illinois law in 1819 discouraged Illinoisans from freeing their slaves or indentured servants by invalidating an act of manumission or the termination of a contract of indenture unless the master posted a $200 bond. Negroes without free papers could be apprenticed, for an indefinite period, to a white man.[55] During the next several years, as Hoosiers and Suckers became embroiled in the final struggle to legalize slavery, they grew more disturbed about the presence of free Negroes.

Morris Birkbeck's "Appeal," written to persuade the electorate in Illinois to vote against a constitutional convention in 1824, was primarily an economic argument against slavery. But he also stressed the social disadvantages of the slave system and declared that slavery would lead to the introduction of a class society similar to that existing in the South. If slavery were introduced, Birkbeck wrote, free labor would be degraded and nonslaveholding Illinois farmers would find themselves

---

[54] *Ibid.,* July 1, 19, 1818.
[55] *Laws of the State of Indiana, 1817-1818* (Corydon, 1818), 39-40, 94; *Laws Passed by the First General Assembly of the State of Illinois, at their Second Session* (Kaskaskia, 1819), 354-361. The marriage law in Indiana was not enforced. In 1820 a white man and his Negro wife settled in Randolph County and lived there without incident. James Eastman of Bloomingburg wrote that his white neighbor had a Negro wife and that local residents considered them "first rate" neighbors. *Indianapolis Recorder,* July 7, 1945; Eastman to Daniel Hoit, Mar. 31, 1849, James Eastman Papers (Indiana State Historical Society Library).

scorned and despised by "petty tyrants" riding around "mighty grand" in their slave-driven carriages. "They would have all their own way," he predicted, "and rule over us like little kings; we should have to patrol round the country to keep their negroes under, instead of minding our own business." Appealing to the southerner's dread of servile insurrection, Birkbeck insisted that the Negro population multiplied faster than the white and that this increase would lead to demands by them to be relieved from subjugation or possibly cause slave revolts. Indeed, he hinted that Illinois might become another Santo Domingo if slavery were legalized.[56]

Birkbeck's writings also revealed a strong anti-Negro bias by incorporating many of the current ideas white people held about Negroes. In one letter, written under the pseudonym of Jonathan Freeman, he declared, ". . . as to neighbors, give me plain farmers . . . for negroes are middling light-fingered, and I suspect we should have to lock up our cabins when we left home, and if we were to leave our linen out all night, we might chance to miss it in the morning. Then, too, would arise an overwhelming flood of gross immorality, carrying all decency before it — But I restrain my pen."[57]

Other antislavery writers predicted that the social conditions of the South would be re-created if Illinois adopted slavery. They further maintained that nonslaveholders in a slave society had little expectation for economic advancement and were almost leveled to the Negro's living conditions. One former southerner warned that "the poor white" would be forced to work with Negroes on public work projects, "while the haughtly slaveholders· [sat] in the shade and [drank] their grog." Former southerners constantly referred to the thievish tendencies of Negroes. One man born in North Carolina recalled that "these petty thefts are generally practised upon the poor people . . . and these are great trials and vexations to the poor, who are perpetually harassed and fatigued with the servile drudgery of patroling through the neighborhood of a night, in order to keep rich people's slaves at home." A

---

[56] *Illinois Gazette,* June 21, 1823, Apr. 3, 1824; Birkbeck, "Appeal," 152-160; Dillon, "Anti-Slavery Movement in Illinois," 97; Flower, *English Settlement,* 211. The "Appeal" also appeared in the *Edwardsville Spectator,* Oct. 11, 18, 1823.

[57] *Illinois Gazette,* Apr. 3, 1824. Birkbeck was born in England in 1763 and settled at Albion, Illinois, in 1818. De Tocqueville noted: "Of all Europeans, the English are those who have mixed least with negroes." De Tocqueville, *Democracy in America,* I, 374.

citizen of St. Clair County summarized the attitude of those who wrote about crimes committed by slaves, saying: "Well, then, let them remain where the people are willing to be answerable for their crimes."[58]

The proslavery element in Illinois made a fatal mistake by suggesting a limited form of servitude: slaves might be held until a certain age and then freed, or slavery might be legalized for only a short period of time. Their purpose, of course, was to overcome antislavery objections to a permanent slave system, but the storm of protests the suggestion caused only weakened the success of the referendum. The antislavery bloc, vigorously attacking the concept of partial slavery, played upon the public dislike of free Negroes. Limited slavery, declared one writer, was most undesirable because it would leave too large a population of free Negroes in the state. Their presence would encourage other Negroes to immigrate and Illinois would become a refuge for free Negroes. In time the Negro population might equal the white, and Negroes might demand full political and social equality. He condemned as inexpedient any form of limited slavery because "it would be sowing the seeds of . . . pestilence which no human power could afterwards exterminate." Besides increasing the number of free Negroes in Illinois, claimed George Flower, the adoption of partial slavery would also inflict a Negro population upon the entire Northwest because manumitted slaves would move into the adjacent states and become a "pest" to the people there. Another antislavery writer believed that the proslavery element had suggested the plan of limited servitude simply to permit Illinois slaveholders (if slavery were introduced) to utilize their chattels until they became old and worn out and then set them free. He was certain that these manumitted Negroes would become public charges or gain their livelihood by pilfering. "What a delightful state of society!" he wrote. "If we have more free negroes in the state than are desirable, let us not, by supporting the convention, open the door for . . . more. . . . We want neither slaves or [sic] free negroes. They are both unprofitable members of society, and ought both to be avoided rather than invited. Let us therefore oppose the Convention, the object of which is to introduce both." A staunch hater of the antislavery principle surmised that even if provisions were made to send Illinois slaves to Africa after they were freed, the antislavery men would encourage them to return. "I tell you," he informed his readers, "I dread

[58] *Edwardsville Spectator,* May 18, 24, Sept. 6, Oct. 4, 1823.

a population of free negroes" scattered throughout the region north-west of the Ohio River. Just before the election, "Spartacus" warned the voters that limited slavery would increase the Negro population in the future and that the antislavery element in the state would pur-chase slaves before their terms of servitude expired and liberate them. He concluded with an appeal to "let those who dislike free negroes, vote against a convention, as the only door through which slavery and this consequent evil can be introduced into this state."[59]

Racial antagonism was, undoubtedly, a prime factor in causing the rejection of a constitutional convention in Illinois. The early and later restrictive laws were certainly proof that free Negroes were unwelcome. At the beginning of the referendum campaign the proslavery element minimized the fact that a revised constitution might permit slavery. When the legalization of slavery was mentioned, naturally its advan-tages were stressed. The refutation of such arguments, especially the point that chattel servitude on a permanent basis would be more detri-mental to Illinois than the immediate prosperity it might bring, forced the proslavery men to compromise their position and to suggest partial slavery. But the failure to make concrete suggestions about the disposi-tion of manumitted slaves left the impression that the freed Negroes would remain in the state. If the majority of the people objected to the small number of free Negroes residing in Illinois in 1824, they cer-tainly would not have sanctioned a plan that would increase the free Negro population ten or twenty years hence. Morever, the procedure of submitting state constitutions for popular approval had not, in 1824, become a generally accepted practice. The probability that a proslavery convention, without any restrictions placed upon it by the federal gov-ernment, might incorporate an article legalizing partial slavery had to be considered. Nor was the fear of such a step imaginary, for even as late as the 1850's it was "believed that in the south part of Illinois, a portion of the population" still favored the adoption of slavery in the state.[60]

The inflexibility of Congress over Article 6 provided time for an antislavery population to file into the southern portion of the Old Northwest and to prevent the introduction of bondage. These pioneers came in mainly from the slave states but "now and then, a more sub-

[59] *Illinois Intelligencer,* July 5, 16, 1824; *Illinois Gazette,* Nov. 25, 1822; *Ed-wardsville Spectator,* June 29, 1824; *Kaskaskia Republican,* Mar. 20, 1824.
[60] (Springfield) *Illinois State Journal,* Feb. 15, 1853.

stantial farmer from New York [or] Pennsylvania" settled.[61] Their convictions, congressional firmness, and time kept slavery from spreading northwest of the Ohio. Yet, the people, Congress, and time were not as kind to free Negroes. Congressional disregard of the first black laws encouraged the enactment of further restrictions. The majority of the people did not oppose discriminatory legislation because they believed that free Negroes should be discouraged from migrating to the Old Northwest. After the failure of the constitutional referenda in Indiana and Illinois, the intensification of anti-Negro prejudice produced even more severe measures to confine the free Negro now that slavery had been rejected.

---

[61] Flower, *English Settlement,* 184.

Northwest of the Ohio, 1824-60

"A most unparalleled prejudice" developed in the Old Northwest following the referenda struggles in Indiana and Illinois. One traveler left Indiana in 1826 with the distinct impression that the constitutional guarantees of personal safety were not extended to men whose "skins [were] black." Although Indianians sanctimoniously admitted that they had been willing to forego the benefits of slavery, they insisted on protection from the principal inconvenience of the system — the settlement of free Negroes. An "Indiana Farmer" argued that Negroes could not be good citizens because their mental inferiority prevented them from assuming the responsibilities of citizenship. Much to his amazement, George Flower of Illinois was ostracized by his neighbors until he terminated a contract by which he had rented land to two Negroes in 1825. When Flower raised the matter of his contractual obligations, his neighbors, who had lived in the eastern as well as the southern portions of the United States, informed him that "black men had no rights that white men need respect." In central Illinois, recalled an early settler, most people considered Negroes little more than sheep with wool on their heads; any talk of the Negro as a human being made little impression upon the local population. One editor from the same section of the state, lauding measures taken in St. Louis County, Missouri, to prevent free Negroes and mulattoes not born there from residing in the county, proposed that communities in Illinois take similar action: "We do not want the negroes . . . thrown upon us; they should be sent to *N. York!*"[1]

---

[1] Harlow Lindley (ed.), *Indiana as Seen by Early Travelers: A Collection of Reprints from Books of Travel, Letters, and Diaries Prior to 1830* (Indianapolis,

Public officials and legislative committees, increasingly concerned about the public excitement over the growing Negro population, advocated measures to limit it. While the ratio of Negroes to whites in the Ohio River states in 1830 was not high, 14,834 Negroes to 1,431,099 white people, the percentages of growth in the Negro population were greater than the percentages in the white. During the 1820-30 decade the Negro population increased 102 per cent in Ohio, 195 per cent in Indiana, and 258 per cent in Illinois. On the other hand, the white population grew by 62 per cent in Ohio, 127 per cent in Indiana, and 185 per cent in Illinois.[2]

Joseph Kitchell, an Illinois state senator, expressed the prevalent attitude among legislators by declaring, "their [Negro] residence among us, even as servants . . . is productive of moral and political evil. . . . The natural difference between them and ourselves forbids the idea that they should ever be permitted to participate with us in the political affairs of our government."[3]

Governor James B. Ray of Indiana assumed the leadership in securing a law which required incoming Negroes to have proof of their freedom and to post a $500 bond for their good behavior and self-support. In his annual message in 1829, Ray announced that a Negro population was pouring into the state, only to become public charges. Because the neighboring states had passed or were considering laws to prevent their immigration, Indiana, in order to protect herself from becoming a dumping ground, must enact the same type of legislation. "Though it might savor somewhat of injustice to interfere with any [Negroes] that are already here," Ray cautioned, "it will still become your prov-

---

1916), 34; (Boston) *The Liberator*, Mar. 29, 1834; *Niles Weekly Register*, XXX (Aug. 12, 1826), 416-417; Flower, *English Settlement*, 260-261; D. N. Blazer, "The History of the Underground Railroad of McDonough County, Illinois," *ISHSJ*, XV (Oct., 1922), 582; (Springfield) *Sangamo Journal*, Nov. 7, 1835.

[2] The increases in numbers were:

	Negro		White	
	1820	1830	1820	1830
Ohio	4,723 to	9,568	576,572 to	937,903
Indiana	1,230 to	3,629	148,851 to	338,020
Illinois	457 to	1,637	53,788 to	155,176

U.S. Bureaus of the Census, *Fourth Census of the United States: 1820, Enumeration of Inhabitants* (Washington, D.C., 1821), n.p.; *Fifth Census of the United States: 1830, Enumeration of Inhabitants,* 142-143, 146-147, 148-149; *1850 Census, Statistics,* 719, 781, 853.

[3] State of Illinois, *Senate Journal, 1828-1829* (Vandalia, 1829), 182.

ince . . . to regulate for the future . . . the emigration [sic] . . . and the continuance of known paupers, thrown upon us from any quarter."[4]

A legislative committee, investigating the problem in Ohio, accepted the conclusions of an earlier report, which stated that "free blacks" were more idle and vicious than slaves, and requested more severe measures to prevent the immigration of free Negroes. The committee described the Negro as a distinct and degraded class that competed with white men for employment, demoralized whites simply by association, and revealed their lack of moral restraint to the younger people.[5]

Ohio, Indiana, and Illinois adopted almost identical statute restrictions against free Negroes by the early 1830's. Defining a Negro as any person with one-fourth or more Negro blood, each state excluded Negroes from the militia, denied them the ballot, and forbade them to give testimony in court cases involving whites. An Indiana exclusion law of 1831, almost an exact copy of the 1804 and 1807 Ohio restrictions, demanded that immigrating Negroes have certificates of freedom and post a $500 bond. Negroes unable to meet either requirement were to be expelled immediately from the state. An Illinois law of 1829 also required incoming Negroes to furnish proof of freedom but raised the bond to $1,000. In addition, slaves and indentured servants in the Sucker State were not permitted to sue for their freedom, and southern slaveholders bringing slaves into the state to free them were subject to extreme fines.[6]

Such legislation was not peculiar to the Ohio River states. The territorial legislatures of Michigan, in 1827, and Iowa, in 1838, passed laws requiring immigrating Negroes to possess certificates of freedom and to post $500 bonds. When Michigan became a state the law remained in force and was applied in one instance. Litigation brought against a Negro, who failed to or could not post bond, resulted in his banishment from the state in 1837. Iowa also banned intermarriage in 1840. The black laws were passed in Michigan to encourage Negroes traveling through the state to Canada to complete their journey. Iowa's proximity to Missouri and the fact that many Iowans considered the "blacks

---

[4] State of Indiana, *House Journal, 1829-1830* (Indianapolis, 1829), 35-36.
[5] (Columbus) *Ohio State Journal*, Feb. 1, 1832.
[6] *The Revised Code of Laws of Illinois, 1827* (Vandalia, 1827), 320; *The Revised Code of Laws of Illinois, 1829* (Vandalia, 1829), 109-112; *Laws of Illinois* (Vandalia, 1831), 101; *The Revised Laws of the State of Indiana* (Indianapolis, 1831), 375-376, 407. In 1840 the Indiana bond law was upheld by the state supreme court in *Baptiste* v. *State*, 5 *Blackf.* 283 (1840).

in the United States . . . the most wretched and miserable" element of the population, guided the actions of the Hawkeye legislators.[7]

Delegates in Michigan and Iowa continued to demand discriminatory measures when the first constitutions of the two states were framed. The Michigan constitutional convention of 1836 prohibited Negroes from voting on the ground that "the negro belonged to a degraded caste of mankind. . . . Nature had marked the distinction [and] Society had . . . recognized and sanctioned it." The people of Michigan, said a convention delegate, presumed that "if the blacks are to be admitted to all the rights of citizens, they will be encouraged to come and fix their residence in the new State. And . . . the consequence would be dangerous to say the least[;] a state of society would be produced, by no means desirable."[8] Many Iowa delegates at the first state constitutional convention in 1844, not content with denying the ballot and membership in the state legislature and militia, also demanded, but did not secure, the incorporation of an outright free Negro exclusion provision in the constitution. One delegate, a former New Yorker, said he would "never consent to open the doors of our beautiful State" to Negroes. If free Negroes were not prevented from settling in Iowa, the neighboring states would drive "the whole black population of the Union" into it.[9]

Discrimination against Negroes intensified during the 1840's and 1850's. Noting the development, Horace Greeley remarked that "the 'Color Phobia,' which prevails so extensively . . . and causes such fear-

[7] Laws of the Territory of Michigan (2 vols., Lansing, 1874), II, 134-135; Arthur Raymond Kooker, "The Antislavery Movement in Michigan, 1796-1840" (unpublished Ph.D. dissertation, University of Michigan, 1941), 60, 262; The Statute Laws of the Territory of Iowa (Dubuque, 1839), 65-67; Wisconsin Territorial Gazette and Burlington (Iowa) Advertiser, Oct. 5, 1837; "An Act to Regulate Blacks and Mulattoes," AI, III (Apr., 1897), 145-147; Louis Pelzer, "The Negro and Slavery in Early Iowa," IJHP, II (Oct., 1904), 471.

[8] Harold M. Dorr (ed.), The Michigan Constitutional Convention of 1835-1836, Debates and Proceedings (Ann Arbor, 1940), 157-159; Constitution of Michigan, 1837, Art. II, Sec. 7.

[9] Constitutions of Iowa, 1844 and 1846, Arts, III, Secs. 1; Arts. VII, Secs. 1; Arts. IV, Secs. 4, in Benjamin F. Shambaugh (ed.), Documentary Material Relating to the History of Iowa (Vol. I, ISHSC, Iowa City, 1897), 153, 155, 164, 194, 204; Benjamin F. Shambaugh (ed.), Fragments of the Debates of the Iowa Constitutional Conventions of 1844 and 1846, Along with Press Comments and Other Materials on the Constitutions of 1844 and 1846 (Iowa City, 1900), 32-33, 52-55. The 1844 constitution was rejected by a popular referendum.

ful spasms on those effected [*sic*] by it, contrasts singularly enough with the politeness to Negroes often exhibited by the Fathers of the Revolution." An Ohio lawmaker remarked in 1850 that "prejudice against the negro [was] worse than it ever [had] been, and it [was] idle to suppose that this sentiment [would] ever decrease as long as the two races remain[ed] together." Even as late as 1859, Henry D. Gilpin of Philadelphia informed Richard Cobden, an English reformer, that racial discrimination was becoming stronger in the free states, and that the "gulf which separates socially the African from the white race is constantly widening and deepening."[10]

The reasons for this increase in racial enmity are, indeed, complex. First of all, economic rivalry between unskilled Negro and white laborers in midwestern urban areas produced tension. Nowhere was this more evident than in Cincinnati, the chief commercial center for the Old Northwest in the 1830's and 1840's. Free Negroes flocked to the city in search of employment, and fugitive slaves found Cincinnati's ghetto, known as "little Africa," a safe refuge from their masters.[11] Between 1820 and 1830 the Negro population rose from 410 to 1,087; by 1850, 3,237 of the city's 115,438 inhabitants were Negro. From the late 1820's there was also a large influx of European immigrants and competition between the two groups for jobs became acute. By 1830 riots broke out and a committee of white citizens petitioned the city council to stem the tide of Negro immigration. Pressures placed upon the Negroes by the municipal authorities forced about half of them to leave the city. The continuing immigration of Negroes caused another riot in 1841; this time, however, Negroes were imprisoned for taking part in the disturbance but were not expelled from the city.[12]

---

[10] *New York Tribune,* Feb. 12, 1846; *Report of the Debates and Proceedings of the Convention for the Revision of the Constitution of the State of Ohio, 1850-51* (2 vols., Columbus, 1851), II, 639; Gilpin to Cobden, Apr. 27, 1859, in Elizabeth Cawley (ed.), *The American Diaries of Richard Cobden* (Princeton, 1952), 176-177.

[11] Frances Trollope, *Domestic Manners of the Americans,* ed. Donald Smalley (New York, 1960), 39-40; Richard C. Wade, "The Negro in Cincinnati, 1800-1830," *JNH,* XXXIX (Jan., 1954), 44.

[12] *Liberty Hall and Cincinnati Gazette,* June 28, 1829; *Cincinnati Advertiser and Ohio Phoenix,* Aug. 18, 1830; Carter G. Woodson, *A Century of Negro Migration* (Washington, D.C., 1918), 57; Charles Cist, *Sketches and Statistics of Cincinnati in 1859* (Cincinnati, 1859), 46; Carter G. Woodson, "The Negroes of Cincinnati Prior to the Civil War," *JNH,* I (Jan., 1916), 5-6; Wade, "Negro in Cincinnati," 49-50; Robert E. Chaddock, *Ohio Before 1850: A Study of the Early Influence of Pennsylvania and the Southern Populations*

Whether or not farmers in the Middle West were apprehensive about economic competition from free Negroes is difficult to determine. So few free Negroes engaged in farming that perhaps farmers were not immediately concerned.[13] Farmers serving as delegates to state constitutional conventions in Illinois and Ohio, two states in which agricultural production was expanding prodigiously, never argued that unlimited free Negro immigration would adversely affect them. In fact, men who listed their occupation as farming seldom engaged in the debates concerning the Negro. At the Illinois convention in 1847 there were 76 farmers among the 162 delegates. Only one of them made extensive remarks on the Negro question, and he opposed discriminatory measures. The most avid supporters of black legislation were lawyers who served as delegates; five of the seven longest speeches in favor of discriminatory laws were made by men from this professional group. At the Ohio convention in 1850, only 28 of the 120 members were farmers. One of them spoke in favor of discrimination and one against it. Again lawyers pushed the discriminatory propositions, giving six of the eight major speeches presented. However, most of the lawyers in both conventions represented rural areas and perhaps they were spokesmen for the farmers.[14]

Increases in the Negro population enlivened the latent prejudice of the white people in Detroit. Delegates representing the city at the 1836 state constitutional convention made the most vitriolic comments against Negroes. As a terminus for the underground railroad, Detroit was confronted by a fairly large concentration of Negroes in southern Ontario and an ever-increasing number of fugitive slaves who remained in the city instead of crossing the river into Canada. By 1835 one editor complained that "our city . . . is infested with thieves, who are for the most part runaway negroes," and he warned the "citizens [to] unite in the task of watching them, for such pests [could] not exist in a com-

---

in Ohio (Vol. XXXI, *Columbia University Studies in History, Economics and Public Law*, New York, 1908), 48; Frank U. Quillin, *The Color Line in Ohio: A History of Race Prejudice in a Typical Northern State* (Ann Arbor, 1913), 26-29.

[13] A more complete discussion on the attitude of Negroes toward farming is found in Leon F. Litwack, *North of Slavery: The Negro in the Free States, 1790-1860* (Chicago, 1961), 174-178.

[14] Arthur C. Cole (ed.), *The [Illinois] Constitutional Debates of 1847* (Vol. XIV, *ISHLC*, Springfield, 1919), 201-205, 208, 210, 213, 218, 224, 855-856, 863; *Ohio Debates, 1850-51*, II, 12, 28-29, 337, 598-599.

munity where the people [were] vigilant, and where justice [was] swift to overtake crime."[15]

The white people, in both the midwestern cities and rural areas, feared that the unlimited immigration of free Negroes would result in miscegenation. The point was too often raised to be overlooked. Indiana, Illinois, Iowa, and Michigan forbade intermarriages and invalidated those that had been performed. Midwestern political leaders continually emphasized the miscegenation idea. At the Illinois Constitutional Convention in 1847, William Kinney vituperatively declared that the lack of a restriction on Negro immigration was tantamount to allowing Negroes "to make proposals to marry our daughters." An increase in the Negro population, wrote an Iowa editor, immediately raised *"thou'ts of amalgamation"* in the minds of Iowans. Nor was the miscegenation bugaboo ignored in Wisconsin, where the only legal restriction against free Negroes was the denial of the franchise. Democrats there warned that giving Negroes the ballot would encourage them to "marry our sisters and daughters, and smutty wenches to [marry] our brothers and sons."[16]

Besides dreading miscegenation, midwesterners also presumed that the lack of restrictions on Negro immigration would cause their states to become a dumping ground for southern free Negroes and manumitted slaves who were forced by the laws of the slave states to emigrate.[17] Apprehension about the matter was the major impetus for the bond laws. Even though the settlement of former slaves had practically ceased by 1840, the dumping ground idea remained strong enough to produce demands for the enforcement of the laws, especially in Indiana.[18] "We presume there is not a nigger in this town [Rich-

---

[15] (Detroit) *Democratic Free Press and Michigan Intelligencer*, Oct. 11, 1832.

[16] *Illinois Debates, 1847*, 217; *Washington Press*, July 29, 1857, in "Contemporary Editorial Opinion of the 1857 Constitution," *IJH*, LV (Apr., 1957), 142; (Madison) *Weekly Wisconsin Patriot*, Sept. 12, 1857.

[17] Virginia laws of 1806 and 1819 stipulated that manumitted slaves remaining in the state could be re-enslaved. By 1831 the Tennessee legislature declared an act of manumission invalid unless the master posted bond to insure the emigration of the slave. A Kentucky law of 1834 required free Negroes and mulattoes to post a bond to remain in the state or face enslavement. *Digest of the Laws of Virginia* (Richmond, 1841), 863; R. L. Caruthers and A. O. P. Nicholson (comps.), *A Compilation of the Statutes of Tennessee* (Nashville, 1836), 279; *A Digest of the Statute Laws of Kentucky* (2 vols., Frankfort, 1834), II, 1220-21.

[18] Northern representatives in Congress usually relied on the dumping ground argument to defend black laws when southerners taunted them about the anti-

mond, Indiana] that has given his bond," declared a Wayne County editor, insisting that if the state bond law were enforced, Negroes from the South would not settle in Indiana. In Cambridge City, another Wayne County community, the city authorities, in 1845, passed a municipal Negro exclusion bill requiring all Negroes to post bond within thirty days or leave. Evidently the bill was not effective because four years later, the townspeople held a mass meeting to devise more stringent means of ridding the city of its Negro population. About the same time a concerted effort to force Negroes to leave was made in Clark County, an antislavery center in territorial days. This action, in turn, caused alarm in neighboring Floyd County, where one of its editors remarked that county officials should take similar action or "we shall soon be overrun with all the worthless, idle and dissolute negroes in the surrounding counties."[19]

Attention was focused on the Negro in the 1840's by the floods of petitions to the state legislatures requesting the repeal of the black laws, and by the rise of the slavery extension question in national poli-

---

Negro restrictions. In the United States Senate, Stephen A. Douglas declared that such legislation was necessary to prevent the free states from becoming asylums "for all the old and decrepit and broken-down negroes that may emigrate [sic] or be sent to [them]." Congressman William Sawyer of Ohio requested three cheers for a group of Ohioans who forced a number of immigrating Negroes to return to the South, and he predicted that, if necessary, the banks of the Ohio River would be lined with armed men to keep "worn out" former slaves in the slave states. However, census information disputes the validity of the theory that Negroes in the Old Northwest were "old and worn out." The age breakdown in the census reports does not indicate that a majority of the Negroes were beyond the employment age. In 1830 there were 14,834 Negroes in Ohio, Indiana, and Illinois. Of this number 901 were over fifty-five years of age and 4,928 under ten years of age. Over half, or 9,005, were between the ages of ten and fifty-five. By 1840 the Negro population increased to 28,105, and only 1,729 were over fifty-five years old. This census clearly reveals that the greatest number of Negroes were between twenty and thirty years of age. Thus, the argument that immigrating Negroes were "old and worn out" did not agree with census figures; the majority of them were of an age group that could have been employed. *Congressional Globe*, 31 Cong., 1 Sess., Appendix, 1664; 30 Cong., 1 Sess., Appendix, 726-728; *1830 Census, Enumeration of Inhabitants*, 142-143, 146-147, 148-149; U.S. Bureau of the Census, *Sixth Census of the United States: 1840, Enumeration of Inhabitants* (corrected, Washington, D.C., 1841), 344, 374, 396; *1850 Census, Statistics*, 719, 781, 853.
[19] *Richmond Jeffersonian*, n.d., in (Newport, Indiana) *Free Labor Advocate*, Jan. 8, 1842, Apr. 26, 1845; *New Albany* (Indiana) *Daily Ledger*, Aug. 10, 1850; (Centerville) *Indiana True Democrat*, Oct. 4, 1850; Thornbrough, *Negro in Indiana*, 62-63.

tics. The petition campaigns, led principally by militant abolitionists, failed to achieve their purpose and, in fact, may have created an adverse effect. Condemning all equal suffrage petitions with the argument that "the two races [could] never live in a state of freedom under the same government," the Michigan legislature in 1846 passed an anti-miscegenation law.[20] A lawmaker in Iowa noted that the petition movement in his state made the people hate "the abolitionist as [much as they] hated the nigger." Petition campaigns were just as unsuccessful in the Ohio River states. Only once, in 1845, did the Illinois legislature consider petitions on the Negro question, and then the lawmakers simply concluded that the black laws "ought not to be repealed." On the other hand, the Ohio legislature wrote rambling reports in defense of the state's discriminatory legislation.[21]

Agitation over the annexation of Texas introduced the slavery extension question into national politics for the first time since the Missouri Compromise. By 1846 the Wilmot Proviso pushed the slavery expansion issue into the limelight; thereafter and until 1860, the status of the free Negro was a never-ending topic in the Old Northwest.

The intensification of anti-Negro sentiment, coming on the eve of constitutional conventions to revise the outmoded state documents between 1847 and 1857, produced extensive discussions on the Negro question during the deliberations. Again these discussions were heightened by a deluge of petitions requesting the relaxation of restrictions. The Negro question was considered the most important matter discussed during the Ohio convention of 1850-51. Almost half of the fifty-two petitions presented to the Indiana delegation in 1850-51 dealt with the Negro in one form or another. In the Michigan convention of 1850, there were six times as many petitions concerning Negro suffrage than any other topic. Henry Clay Dean of Iowa reported, following the Iowa convention of 1857, that the Negro question played

---

[20] State of Michigan, *House Journal, 1843* (Detroit, 1843), 17; *Senate Journal, 1845* (Detroit, 1845), 163; *The Revised Statutes of Michigan, 1846* (Detroit, 1846), 330.

[21] F. I. Herriott, "Iowa and the First Nomination of Abraham Lincoln," *AI,* VIII (Oct., 1907), 199; State of Illinois, *House Journal, 1845* (Springfield, 1845), 156; W. Sherman Savage, "The Contest over Slavery Between Illinois and Missouri," *JNH,* XXVIII (July, 1943), 312; State of Ohio, *House Journal 1840-1841* (Columbus, 1841), Appendix, 1-6.

too important a role in the debates and caused the Democratic party to lose control of the state government.[22]

Comments about the Negro race were vituperative, to say the least. William Kinney of Illinois insisted that people advocating equal suffrage "did not know how lazy, and good-for-nothing" Negroes were. Any leniency on the part of officials, warned a native southern Illinoisan, would cause the people in his section of the state to "take matters into their hands, and commence a war of extermination." Rather than permit equal rights, declared on Indianian, it "would be better to kill them off." David Dobson of Indiana, stunned by the support which Negro suffrage received from one delegate, retorted: "Whenever you begin to talk about making negroes equal with white men, I begin to think about leaving the country." In Ohio, William Sawyer expressed his opposition to petitions and equal suffrage by claiming, "the United States were designed by the God in Heaven to be governed and inhabited by the Anglo-Saxon race and by them alone." Sawyer denied that the doctrine of equality in the Declaration of Independence embraced Negroes because the race was "very little removed from the condition of dumb beasts — they wallowed in the mire like hogs, and there was nothing of civilization in their aboriginal conditions."[23] Moreover, such remarks were not the exception, but revealed instead the general attitude. Even the few delegates who favored a generous policy toward Negroes seldom argued that Negroes were entitled to equal rights because, except for militia and jury duty, they had to fulfill the other obligations of citizenship. More often pro-Negro arguments left the impression that Negroes should be pitied and uplifted by sympathetic action on the part of the white people.

As might be expected, the revised constitutions either continued the restrictions against Negroes or made them more severe. All of the states, except Ohio, submitted as popular referenda separate articles concerning the Negro. Michigan, Wisconsin, and Iowa submitted suffrage articles; Illinois and Indiana, exclusion provisions. On the whole,

---

[22] *Cincinnati Enquirer*, Jan. 19, 1851; Kettleborough, *Constitution Making in Indiana*, I, 221; *Report of the Proceedings and Debates in the Convention to Revise the Constitution of the State of Michigan, 1850* (Lansing, 1850), 284; *Dubuque* (Iowa) *Weekly Times*, Feb. 27, 1858.

[23] *Illinois Debates, 1847*, 216, 860; *Report of the Debates and Proceedings of the Convention for the Revision of the Constitution of the State of Indiana, 1850-51* (2 vols., Indianapolis, 1851), I, 233, 574; *Ohio Debates, 1850-51*, I, 679; II, 553, 639.

public regard toward the referenda procedure was favorable. Only in Wisconsin was the method criticized. There one editor, complaining about the entire constitution, described the referendum process as "one of the most discreditable of many discreditable acts" of the constitutional convention. Rather than foster opposition, the referendum procedure prevented Negrophiles from blaming convention delegates for anti-Negro laws. This is substantiated by the fact that the only extensive comments about the refusal to grant equal suffrage were voiced in Ohio. A letter, appearing in the Free Soil *True Democrat,* denounced the voting restriction as a contradiction of the republican philosophy of government. "There is a sharp clash between the constitution's bill of rights and the suffrage article," wrote an Ashtabula editor. " 'All men by nature are free and independent,' don't look well by the side of 'every White male citizen.' "[24]

The results of the suffrage referenda in Michigan, Iowa, and Wisconsin between 1849 and 1857 proved conclusively that political equality was not popular. In the Wolverine State in 1850, 72 per cent of the voters, 32,026 out of 45,000, refused to concede the franchise. In the latter states the percentages were 86 and 61, respectively.[25]

The denial of Negro suffrage was not limited to any one political party although the Democrats received the blame because of their

---

[24] (Milwaukee) *Sentinel annd Gazette,* Oct. 23, 1846; (Cleveland) *Daily True Democrat,* June 13, 1851, in Works Progress Administration, *Annals of Cleveland* (59 vols., Cleveland, 1936-38), XXXIV, 65; *Ashtabula Sentinel,* n.d., in *Cleveland Plain Dealer,* May 25, 1851. In 1859 the Democratic Ohio legislature denied the ballot to persons with "African blood in their veins." Election judges were empowered to determine who was ineligible under the law, and to prevent leniency on their part, the bill provided a fine and prison sentence for any judge who violated it. The purpose of the act was not to prevent Negroes from voting, for constitutionally they did not possess the right, but rather to make it appear as if mulattoes had elected Chase to the governorship in the recent election. By the end of the year the state supreme court declared the law unconstitutional, and the Republican legislature repealed it the next year. *Revised Statutes of the State of Ohio, 1860* (2 vols., Cincinnati, 1860), I, 548-549; *Cleveland Leader,* Mar. 31, 1859, in W.P.A., *Annals of Cleveland,* XLII, 459; Eugene H. Roseboom, *The Civil War Era, 1850-1873* (Vol. IV, *The History of the State of Ohio,* Columbus, 1944), 341, 343; *Anderson v. Milliken et al.,* 9 Ohio (3 *Critchfield*) 579-581 (1859).

[25] *Whig Almanac and United States Register, 1851* (New York, 1852), 59; Henry M. Utley and Byron M. Cutcheon, *Michigan as a Province, Territory, and State* (4 vols., New York, 1906), III, 334. For the Iowa vote see page 41; the Wisconsin percentage is based on the 1857 referendum — see page 42.

overwhelming majorities in the conventions.[26] David Davis of Illinois, a Whig delegate at the 1847 convention and a staunch friend and supporter of Lincoln, was as opposed to equal suffrage as any Democrat. When the referendum was defeated in Michigan, a disgruntled Whig insisted that Democratic political strength was responsible. "No, Sir," he wrote, "the patent Democracy of this State [would] not vote for universal suffragé. That party thinks 'niggers are very well in their place,' but it would be dangerous to trust them with the elective franchise, because they may not always vote the 'Democratic ticket.' "[27] But the argument loses its force when it is realized that the Democratic party never secured a larger majority than 7,942 votes in its most successful national campaign in the state in 1852; it seems unlikely that Democrats could have been totally responsible for the 12,974 majority vote on this one issue.

Even in Iowa, where the Republican party dominated state politics and the 1857 constitutional convention, the suffrage referendum was decisively defeated by a vote of 49,511 to 8,489.[28] And the Republicans expected the result. In the convention they used the referendum issue only to determine the political solidarity of the Republican delegation. William Penn Clark, a Republican delegate, insisted that his party was not interested in granting equal suffrage to Negroes. Its major principle was against the extension of slavery, and Iowa Republicans had never committed themselves to any type of Negro equality.[29]

---

[26] Democratic membership was so strong in Illinois, 91 Democrats to 71 Whigs, that the constitution was referred to as the "party constitution." There were one-fourth again as many Democrats as Whigs in the Indiana delegation, and the majority of the delegates in Ohio, Michigan, and Wisconsin were Democrats. *Illinois Debates, 1847,* 10; *Alton* (Illinois) *Telegraph and Democratic Review,* June 18, July 2, 1847; Kettleborough, *Constitution Making in Indiana,* I, 22; *Ohio Debates, 1850-51,* I, 15; Utley and Cutcheon, *Michigan,* III, 337; Emil Olbrich, *The Development of Sentiment on Negro Suffrage to 1860* (Vol. III, *Bulletin of the University of Wisconsin,* No. 477, History Series, Madison, 1912), 88.

[27] *Illinois Debates, 1847,* 219; "Wolverine" to Greeley, Oct. 23, 1850, in *New York Tribune,* Nov. 5, 1850.

[28] Twenty-one of the thirty-six delegates in Iowa were Republicans. Herriott, "Iowa and the First Nomination of Lincoln," VIII, 199.

[29] Eric M. Eriksson, "The Framers of the Constitution of 1857," *IJHP,* XXII (Jan., 1924), 57; *The Debates of the Constitutional Convention of the State of Iowa, Assembled at Iowa City, Monday, January 19, 1857* (2 vols., Davenport, 1857), II, 669. Prominent Iowa Republicans fought the enfranchisement of Negroes in the state after the Civil War, demanding that Negro suffrage be granted only in the former Confederacy. Cyrenus Cole, *Iowa Through the Years* (Iowa City, 1940), 314.

Republican editors in Iowa immediately defended the action of their party's delegation at the convention. The policy of referring Negro suffrage to popular vote, which was causing a "wonderful furor," declared one editor, indicated that the Republican party relied on democratic principles of government. "Democratic Michigan and ultra Democratic Illinois submitted the same vote," he wrote. "One would think the idea was born of modern black amalgamation Republicans." While most Republican editors opposed Negro suffrage, they thought the convention had handled the matter correctly. On the eve of the referendum, a Democratic editor admitted that Iowa Republicans did not share the national Republican party's amalgamation attitude. Predicting the defeat of Negro suffrage, he wrote, "There is no man of our acquaintance, be his politics Republican or Democratic, who desires to have negroes come among us."[30]

In regard to the Negro generally, Wisconsin was the most liberal state in the Old Northwest in that no immigration restriction was enacted against Negroes. Yet, even this attitude did not indicate approval of Negro suffrage. A universal suffrage referendum was defeated in 1849.[31] When it was submitted for the second time in the general election of 1857, the electorate rejected equal suffrage by a vote of 40,106 to 27,550, even though Alexander Randall, the Republican candidate, was elected governor. The result was due to the Republican failure to

---

[30] *Washington Press,* July 8, 29, 1857; *Montezuma* (Iowa) *Republican,* May 30, 1857; *McGregor's North Iowa Times,* June 24, July 24, 1857, all in "Contemporary Editorial Opinion," 117-119, 137-138, 140-141, 143-146.

[31] Wisconsin's 1848 constitution empowered the legislature to confer the franchise on Negroes provided popular consent was secured. In 1849 the legislature voted to submit the suffrage question to a public referendum at the next general election. Although 31,759 people voted in the election, only 5,265 voted for Negro suffrage and 4,075 against it. The constitutional provision as written caused the state board of canvassers to decide that a majority of the votes cast in the election was needed for approval of the measure. Because 5,265 obviously was not a majority of 31,759 the proposition was considered defeated. In 1866 the state supreme court declared that the article as written did not mean a majority of the total votes cast in the election, but rather a majority of the total votes on the proposition. The supreme bench therefore decided that Wisconsin Negroes had legally possessed the elective franchise for seventeen years. *Journal of the Convention to Form a Constitution for the State of Wisconsin, with a Sketch of the Debates* (Madison, 1848), 180, 185, 192-193; State of Wisconsin, *Senate Journal, 1849* (Madison, 1849), 440; *Southport* (Wisconsin) *Telegraph,* Nov. 9, 23, 1849, in Leslie H. Fishel, Jr., "Wisconsin and Negro Suffrage," *WMH,* XLVI (Spring, 1963), 185; *Gillespie* v. *Palmer et al.,* 20 *Wisc.* (15 *Vilas and Bryant*) 572 (1866).

support the issue in order to secure the governorship. Democrats even hinted that Republicans would have publicly opposed equal suffrage except for the insistence of Sherman Booth "and his old abolition guard." Inasmuch as Republican editors remained strangely silent about Negro suffrage, there was some truth in this contention. All things considered, the Democratic charge that universal suffrage had "not a friend to support it as as political measure," and that "a Republican dare not endorse it, or a Republican candidate go before the people upon it," expressed the situation correctly.[32]

Iowa reanimated the idea of excluding free Negroes by means of a constitutional provision. Missouri's 1820 constitution had contained a free Negro exclusion clause, but Missourians had agreed not to enforce it it against Negroes from the free states. The 1844 constitutional convention in Iowa incorporated a similar provision in its constitution, but the federal officials in the territory, citing possible congressional disapproval, persuaded the convention to remove the article. Later, in 1851, after statehood was achieved, the state legislature passed an exclusion law.[33]

This action, and the fact that Congress admitted Florida in 1845 with a free Negro exclusion clause in its constitution, had a decided influence in the Ohio River states where the old bond laws proved ineffective and where the Negro population increased 50 per cent between 1840 and 1850.[34] Following Iowa's example, Ohio attempted to prohibit free Negro migration by a constitutional provision in 1850. Illinois and Indiana, like Florida, adopted exclusion provisions in 1847 and 1851.

Despite the repeal of Ohio's 1804 and 1807 black laws in 1849, Negro exclusion remained a popular subject during the 1850's.[35] Peti-

---

[32] *Whig Almanac and United States Register, 1858* (New York, 1858), 62-63; (Madison) *Argus and Democrat,* July 21, Aug. 13, Sept. 5, 19, Oct. 1, 1857; (Madison) *Wisconsin State Journal,* Aug. 20, Sept. 4, 7, 1857; *Milwaukee Sentinel,* Nov. 5, 1857; Fishel, "Wisconsin and Negro Suffrage," 185-186.

[33] Shambaugh (ed.), *Fragments,* 115-116, 165; *Laws of Iowa, 1850-51* (Iowa City, 1851), Chap. 72.

[34] The increases in the respective states were: Ohio, 17,342 to 25,279; Indiana, 7,165 to 11,262; Illinois, 3,598 to 5,436. *1850 Census, Statistics,* 719, 781, 853.

[35] The repeal of the black laws was achieved because of an extremely complicated situation in the state legislature which gave the eleven Free Soil senators and representatives the balance of power. After a month of political maneuvering the Free Soilers agreed to support the Democratic party's state measures on

tions demanding a constitutional exclusion provision caused prolonged discussions during the 1850 constitutional convention. Exclusionists approved of the petitions, insisting that the framers of the 1802 constitution had intended Ohio "for the white man, and the white man only." William Sawyer, always in the front ranks when the Negro question was considered, spoke eloquently on the glories of exclusion as the only means of preventing the state from becoming a focal point for former slaves. The opposition of the delegates from the northern part of the state, however, forestalled the adoption of an exclusion article. Nevertheless, the matter did not end with the convention; three exclusion attempts were made in the state legislature during the 1850's. The first came one month after the repeal of the 1804 and 1807 laws. The Illinois black law of 1853 influenced the second reconsideration. Shortly after the Illinois act became a nationwide topic, a bill restricting Negro immigration was again introduced in the legislature, but it was pushed aside for more pressing matters. The last attempt in 1859 failed because the Republican majority in the judiciary committee refused to bring the proposal before the lower house.[36]

The exclusion hassle in Illinois began at the constitutional convention of 1847 when Benjamin Bond, from Clinton County in the central part of the state, proposed a resolution prohibiting the immigration of free Negroes. Delegates from the southern counties immediately came to Bond's aid, arguing that their constituents had left the South to escape the evil effects of slavery and the Negro. Southern Illinoisans, they maintained, preferred the society of white men and settled in the free states "to get rid of this intolerable nuisance." Strongly advocating exclusion, William Allen of Marion County declared that the Negro race was "good for nothing, either to the state, the church, or themselves"; they were idle and lazy and the people of his district wanted "to get rid of those there." Liberal delegates temporarily frustrated the

the condition that the Democrats back their proposal to repeal the black laws and to help them elect Salmon P. Chase to the U.S. Senate. More detailed coverage can be found in Theodore Clarke Smith, *The Liberty and Free Soil Parties in the Northwest* (New York, 1897), 92-97; Francis P. Weisenburger, *The Passing of the Frontier, 1825-1850* (Vol. III, *The History of the State of Ohio*, Columbus, 1941), 471-472. Far more titillating, however, are the newspaper accounts from January to March, 1849. See especially the *Ohio State Journal, Cleveland Plain Dealer,* and *Cincinnati Enquirer.*
[36] *Ohio Debates, 1850-51,* I, 28-29; II, 337-338, 598-599; *Ohio State Journal,* Mar. 7, 8, 1849; *African Repository,* XXIX (1853), 110-111; State of Ohio, *Senate Journal, 1858* (Columbus, 1858), 68, 79, 108, 282.

issue by insisting that the convention would be "shame[d] . . . in the face of the world" if it adopted an exclusion provision, and the people would be forced to reject the entire constitution to save the reputation of the state. Still the exclusionists could not be dissuaded, and they finally mustered enough support for the submission of a separate exclusion article along with the constitution to a popular referendum.[37]

Indianians justified exclusion by referring to a Kentucky law of 1850 which subjected any free Negro immigrating into the state or any emancipated slave remaining in the state to a five-year penitentiary sentence. "What is our situation in the State of Indiana?" cried one delegate, maintaining that the Kentucky law made the free states along the Ohio River receptacles for the Negroes from the slave states. "Now what I say is, that we should, in order to protect ourselves, enact stringent laws, or insert a clause in the new Constitution prohibiting the future emigration [sic] of blacks into this State." Relying solely on public sentiment, another delegate concluded "that a stop should be put to the immigration of negroes into our State, I believe to be the will of almost the entire people. I believe that there is no question on which the will of the people has been so clearly and definitely given, as on this." Such agitation produced Article XIII of the revised constitution which declared that after the adoption of the document, no Negro or mulatto could settle or enter the state, all contracts with Negroes were void, persons hiring or encouraging Negroes to settle in Indiana were subject to a $500 fine. Finally the article empowered the legislature to appropriate funds for the colonization of Negroes. As in Illinois, the article was submitted to a public referendum.[38]

The Illinois electorate approved the prohibitory clause by a vote of 60,585 to 15,903 on March 6, 1848. The results of the Indiana referendum, held in August, 1851, were more startling; Article XIII was approved by a vote of 113,628 to 21,873.[39]

---

[37] *Illinois Debates, 1847*, 201-203, 208, 218, 224-227, 856, 863; *Chicago Journal*, June 19, 1847; *Sangamo Journal*, July 1, 1847; (Springfield) *Illinois State Register*, June 26, Aug. 24, 26, 1847; Ameda Ruth King, "The Last Years of the Whig Party in Illinois, 1847 to 1856," *ISHST* (1925), 116.

[38] *Revised Laws of Kentucky, 1852* (Frankfort, 1852), 647; *Indiana Debates, 1850-51*, I, 247, 249, 445; II, 1406, 1586, 1931; Kettleborough, *Constitution Making in Indiana*, I, 360-362; Thornbrough, *Negro in Indiana*, 64.

[39] Pease (ed.), *Illinois Election Returns, 1818-1848*, 173-180; *Chicago Journal*, Mar. 30, 1848; (Indianapolis) *Indiana State Sentinel*, Sept. 18, 1851; (Indianapolis) *Indiana Statesman*, Sept. 3, 1851.

Opposition to the exclusion policies existed, but the referenda indicated that the majority of the people favored the propositions. On the other hand, approximately 5,000 men in each state were too apathetic about the exclusion provisions to vote on them. This situation occurred in Illinois because editors and politicians practically ignored the exclusion article in the pre-referendum campaign. The Democratic *Illinois State Register* in Springfield reported the provision without comment. Although the Whig editor in the same city opposed the Democratic "party constitution," he did not mention the exclusion article as one of his reasons. After the provision was adopted, he poetically wrote: "Sound the Loud trumpet 'oer Egypt's dark sea, The people have spoken, — and Egypt is free!" The only pre-election protest of note was written by a Peoria editor who clearly stated that while he favored discriminatory legislation against Negroes, he would not support the exclusion provision because it was a "gross outrage upon the rights of humanity. We do not speak as abolitionists, but we cannot consent to placing a human form below our cows & horses." Gershom Flagg, a contemporary, explained the lack of editorial comment: members of the convention, whether Democrats or Whigs, favored the constitution, and they used their influence with their political editors to advocate its acceptance, or if they could not do that, to "lie low & keep dark."[40]

Opposition to Article XIII in Indiana was fierce, but it came primarily from Free Soilers. The people of northern Indiana, Samuel Benton of Fort Wayne incorrectly presumed, could not possibly approve a constitution containing such a harsh provision against the Negro. The exclusion article would have failed had it been submitted as a separate measure and not with the constitution, wrote William Merrill of Indianapolis. Indiana politicians, however, realized that an exclusion policy would be successful. In his election campaign as a delegate to the convention, Higgins Lane was cheered when he advocated the adoption of an exclusion measure. Lane concluded "that . . . whether free negores [sic] or salves [sic] are a blessing or a curse[,] the Free States are determined they shall spread no farther." A resident of

---

[40] *Illinois State Register*, Sept. 3, 1847; *Sangamo Journal*, June 3, Sept. 11, 1847; *Illinois State Journal*, Mar. 16, 1848; *Peoria* (Illinois) *Weekly Democratic Press*, May 26, June 9, Nov. 3, 1847; Gershom Flagg MS article on the new constitution written for the *St. Louis Republican*, Jan., 1848; J. R. Stanford to Flagg, Mar. 12, 1848, Gershom Flagg Papers (Transcripts, Illinois Historical Survey).

Fort Wayne summarized the general attitude by writing that exclusion was not discussed among his acquaintances, but he was certain that the majority of them felt as he did: "Kentucky and other States, when the labor of their aged and superannuated Slaves ceased to be profitable . . . would gladly free them and send them over to our State, to become a charge on our free population. . . . To prevent such occurrances [sic], I would say it would be well [to adopt a measure] that will prevent them from emigrating [sic] to the State hereafter."[41]

Free Soil newspapers printed caustic comments against Article XIII. One remarked that the convention's declaration, "all men are created equal," really meant "all men are created equal — except niggers." A Free Soil editor in Centerville wrote that the "people of Indiana have voluntarily and gratuitously published to the world, through their fundamental law, that they are barbarians"; the adoption of the article was "a burning shame . . . even in a land of Hottentots." In a letter to the same editor, "Tobit" wondered how the people of Indiana could approve an exclusion provision and still "wish to be considered followers of the meek and lowly Jesus."[42] Scathing as these comments may be, they were few and far between.

Article XIII conveniently provided a means to attack the developing antislavery feeling. Both Whig and Democratic editors outside of Indiana took great delight in blaming antislavery Indianians for the provision and labeling them bigots. A Chillicothe, Ohio, editor charged that Indiana abolitionists, "by their officious and disgustful intermeddling," were responsible for the article. The Whig *Ohio State Journal* snidely remarked that even in Ohio Salmon P. Chase, then a Free Soil senator, was thrown into a "spasm of joy" over Indiana's exclusion provision. If the South freed its 3,000,000 slaves, another editor claimed, "and they should begin to arrive freely in the State of New York, we should expect that free soilers and abolitionists would be among the first to oppose them. Seward, Weed, Greeley & Co., would

---

[41] A. Harlan to William F. Jones, Feb. 24, 1850, William F. Jones Papers (Indiana State Library) ; Samuel Benton to Allen Hamilton, Dec. 27, 1850; P. Hoagland to Hamilton, Dec. 7, 1850, Allen Hamilton Papers (Indiana State Library) ; William M. Merrill to Hazen Merrill, Feb. 28, 1851, Hazen Merrill Papers (Indiana State Historical Society Library) ; Higgins Lane to General S. Stone, Oct. 17, 1849, Henry S. Lane Papers (Indiana State Historical Society Library).

[42] *New York Tribune*, Dec. 13, 1850, Feb. 17, 1851; *Indiana True Democrat*, Aug. 28, Sept. 4, 1851.

probably lead the van, [for] *the fact is, that in no part of the country is a large, free colored population wanted.*[43]

This line of attack against antislavery political groups, although rarely heard in 1850, became commonplace by 1860. Its purpose, of course, was to equate racial equality with antislavery sentiment. While numerous antislavery men objected to equal rights, many militant abolitionists or philanthropic groups, such as Quakers, were more liberal. The efforts of the abolitionists to improve the Negro's conditions, especially those of the Lane Seminary students, and the early attempts of Quakers to settle manumitted slaves in Ohio and Indiana, gave to the less informed white people the impression that persons opposed to the extension of slavery also favored full equality of the races. Therefore, Whigs and Democrats alike declared that the midwestern exclusion policies were reactions against Free Soil and abolitionist efforts to improve the Negro's status.

The most vocal advocate in favor of exclusion in Indiana was the editor of the *State Sentinel.* After the adoption of Article XIII, he kept prodding the legislature to pass implementing legislation. If the article were not enforced, he prophesied, the poorhouses of the state would soon be filled with Negro immigrants. In 1852 the lawmakers adopted a measure enforcing Article XIII but, for all practical purposes, it was a restatement of the article and caused very little comment.[44]

The exclusion provision of the 1847 Illinois Constitution was not implemented until 1853. The Illinois legislative sessions of 1849 and 1851 failed to enact an enforcement measure. This lack of action may have caused Illinois Negroes and abolitionists to presume that the lawmakers had become less rigid about anti-Negro restrictions. The Chicago Literary and Debating Society, a Negro organization, passed resolutions in December, 1852, requesting repeal of the law which prohibited them from testifying against a white person. Simultaneously abolitionists sent a petition with 3,000 signatures to the state legislature, requesting the repeal of the same restriction. However, under the leadership of John A. Logan, the lower house tabled the petition.[45]

---

[43] *Ohio State Journal,* Aug. 15, 1851; *Scioto Gazette,* Feb. 21, 1851; *New York Journal of Commerce,* n.d., in *Indiana State Sentinel,* Sept. 4, 1851.
[44] *Indiana State Sentinel,* Feb. 19, 22, Sept. 3, 1851; *The Revised Statutes of Indiana, 1852* (2 vols., Indianapolis, 1852), I, 375-376.
[45] State of Illinois, *House Journal, 1853* (Springfield, 1853), 5, 22-23; *Daily Alton* (Illinois) *Telegraph,* Jan. 31, 1853; *Illinois State Journal,* Jan. 1, 1853.

Always an aspiring politician, Logan even as an assemblyman revealed his knack for assuming the most advantageous political position. On January 29, 1853, solely to improve his political stature, Logan introduced "An Act to Prevent the Immigration of Free Negroes into This State."[46] Debate on the bill lasted for three days, during which time northern representatives attempted to nullify it by attaching amendments. Demanding that his bill "stand or fall upon its own merits or demerits," Logan fought all changes. Discussion reached such a pitch that one reporter remarked: "Not only abolitionism . . . but physiology, anatomy, and even theology" entered into the arguments. And only the Negro question could have raised such a discussion, he insisted. Notwithstanding the opposition, the bill passed the house by the overwhelming majority of 45 to 23 votes. The senate quickly passed it by a bare majority.[47]

The law, undoubtedly the most severe anti-Negro measure passed by a free state, stipulated that any person bringing a Negro or mulatto into Illinois, other than someone traveling through with his slaves, was liable to a fine of from $100 to $500 and a one-year prison sentence. Moreover, the act required the governor, if such a person was not a resident, to request his extradition to face charges and trial. Negroes entering and remaining in the state for ten days were to be tried for high misdemeanor. Conviction meant a fine of $50, payable immediately. If the fine could not be paid, the Negro's labor was to be publicly auctioned; the period of service was determined at the time of purchase. Any Negro punished under the act was to be apprehended again if he did not leave the state within ten days after his service ended. The fine was increased $50 for each subsequent offense.[48]

---

[46] A letter from William Parrish, Logan's law partner, clearly indicated the political basis of the act. Logan must have discussed the possibility of introducing the bill with Parrish because two weeks before Logan introduced the bill, Parrish wrote: "The move or resolution in relation to the immigration of free negroes into this state is one that will reflect credit and distinction. . . . The harder the fight on such a measure[,] the greater will be the distinction. . . . I have no fears but what we will be able to exert an influence in the political arena in Egypt sufficent [sic] for all practical purposes." Parrish to Logan, Jan. 16, 1853, John A. Logan Family Papers (Manuscript Division, Library of Congress).
[47] State of Illinois, House Journal, 1853, 67, 271, 356; State of Illinois, Senate Journal, 1853 (Springfield, 1853), 974-975; Alton Daily Morning Courier, Feb. 4, 1853; Illinois State Journal, Feb. 2, 8, 1853.
[48] Samuel Treat, Walter Scates, and Robert Blackwell (comps.), The Statutes of Illinois in Force, 1857 (2 vols., Chicago, 1858), II, 824-827.

An immediate reaction to the bill came from newspapers in all sections of the state regardless of political affiliation. Of the one hundred newspapers in Illinois, only two, the Democratic *McDonough Independent* and the Democratic *State Register,* favored the bill. In central Illinois, Bloomington's only newspaper (Whig) declared that "even down in 'Egypt' some of the papers are giving it all sorts of thunder." Its provisions were "utterly at variance with the dictates of justice and humanity," screamed a Peoria Whig editor, and Chicago Whigs demanded to know why "free negroes [were continually made] the scapegoat race for the sins of the round world." Taking the opportunity to severely scold the Democratically controlled legislature, the staunchly Whig *State Journal* insisted that political ambition produced the bill and that the legislators who voted for it did so for their own political advancement. The Whig *Alton Telegraph* declared that the members of the legislature were no better than the Spartans who were accused of keeping down the Helots by mass murder. Even the editor of the *Ottawa Free Trader,* an avid Democrat, wrote: "We should like to see the man that would mount the auctioneer's block in this town and sell a freeman to the highest bidder, and we should like to see the bidder." The Democratic, and later Copperhead, *Jonesboro Gazette* wondered how long the people "of this hitherto 'free state' [would] suffer this shameful enaction to disgrace their statute book?"[49]

Although Illinois editors bitterly condemned the black law, most of them did not oppose Negro exclusion. The *Chicago Democratic Press* abhorred the stringency of the act but approved of its object. The *Quincy Whig* admitted the power of the legislature to prohibit Negro

[49] *Quincy* (Illinois) *Whig,* Apr. 15, 1853; *Bloomington* (Illinois) *Intelligencer,* Mar. 16, Apr. 20, 1853; *Peoria* (Illinois) *Weekly Republican,* Feb. 25, Mar. 11, 1853; *Illinois State Journal,* Feb. 15, 1853; *Chicago Journal,* Feb. 9, 1853; *Daily Alton Telegraph,* Feb. 28, 1853; *Ottawa Free Trader,* n.d., in *Daily Alton Telegraph,* Mar. 5, 1853; *Jonesboro Gazette,* n.d., *Alton Daily Morning Courier,* Apr. 14, 1853. The black law was also bitterly denounced by editors outside of Illinois. Horace Greeley thought it was "punishment enough" for Negroes "to live among such cruel, inhospitable beings" as the residents of Illinois, let alone have such a law inflicted on them. The *Charleston Mercury* offered to publish periodically the prices of Negroes so Illinoisans would know how much to pay for them. A small Texas newspaper printed the most caustic and probably the most truthful comment: "Illinois is honest. She stands no longer behind the veil of false philanthropy. She wants no free Negroes to pour out her sympathetic tears upon — and plainly says so." (Washington, D.C.) *National Era,* Mar. 17, 1853; *New York Tribune,* Mar. 7, 1853; *Charleston Mercury,* n.d., *Henderson* (Rusk County, Texas) *Flag,* n.d., both in *Alton Daily Morning Courier,* Mar. 1, 22, Apr. 5, May 28, 1853.

immigration, stating that the members of the legislature were not properly fulfilling their duty "if they neglected to pass effectual laws" to enforce the constitutional provision. The main objection of most editors to the black law was not that it excluded Negroes but rather that it did not contain provisions to prevent slaveholders from coming into Illinois, paying a Negro's fine, and taking him South into slavery.[50]

The exclusion laws of Indiana and Illinois were not effective.[51] True, the number of Negroes in Indiana declined slightly, by 166, during the 1850's. This was not due to Article XIII but rather to the fact that Indiana lagged behind the rest of the Northwest in population growth during the ante-bellum period. The lack of industry and the general impression that the swampy grasslands in the central part of the state were not conducive to agriculture caused settlers to seek more favorable areas. In Illinois the Negro population increased from 5,436 to 7,628 between 1850 and 1860, and this growth occurred primarily in the northern section of the state.[52] Chicago had by 1860 surpassed Cincinnati as the commercial center in the Northwest. Negroes still sought employment in the Ohio city, but Chicago offered greater advantages. For fugitives the lake city was a better location because escape to Canada was easier. Furthermore, the people in northern Illinois, most of whom had opposed the 1853 law, had little inclination to enforce it, and Negroes in the area were safe from being punished for violating its provisions.

Colonization of the Negro in Africa, going hand in hand with exclusion, was often portrayed as a magnanimous undertaking to improve the lot of the Negro. To the degree that colonization efforts encouraged slaveholders to liberate their chattels, this concept is partly substantiated. But in the Old Northwest, where colonization propaganda was directed solely at free Negroes, its benevolence can surely be ques-

---

[50] *Chicago Democratic Press*, n.d., in *Alton Daily Morning Courier*, Mar. 1, 12, 1853; *Quincy Whig*, Feb. 21, Mar. 5, 25, 1853.
[51] Article XIII and the 1853 black law were enforced on a number of occasions. In 1864 the Illinois Supreme Court declared the 1853 law constitutional. See Gustave P. Koerner, *Memoirs of Gustave P. Koerner, 1809-1896*, ed. Thomas J. McCormack (2 vols., Cedar Rapids, Iowa, 1909), II, 31; "Pardon of Six Men of the Crime of Being Negroes," *ISHST* (1910), 50; James N. Gridley, "A Case Under an Illinois Black Law," *ISHSJ*, IV (Jan., 1912), 401-425; *Nelson v. the People*, 33 *Ill.* (2 *Ewell*) 398 (1864); Thornbrough, *Negro in Indiana*, 131, *et passim*.
[52] *1850 Census, Statistics*, 719, 781; U.S. Bureau of the Census, *Eighth Census of the United States: 1860, Population* (Washington, D.C., 1864), 34, 111.

tioned. Whereas the exclusion laws attempted to prevent Negro immigration, both Negrophobes and antislavery men considered colonization an excellent means of removing the existing Negro population.

The colonization movement in the Old Northwest fell into two distinct phases. The first began in the mid-1820's and continued for approximately ten years. From its inception, early colonization supporters declared the effort would reduce the Negro population. This type of propaganda caused the movement to receive effective support in Ohio where anti-Negro sentiment was most acute in the 1820's. "The people of this state are deeply interested in the success of this society," declared a Columbus editor in 1827, because too many Negroes were moving into the state where "they are worse than drones to society." Presuming that colonization was the only recourse for Ohio to free herself from the burden of supporting the Negro race, he urged the legislature to "assist in this benevolent measure."[53]

Isaac Newton Blackford, an Indiana Supreme Court judge, ominously warned in 1829 that "a low, ignorant, degraded multitude of free blacks" soon would swarm into Indiana unless the colonization movement received support. "Our black population adds nothing to the strength, and little to the wealth of the nation," the Indiana Colonization Society reported several years later. "Let them be removed and their places be supplied with intelligent freemen, and we venture to say that a saving equal to the cost of their removal would be gained in the expense of courts of justice and poor houses." In his address to organize the Illinois Colonization Society at Vandalia in 1830, Cyrus Edwards flatly stated that the laws of the southern states forced free Negroes to find new homes. "Illinois does not now have too many negroes, but can't you see the effect if the other states pass laws?" he asked. "All the negroes will come here." Describing Negroes as a "dangerous and baneful influence" on the white people around them and insisting that no matter how great their industry or how abundant their wealth and attainments, Edwards declared that Negroes could never achieve equality or "even a familiar intercourse with . . . society!"[54]

---

[53] Philip J. Stadenraus, *The African Colonization Movement, 1816-1865* (New York, 1961), 177-180, 182-183; *Ohio State Journal*, July 12, Dec. 7, 1827.
[54] (Indianapolis) *Indiana Journal*, Nov. 12, 1829, Jan. 5, 1833; Cyrus Edwards, *An Address Delivered at the State House in Vandalia, on the Subject of Forming a State Colonization Society, Auxiliary to the American Colonization Society* (Jacksonville, Illinois, 1831), 9-19; (Vandalia) *Illinois Intelligencer*, Mar. 19, 1831.

Despite successes, however, the early colonization movement waned in the 1830's. The decline was due, in part, to the withdrawal of midwestern abolitionists and Quakers from the effort. John D. Russ of Indiana, strongly criticizing abolitionists for their increasing lack of support, declared that they were indifferent about free Negroes and only concerned about the slave. If abolitionists "offered their all in the cause" of colonization, Russ concluded, the South might follow their example.[55]

The second phase of colonization activity in the Old Northwest, beginning in the mid-1840's, was stimulated by the increase in racial enmity. In Illinois the new interest was revealed by D. J. Pinckney during the constitutional convention of 1847: "I am in favor of removing [Negroes] not only from this State, but from all the States." Alexander Stevenson carried the argument further in Indiana, declaring that the Negro was physically and mentally inferior and that the only remedy to rid the white American of the evil of the colored race "is to be found in colonizing the negroes in their native Africa." Stevenson considered it impolitic for "a refined and superior class to keep in their midst an uncultivated, degraded and inferior race." To encourage colonization, white people should continually raise the cry of *"emigrate, emigrate* to your native country."[56]

People in Michigan, Iowa, and Wisconsin, unaffected by the first phase of the colonization movement, became interested in the possibilities offered by the revived scheme. Reviewing the colonization activities in the Ohio River states, a Michigan resident, in 1851, asked why Michigan's Negroes were not encouraged to emigrate. If they appealed to the white citizens for aid, their request would not be ignored because the whites did not want Negroes as residents. "When [Negroes] come to know the truth," he wrote, "they will take that forward step toward a great and happy destiny, to which they are invited by every inducement." In 1855 a Wisconsin State Colonization Society was formed, but it accomplished little except to pass resolutions requesting legislative appropriations and recommending an organized transportation system to make colonization effectual.[57] Colonization sentiment

---

[55] Thomas E. Drake, *Quakers and Slavery in America* (New Haven, 1950), 139; Litwack, *North of Slavery*, 27 *et passim*; John D. Russ to Henry Clay, Dec. 22, 1838, William Henry Smith Collection (Indiana State Historical Society Library).

[56] *Illinois Debates, 1847*, 107; *Indiana Debates, 1850-51*, I, 247-248, 443, 448.

[57] *Detroit Free Press*, Feb. 26, 1851; *African Repository*, XXXI (1855), 144.

this far north, however, lagged. For one thing, the project cost money and many Wisconsin and Michigan advocates could not afford to be or hesitated at being too generous. Nor was the influx of free Negroes, except in Detroit, a matter of overwhelming public concern in those states.

Iowa's short-lived and unsuccessful colonization society simply agitated for diplomatic recognition of Liberia, hoping that recognition would encourage more Negroes to emigrate. The society began in 1855, but the organization remained weak because it had no well-regulated agency to collect funds and disseminate information. In January, 1857, a statewide meeting was held at Iowa City; thereafter the society disintegrated. The impetus for the organization was its anti-Negro bias which was revealed by J. C. Hall, the principal speaker at the 1857 meeting. He opened his speech with the supposition that the Negro had been considered repulsive and inferior during the entire scope of written history and only "wild and deluded fanaticism" encouraged moral, social, or political equality. "They are here; they can never have a home or a country here," he declared. "As long as they remain, they must be outcasts and inferiors. They can have no aspirations [except] as the objects of an unwelcome, hesitating and noisy charity." Hall insisted that sending the American Negro across the Atlantic would improve the Negro race in Africa, for the Negro in America had been elevated simply by his association with the whites and his introduction to the Christian religion. Iowans, he concluded, favored giving the Negro a home as long as that home was not in Iowa.[58]

The most extensive colonization propaganda during the second phase of the movement occurred in Ohio. It began when various philanthropists promised to donate $11,000 to an "Ohio in Africa" project in 1849. The American Colonization Society immediately exerted its influence in the affair by creating a "Committee of Correspondence for Ohio" to publicize the project and by appointing David Christy, the state agent and, later, the author of the phrase "cotton is king," to memorialize the state legislature for financial support. Christy zealously undertook his assignment. Pointing out to the legislators that there had been a continuous stream of Negro migration into the Old Northwest, he boldly announced that "the Ohio Valley [would] soon become the home of a large proportion of the free colored population." In an

---

[58] *African Repository*, XXXIII (1857), 119-121; *Annual Report of the Colonization Society of the State of Iowa* (Iowa City, 1857), 7-11.

elaborate colonization plan Christy predicted that if the legislature would prohibit the further immigration of free Negroes and appropriate enough money to send 600 Negroes a year to Africa, the state would soon be devoid of Negroes. Stressing *"that a separation from the whites* [was] *essential to the prosperity of the colored man, and that colonization at some point* [offered] to him his only hope of deliverance," Christy insisted that the abolitionist plan of emancipating Negroes and granting them equal rights was unworkable.[59]

The immediate impact of Christy's remarks produced a bill which appropriated $25 for each Negro, not to exceed 50 a year, who would emigrate to Liberia. Upon reflection, however, the measure was defeated because the state was in debt and the bill did not provide an effective means for preventing Negroes from other states from moving into Ohio and taking advantage of the offer. The legislature contented itself by passing a resolution that the federal government set aside a part of the Mexican cession for Negro colonization. One editor thought that the resolution was not as satisfactory as "Ohio in Africa" but at least the lawmakers had made a "sensible move" to dispose of the vexing Negro question. G. M. Gibson criticized a similar resolution passed by the Indiana legislature because it would give to Negroes land for which white men had fought.[60]

The renewed colonization effort in Indiana, beginning in the mid-1840's, was characterized by strong prejudicial attitudes. The Williamsport Literary Society, debating the proposition that all men are created equal, decided the question in the negative inasmuch as "all men" included Negroes. By 1845 Sunday school teachers throughout Indiana encouraged Negro children to urge colonization on their parents. However, one Sunday school teacher reported in despair that it was impossible to teach young Negroes the advantages of colonization for "their brain pans seem full of starch and water." Such sentiment proved advantageous to Benjamin Kavanagh when he arrived in the state to revitalize the colonization movement in December, 1845. In his first address, Kavanagh declared that the Negro was an outcast and that colonization was the only scheme promising to rid Indiana of its

---

[59] (Cincinnati) *Cist's Weekly Advertiser*, Jan. 3, 1849; David Christy, *A Lecture on African Colonization, Delivered in the Hall of the House of Representatives of Ohio, January 19, 1849* (Cincinnati, 1849), 22 pp. — see especially 25-29; *African Repository*, XXV (1849), 69, 323, 362.

[60] *African Repository*, XXVI (1850), 126, 166; *Cist's Weekly Advertiser*, Apr. 14, 1849; G. M. Gibson to Henry S. Lane, Mar. 6, 1860, Lane Papers.

Negroes. On the whole, Indianians regarded the new effort favorably. Some realized the true meaning of the revitalization and Kavanagh's speech. For example, the author of a letter in the *Indiana Freeman* wrote that he understood the citizens of Indianapolis had recently met "to exhume the Society for manufacturing *prejudice against color.*"[61]

The Indiana legislature revealed its interest in the renewed development by passing a resolution in February, 1848, which praised the effort. During the next session a house committee report threatened that internecine warfare would erupt if the two races were not separated by colonization, but the lawmakers rejected a request for monetary aid from the state society on the ground that they lacked authority to make such an appropriation. Reassuring the legislators that they did, Governor Joseph Wright encouraged them "to look into this subject in the right light, and in the proper spirit." Other states had their own settlements in Liberia, and Wright felt that Indiana should have hers. After the adoption of Article XIII of the 1851 constitution, which also provided that fines collected in violation of the article were to be paid into a colonization fund, the governor became more explicit. Informing the legislators that "it is very desirable that the subject of colonization should receive . . . attention," Wright declared that the cause of colonization was advancing and it was important for Indiana to extend her influence, no matter how limited her contribution might be.[62]

Pressure was exerted on the Democratic legislature from other sources. The *Sentinel,* the Democratic organ in Indianapolis, printed numerous editorials in support of colonization. Declaring some sympathy for the Negro, the editor acknowledged that there was a "gulf of separation, which cannot be passed." For that reason, colonization was in accord with justice and humanity. As long as Negroes remained in the United States, they would have to contend with the prejudices of

[61] *African Repository,* XXXI (1855), 23; *The Counties of Warren, Benton, Jasper and Newton, Indiana: Historical and Biographical* (Chicago, 1883), 129; Edward S. Abdy, *Journal of a Residence and Tour in the United States of North America from April, 1833, to October, 1834* (3 vols., London, 1835), II, 365-366; Betty Bates to Meg W. Moore, Sept. 11, 1853, Meg W. Moore Papers (Indiana State Library); *Eleventh Annual Report of the Indiana Colonization Society, 1845* (Indianapolis, 1846), 20-27; *Indiana Freeman,* Jan. 24, 1846, in *Indiana State Sentinel,* Apr. 2, 1846.
[62] *Laws of Indiana, 1847-1848* (Indianapolis, 1848), 111-112; State of Indiana, *House Journal, 1849-1850* (Indianapolis, 1850), 598-602; State of Indiana, *House Journal, 1850-1851* (Indianapolis, 1851), 39; *Indiana State Sentinel,* Dec. 4, 1851.

color and caste which the white man held for them. Colonization, he finally stated, was a subject "we can enter into with heart and soul, and one upon which we love to dwell [because] they must go." Governor Wright received numerous letters in favor of colonization and undoubtedly the legislators were made aware of their contents. Moreover, James Mitchell, a Negro Methodist minister and the new agent of the state society, constantly requested money and presented elaborate schemes to the lawmakers. Mitchell also played upon their prejudices, insisting that the United States should remain a "pure republic," that there was no salvation for another race when it came into conflict with the Anglo-Saxon race, and that if the Negro race remained, it could be nothing other than a class of peasants excluded from white society. Mitchell's *coup de grâce* was to announce that the region around Grand Cape Mount, about fifty miles from Monrovia, could be purchased for $5,000 and established as the "Indiana Colony."[63]

In 1853 the lawmakers capitulated. They revoked the charter of the state colonization society and replaced it with a state board of colonization, consisting of the governor, the secretary of state, and the state auditor. The governor received the authority to promote colonization and to supervise the work of the agent of the board, Mitchell. In addition, $5,000 and all fines collected in violation of Article XIII were appropriated to colonize Negroes who were residents of the state before the 1851 constitution became effective. Of the money appropriated, $3,000 was set aside to purchase Grand Cape Mount. Each Negro who emigrated was rewarded with a grant of 100 acres of land and $50. The legislature appropriated another $5,000 during each of the next two sessions, and in 1855 Governor Wright recommended that the annual appropriation be continued on an indefinite basis.[64]

---

[63] *Indiana State Sentinel,* Feb. 5, July 3, 1851, May 13, 1853; (Indianapolis) *Indiana State Journal,* July 1, 1852; State of Indiana, *House Journal, 1851* (Indianapolis, 1851), 1021-24; State of Indiana, *House Journal, 1852* (Indianapolis, 1852), 397; James Mitchell, *Answer of the Agent of the Indiana Colonization Society to the Resolution of Inquiry on the Subject of African Colonization* (Indianapolis, 1852), 5-6, 18; in the Wright papers see especially S. T. Ensey to Wright, Feb. 25, 1854, Joseph A. Wright Papers (Indiana State Library).

[64] *Indiana State Sentinel,* Feb. 24, Mar. 21, 1853; State of Indiana, *House Journal, 1853* (Indianapolis, 1853), 556-557, 570-571; *Laws of the State of Indiana, Passed at the Thirty-Seventh Session of the General Assembly* (Indianapolis, 1852), 23; *African Repository,* XXIX (1853), 129-130; **XXXI**

The *African Repository,* the organ of the national colonization society, and Indiana colonization supporters lauded the effort but failed to note that it was unsuccessful. Mitchell miscalculated the amount of money needed to purchase Grand Cape Mount. The natives demanded more money than he estimated, and he had neither the money nor the authority to pay a larger amount. During 1853 and 1854 a total of 47 Negroes took advantage of the law. The following year 50 more indicated that they were willing to emigrate but later refused to go. From that time, no Negroes left Indiana under the auspices of the law to settle in Africa. In 1859 several Negroes filed applications, but the state finances were so badly strained that they were told to wait until money could be found for the purpose. Of the $15,000 appropriated, only $5,063 was spent. The American Colonization Society received $3,000 to purchase Grand Cape Mount and the remaining sum was expended mainly in salaries.[65]

Some colonization supporters contended that the Indiana colonization effort failed because of the abolitionists. Mitchell assumed this, writing that abolitionists were determined to secure the emancipation of slaves in the South and to force Negroes into white society. Therefore, they discouraged Indiana's Negroes from colonizing. Another colonization supporter, L. L. Hintner, presumed as much and added that abolitionist fanaticism would lead to miscegenation. The abolitionist demand for political equality was a disgraceful step, wrote Hintner, which would "make a baboon his equal" and would cause a mixture "of our children's blood."[66]

(1855), 145; *Thirty-Sixth Annual Report of the American Colonization Society, 1853* (Washington, D.C., 1853), 10.

[65] *Report of the Agent of the State Board of Colonization of the State of Indiana for 1853* (Indianapolis, 1853), 9; *Report . . . 1855* (Indianapolis, 1855), 6; *Report . . . 1857* (Indianapolis, 1857), 333-335; *Report . . . 1859* (Indianapolis, 1859), 4.

[66] James Mitchell, *Letters on the Relation of the White and African Races in the United States, Showing the Necessity for the Colonization of the Latter* (Springfield, Illinois, 1860), 6-7; L. L. Hintner to Elisha Embree, Apr. 4, 1849, Elisha Embree Papers (Indiana State Library). It does not fall within the scope of this book to discuss completely the complex question of why the midwestern colonization movement failed. Interested readers should see Stadenraus, *Colonization Movement;* Louis Mehlinger, "The Attitude of the Free Negro Toward African Colonization," *JNH,* I (July, 1916), 276-301; Howard H. Bell, "A Survey of the Negro Convention Movement, 1830-1861" (unpublished Ph.D. dissertation, Northwestern University, 1953). A shorter analysis is found in August Meier and Elliott Rudwick, *From Plantation to Ghetto: An Interpretive History of American Negroes* (New York, 1966), 95-101.

Negroes watched with dismay this procession of events meant to restrict or exclude them or to encourage them to leave the country. Augustus Washington, noting the midwestern restrictive laws, wrote that his race had been a "political football" since the founding of the United States. Political parties used the Negro question to gain votes, but no matter which party won the elections the Negroes were "the losers." Whites openly declared the moral and intellectual inferiority of the Negro race, and it was this idea, Washington presumed, more than their humanitarian ideals that prompted their antislavery sentiment. John Kirk, an abolitionist, asked one of his Negro friends if he would not rather emigrate to Africa where he would be beyond the reach of the numerous restrictions. The Negro replied, "I would die first, before I would leave the land of my birth. I will stay and fight it out, as long as whites look down upon me I can look up to them."[67]

The white people in the Old Northwest also watched this process which further imbued race prejudice and attempted to confine the Negro to the South. And herein lies the importance of the whole procedure, for it was the people of the Old Northwest or those slowly pushing through the region who became the principal settlers of the Great Plains and the Pacific Northwest. They absorbed and transferred midwestern ideals and sentiments. Bombarded with antagonistic statements about Negroes from lawmakers and editors, requested to vote for or against restrictive measures, and faced with an almost constant agitation against the expansion of slavery, these pioneers pushed westward with an increased determination to keep the Negro, free or slave, out of the new lands. In 1850 an observant Indianian surmised as much when he wrote: "The 'Negro Question' is one that has engaged the attention of American[s] for the past few years . . . and is likely to be the Subject of continued discussion, for a few years at least, throughout the country."[68]

---

[67] Augustus Washington to William McLain, July 3, 1853, in Carter G. Woodson (ed)., *The Mind of the Negro as Reflected in Letters Written During the Crisis, 1800-1860* (Washington, D.C., 1926), 135-140; John Kirk to "Brother" Calvin, Mar. 13, 1853, John Kirk Letter Books (MSS, Chicago Historical Society).
[68] P. Hoagland to Allen Hamilton, Dec. 6, 1850, Hamilton Papers.

In Eldorado

Early American settlers in California described the small number of Negroes there as a "mixture of every color, description and grade." According to accounts, white Californians and Indians accepted Negroes as equal individuals before 1848 and even intermarriage among the three groups was not frowned upon.[1] This situation quickly changed, however, with the arrival of large numbers of Americans after 1848. Prejudice against Negroes resulted in the incorporation of the voting and militia restrictions, so common in the Middle West, into the California Constitution of 1849. Negrophobe delegates at the constitutional convention, mainly from the mining districts, succeeded in securing an exclusion provision but following a change of opinion it was withdrawn. Negro exclusion remained a popular subject with the state legislature until 1852; thereafter, sentiment against Negroes became less pronounced due to the more weighty problem of Chinese immigration. Although anti-Negro feeling remained strong, the Orientals received the brunt of racial enmity for the next several years.

Noticeable anti-Negro prejudice in California was at first predominant in the mining regions where slaveholders and free Negroes, like other early immigrants, sought wealth. The slaveholders, coming in groups with their slaves, remained together in the mining areas; free Negroes converged on certain locales and cooperated in their mining efforts. So numerous were free Negroes in one mining section along the American River that it was nicknamed "Nigger Bar." Moreover, the concentration of slaves and free Negroes in specific areas gave the impression that there was a large Negro population in the mining regions. Yet, only about one-third of California's 962 Negroes lived in

---

[1] *New York Tribune*, Apr. 5, 1844; John Walton Caughey (ed.), *The Jacob Y. Stover Narrative: Southwest from Salt Lake City in 1849* (San Francisco, 1937), 177.

the mining districts in 1850. The number of slaves is unknown, however, because the census did not differentiate between free and slave Negroes.[2]

For an inexplicable reason, white miners thought Negroes were "proverbially lucky" in discovering gold fields. The stories of their good fortune spread east and, as a result, several New York merchants provided travel expenses for Negroes who would prospect in gold for them. Southerners also took advantage of the Negro's rumored luck. Thomas Gilman of Tennessee allowed one of his slaves to leave for California provided the Negro would pay for his freedom in gold. The slave met his original obligation so quickly that Gilman continued to extort money from him. Another slave's intuition about the location of a large gold deposit enabled the Negro and his master to acquire a $20,000 fortune in a short time. William Manney's four slaves panned $4,000 worth of gold in one week.[3] Slaves, moreover, served in other capacities, usually as domestic workers, to acquire money for their masters. One of William Marmaduke's slaves worked with Marmaduke in the mines while the other was employed as a cook. Marmaduke informed his wife that if he continued to accumulate large amounts of money with the help of his two slaves, he would return home in five months a very rich man.[4]

Independent miners considered slave labor unfair competition no matter how valuable it was for the master. Walter Colton noted, while traveling through the mining districts, that white miners refused to work among slaves. The miners were not concerned about "slavery in the abstract," Colton wrote, "or as it exists in other communities; not one in ten cares a button for its abolition, nor the Wilmot Proviso either; all they look at is their own position; they must themselves swing

[2] *1850 Census, Statistics*, 968-969.
[3] *New York Tribune*, Nov. 21, 1849; W. Sherman Savage, "The Negro on the Mining Frontier," *JNH*, XXX (Jan., 1945), 32; J. D. Borthwick, *Three Years in California* (London, 1857), 163, 165; David Cosad, "Journal of a Trip to California by the Overland Route and Life in the Gold Diggings During 1849-1850," MS (California Historical Society Library), Aug. 11, 1849 entry.
[4] Daniel B. Wood, *Sixteen Months in the Gold Diggings* (New York, 1851), 32; Marmaduke to his wife, Mar. 6, 1850, William D. Marmaduke Papers (typewritten, California Historical Society Library). Some slaveholders in California voluntarily freed their slaves. District court records for San Diego County reveal that James R. Holman indentured his slaves, stipulating that they were free to go where they wished when their indenture period ended. *History of San Diego County, California* (San Francisco, 1883), 70.

the pick, and they won't swing it by the side of negro slaves." California, to most of them, was a "new world, where they [had] a right to shape and settle things in their own way," and this did not include competing with slave labor. During the constitutional convention of 1849 a delegate from the mining region, bitterly complaining about the presence of both slaves and free Negroes at the mines, insisted that miners were intelligent and respectable people, and they would not dig with Africans: "No, sir, they would leave this country first." Although industrious miners did not regard their labor as undignified, it was degrading to "swing a pick side by side with the negro," another delegate argued. Bands of Negroes, slave or free, he maintained, created "a monopoly of the worst sort." Slave labor shunted the profits of the mines into the pockets of single individuals, and free Negroes, by cooperating with each other, acquired larger fortunes than individual white miners.[5] The speaker exaggerated his point in order to sway his audience. A few Negroes became rich from mining but the majority did not. Actually, both delegates seemed unaware that free Negroes were merely continuing their stateside living pattern. Faced with prejudice and restrictions, Negroes in the East were forced into ghetto areas; Negroes who migrated to the West Coast simply re-established this pattern.

The resentment against slave labor led, in a few recorded instances, to acts of near violence. Early in 1850 nonslaveholding miners in a southern mining region drove the slaves out of the area. When Thomas Green and several other Texans arrived with their fifteen slaves at Rose's Bar and staked out claims for themselves and their slaves, they immediately encountered opposition. At a mass meeting the nonslaveholding prospectors protested that the Negroes' claims violated the federal land laws, which forbade Negroes from acquiring public land, and they passed a resolution stating that "no slave or negro should own claims or even work in the mines." Informing Green and his companions that the mines were for "white men, *only,*" the miners demanded the removal of the Negroes. Following the Texans' refusal to leave, the nonslaveholders held another meeting. This time they notified the Texans that their slaves would be forcibly expelled from the area if

---

[5] Walter Colton, *Three Years in California* (New York, 1860), 374; J. Ross Browne, *Report of the Debates in the Convention of California, on the Formation of the State Constitution, in September and October, 1849* (Washington, D.C., 1850), 144, 333.

they remained. Evidently the second threat was effective because the Texans left.[6]

Free Negroes in territorial California encountered restrictions similar to those found in the East. In the larger mining towns and in San Francisco special rooming houses, hotels, and restaurants were established for them. In areas where Negroes were less prominent, they were permitted to use the same facilities as the white people but could not share the same rooms or eat at the same tables with white men. Saloonkeepers catered to Negroes but segregated them at their own tables or at their own section of the bar. Independent gamblers and gambling houses openly encouraged Negroes to gamble because their "proverbial luck" in finding gold did not follow them to the gaming tables.[7] On the whole, it appears that white Americans in California did not object to associating with Negroes if the association was monetarily advantageous.

The questions of slavery and the residence of free Negroes became open issues when Californians established their state government in 1849. Mass meetings, which preceded the constitutional convention, passed numerous resolutions regarding the Negro. Some demanded the prohibition of slavery and others called for a constitutional restriction against the immigration of free Negroes. The opposition to slavery was most intense in the mining districts, but R. G. Gilbert, editor of the *Alta California,* feared that the desire for statehood in these districts might cause the miners to become tools in the hands of the small but vocal proslavery element who talked of obstructing the formation of a free state government. On the other hand, the antislavery element in San Francisco declared that it would not be intimidated and proposed the creation of a separate state, including the city and the surrounding area, if the future state constitution permitted Negro servitude.[8]

San Franciscans also ardently objected to the residence of free Negroes. Whether or not an accretion in the Negro population was responsible for their attitude cannot be determined. The 1850 census for

---

[6] *History of San Diego County,* 70; Allen B. Sherman (ed.), "Sherman Was There: The Recollections of Major Edwin A. Sherman," *CHSQ,* XXIII (Dec., 1944), 351.

[7] Borthwick, *Three Years in California,* 165.

[8] (San Francisco) *Daily Alta California,* Jan. 11, 1849; *New York Tribune,* Sept. 17, 25, Nov. 12, 15, 1849.

California was inaccurate and no statistics were given for San Francisco. Nevertheless, the editor of the *Californian* declared, "We desire only a white population in California." Although he "dearly loved" the Union and wanted California to be part of it, he preferred complete independence from the United States unless Congress approved the prohibition of both slavery and "free Blacks." Because he had left the slave states to escape competition with slave labor and association with Negroes, the editor announced that he strongly opposed the presence of Negroes, free or slave. Agreeing with the *Californian,* Samuel Brannan of the *California Star* wrote that any type of Negro labor would drive away the "sober and industrious middle class" because it was not respectable for white men to work with Negroes. Inasmuch as the majority of the people opposed the presence of Negroes, Brannan predicted that both slavery and free Negroes would be excluded from the future state.[9]

Local sentiment and newspaper agitation caused these questions to play an important role in the election for delegates to the constitutional convention. When Brigadier General Bennett Riley, the local military commander, approved of the election, he recommended that all men over twenty-one be allowed to vote. The San Francisco district refused to accept his suggestion. The town council had previously decided that only white men could vote in municipal elections and the district adopted that ruling. Although the general anti-Negro attitude in the other districts would indicate that Negroes did not participate in the elections, evidence to prove the fact is lacking.

On the whole, the elections proceeded without incident. While the mining districts had difficulty finding men who were willing to stop temporarily the search for gold and devote time to the duties of a delegate, miners insisted that any candidate accepting a nomination must advocate the prohibition of slavery. A mass meeting at Mormon Island specifically resolved that slave labor was too competitive to be tolerated and that any candidate not pledging himself to prohibition should not be elected. Candidates from the Los Angeles district were required to give similar pledges but for a different reason. The majority of the Americans in the district, "although Southern men, were positive that [they] wanted no slavery. [They] had enough of a variety of

---

[9] (San Francisco) *Californian*, Mar. 5, 1849; (San Francisco) *California Star*, Mar. 25, 1848.

races, and the character of the country was not favorable to any but free labor."[10]

Negro exclusion was the only topic that produced prolonged debate during the constitutional convention meeting at Monterey in September, 1849. Apparently, the delegates unanimously agreed to accept the same constitutional restrictions found against free Negroes in the Middle West. Without opposition or debate, Negroes were debarred from voting and excluded from the militia. The delegates also unanimously approved the slavery prohibition clause copied from the recently framed Iowa Constitution.[11] Some delegates from the slave states fa-

---

[10] *Daily Alta California*, Jan. 4, June 14, 1849; Samuel H. Willey, "Personal Memorandum," MS (Bancroft Library), 122, 127; U.S. Congress, House of Representatives, *House Executive Documents*, 31 Cong., 1 Sess., No. 59 (ser. no. 577), 6; Cardinal Goodwin, *The Establishment of State Government in California, 1846-1850* (New York, 1914), 110; Benjamin David Wilson, "Observations of Early Days in California and New Mexico," MS (Bancroft Library), 110.
[11] Browne, *California Debates*, 70; Merrill G. Burlingame, "The Contribution of Iowa to the Formation of the State Government of California in 1849," *IJHP*, XXX (Apr., 1932), 189; *Constitution of the State of California, 1849* (San Francisco, 1850), Art. II, Sec. 1. Slavery continued to exist after 1849, however, chiefly because white settlers did not demand the enforcement of the prohibition article and because many slaves were unaware that they could claim their freedom. Moreover, the prohibition of slavery did not discourage further attempts to introduce it. In December, 1851, James Gadsden of South Carolina wrote to Thomas J. Green, a California state senator, suggesting that the legislature pass a law permitting the establishment of a slave colony in southern California. Simultaneously, 1,218 people in Florida and South Carolina sent a petition to the California legislature, requesting permission to settle in the state with their slaves. These requests came at the same time that southern Californians were agitating for a division of the state because of unequal legislative representation, unequal taxation, and the lack of internal improvements in their area. Antidivisionists equated the requests, but editors in California and correspondents of eastern newspapers found little evidence that the division demands and the slaveholders' requests were connected. The editor of the *Los Angeles Star* objected to the rumors that division was being advocated to introduce slavery, declaring, "that ol Mare's nest — Slavery in Southern California — was constantly being raked over" in the northern part of the state in order to defeat division. The legislatures of 1852 and 1853 rejected bills for conventions to discuss a division. Succeeding legislatures adopted measures eliminating the complaints of the southern Californians, and by the late 1850's a referendum for a convention to consider division was defeated. Clyde A. Duniway, "Slavery in California After 1848," *AHAAR* (1905), I, 244; James Gadsden to Thomas J. Green, Dec. 7, 1851, in John C. Parish (ed.), "A Project for a California Slave Colony in 1851," *HHLB*, VIII (Oct., 1935), 173-175; *Daily Alta California*, Aug. 9, Sept. 25, Oct. 27, 1851, Jan. 17, Feb. 7, 19, 28, 1852; *New York Times*, Dec. 1, 1851, Mar. 23, 31, 1852; State of California, *House Journal, 1852* (San Francisco, 1852), 159; *Senate Journal, 1860* (Sacramento, 1860), 27.

vored slavery but, realizing that the opposition against the institution was too strong, they voted to reject it. Moreover, the assumption of a rigid proslavery position might thwart their political aspirations for the future. When the constitution was presented to Congress, the prohibition of slavery was defended by citing both Cass's squatter sovereignty principle and Calhoun's Senate resolution of 1847 which stated that "a people . . . have the unconditional right to form and adopt the government . . . which they think best calculated to secure their liberty, prosperity, and happiness."[12]

Antislavery delegates at the convention circulated rumors that the proslavery members secretly planned to save California for slavery by extending the boundaries of the inchoate state to the crest of the Rocky Mountains. They presumed that Congress would reject a constitution containing such extreme boundaries and, during the interim before another convention met, a large proslavery element might migrate west and produce a change in the attitude regarding slavery. According to the rumors, William Gwin, a future United States Senator, devised the plan. Gwin denied the fact, however, insisting that he had always been opposed to slavery. Later he wrote that the extended boundary was suggested to provide law and order and protection from the Indians for those settlers migrating by land to California.[13]

M. M. McCarver introduced the Negro exclusion topic. Although his proposal forbade the immigration of all Negroes, McCarver declared that he was primarily interested in preventing the importation of slaves who would temporarily work at the mines and then, after they were freed, remain in the state as free Negroes. An exclusion provision, he argued, was essential in order to protect California from "an evil so enormous as this[,] for . . . no population on the globe [was] more repugnant to the feelings of the people than idle, thriftless free Negroes thrown into the state." Numerous anti-Negro delegates supported McCarver's motion. Most of them, by referring to the exclusion provision of the 1847 Illinois Constitution, revealed their knowledge of that document and its influence on them. Not a single delegate, however, was a native of Illinois, and only one of the 48 delegates had been

---

[12] Daniel Knower, *The Adventures of a Forty-Niner* (Albany, New York, 1894), 114-115; *House Executive Documents*, 31 Cong., 1 Sess., No. 59, 3-4; *Daily Alta California*, Oct. 1, 1849.

[13] J. M. Guinn, "How California Escaped State Division," *SCHSAP*, VI (1905), 226; William H. Ellison (ed.), "Memoirs of Hon. William M. Gwin," *CHSQ*, XIX (Mar., 1940), 8; *California Debates*, 43.

born in the Old Northwest. The delegates were aware of the Illinois prohibitory clause because of their former residence in the Middle West. These so-called "Westerners — people who regardless of their origin, had spent much of their [lives] on those older frontiers of the Missouri and Mississippi valleys or in the lands immediately fronting on the Ohio River" — were numerous in California, and they embodied the frontier spirit and political ideals found there.[14]

Jacob R. Snyder placed the exclusion issue before the convention in purely economic terms, calculating that during the lifetime of a slave in the southern states, a slaveholder could realize a $6,000 profit from each slave's labor. This amount, Snyder presumed, was reduced by the slave's periodic inability to work because of illness or old age. In the mines a slaveholder could expect an equal monetary return in four years and then liberate the slave, having no further obligation toward him. "Do you suppose this will not be tried?" asked Snyder. "It will, sir, and . . . you will find the country flooded with a population of free Negroes — the greatest calamity that could befall California." Robert Semple announced that the people in his district, Sonoma, feared that if an exclusion provision were not incorporated into the constitution, indentured "negroes [would be] brought . . . by the thousands and the whole country [would later be] filled with emancipated slaves — the worst species of population — prepared to do nothing but steal, or live upon our means as paupers." Other delegates predicted that unlimited Negro immigration would drive away the white population and would result in "a black tide [sweeping] over the land . . . greater than the locusts of Egypt." Arguing that free Negroes in the eastern states did not have the financial means of traveling to California, the more liberal delegates introduced a proposal to restrict only the importation of indentures and slaves, not all Negroes. The convention rejected this amendment, adopting the original proposition on September 20, 1849.[15]

The prohibitory measure received support solely because of anti-Negro prejudice. At least three delegates made their positions quite evident, saying: "I [am] against the admission of all colored men of the African race"; "I am opposed to the introduction of negroes . . . free or bond"; and "Let us not receive [Negroes] at all." Yet, the apprehension regarding the profitability of mine slavery was not an idle

---

[14] *California Debates*, 139, 478-479; Rodman W. Paul, *Mining Frontiers of the Far West, 1848-1880* (New York, 1963), 26.
[15] *California Debates*, 143-144, 146-147, 237, 334.

argument. In fact, the interest of some slaveholders in California's gold mines clearly indicated that they did not consider slavery to be limited to an agricultural economy. Several delegates said they had received letters from slaveholders inquiring about the attitude toward slavery in California and stating their intentions of traveling west if they could be assured of retaining their chattels. Jefferson Davis recognized the value of slave labor in the mines when he declared, "I hold that the pursuit of gold-washing and mining is better adapted to slave labor than to any other species of labor recognized among us." Equally emphatic about the opportunity for slavery in the mines, Thomas L. Clingman of North Carolina said: "But for the anti-slavery agitation, slaveholders would have carried their negroes into the mines of California in such numbers, that I have no doubt but that the majority there would have made it a slave holding State." Possibly more than anything else, these statements refute the contention that slavery had reached its "natural limits" in the 1850's. Slaveholders did not stay away from the California mines because of their inability to adapt slave labor to mining. As in the Old Northwest, they simply refused to migrate to an area where their chattels were not secure.[16]

Although his remarks were not immediately effective, Edward Gilbert, just before McCarver's motion was passed, made the most influential speech in the entire exclusion debate. Gilbert began by declaring that the assembly had "several hobbies," namely the immigration of free Negroes and the possibility of mine slavery. As far as Negro immigration was concerned there was little likelihood of Negroes coming in great numbers. Slaveholders might transport slaves to work at the mines, but such cases would be rare. With considerable astuteness, Gilbert argued that the exclusion article was unfair and could not be defended logically because there was no provision to restrict the "miserable natives [from] the Sandwich Islands and the other Islands of the Pacific [or] the degraded wretches of Sidney, New South Wales, or the population of Chili, Peru or Mexico." These people, thought Gilbert, were just as much of a pollution to the "soil of California" as Negroes, and "most of them [were] as bad as any of the free negroes of the North, or the worst slaves of the South." The exclusion article was based solely on race prejudice directed against the Negro, said Gilbert,

---

[16] *Ibid.*, 142-143, 145, 147, 335; *Congressional Globe*, 31 Cong., 1 Sess., 202, 731; Eugene D. Genovese, *The Political Economy of Slavery* (New York, 1965), 256-260. The natural limits theory was proposed by Charles W. Ramsdell, "The Natural Limits of Slavery Expansion," *MVHR*, XVI (Sept., 1929), 151-171.

and unless all other races were also excluded from California, it was completely indefensible. Calling attention to the objections raised by Congress over the Negro exclusion provision in the 1820 Missouri Constitution, Gilbert suggested that Congress would also object to a similar provision in the California document. "I believe," he warned, "your constitution will be rejected by the revisory power which it must pass at Washington [if an exclusion article is inserted]. Sir, if there is any one consideration more than another that would tempt me to forego all my feelings and principles, it would be that of securing to California, with as little delay as possible, a proper form of State Government."[17]

Gilbert's speech produced a delayed reaction ten days after McCarver's motion was adopted. Fearing that the exclusion article would jeopardize the acceptance of the constitution by Congress, a number of delegates spoke of reconsidering the proposition. By October 3, the provision was reconsidered and removed by a vote of 31 to 8.[18]

The proceedings of the convention and the reconsideration vote indicated that Negro exclusion received its strongest support from the mining districts, the areas most concerned about the Negro question. For example, six of the eleven major speakers favoring exclusion represented the mining districts of Sacramento and San Joaquin, which had a total of fourteen delegates. The first vote on McCarver's proposition was not recorded, so it cannot be determined how the mining delegates voted. But on the reconsideration, 28 of the 31 votes for removing the provision from the constitution were cast by nonmining delegates. The delegates from the mining districts were split on the reconsideration vote — three to retain and three to remove the article. Moreover, eight of the fourteen delegates from the mining districts abstained from voting. Because the arguments for removing the exclusion provision emphasized possible congressional disapproval, their failure to vote hinted that although they favored Negro exclusion, they desired statehood more. During the convention most of the petitions demanding exclusion came from the mining districts. Thus, faced with the dilemma of voting contrary to the wishes of their constituents or possibly jeopardizing statehood, the majority of the delegates from the mining districts simply abstained on the reconsideration vote.[19]

[17] *California Debates,* 149-152.
[18] *Daily Alta California,* Oct. 1, 1849; *New York Tribune,* Nov. 12, 1849; *California Debates,* 330-331, 339, 340-341.
[19] *California Debates,* 338-339, 478-479; Goodwin, *Establishment of Government in California,* 128-132.

The omission of an exclusion provision had no appreciable effect on the adoption of the constitution; Californians accepted the document by an overwhelming majority.[20] And after California became a state, Negro exclusion became one of the first issues the legislature faced.

Peter Burnett and John McDougal were the first two governors of California. Burnett, elected in 1849, resigned after a year in office, and McDougal, the lieutenant governor, succeeded him. Both men were decidedly anti-Negro. Burnett had lived in Oregon before coming to California, and there he had advocated incorporating a restriction against Negro immigration into the laws of the Oregon provisional government. McDougal's statements during the constitutional convention revealed his dislike of the Negro. Moreover, as chairman of the board of state prison inspectors during his term as governor, he inserted a statement in the annual report that Negroes were degraded and conspicuous for their drunkenness and improvidence and, for these reasons, he refused to pardon any of the Negroes serving sentences in the state prison.[21]

Burnett wrote that his main reason for migrating to the West Coast was to help build a great American community on the Pacific Ocean. Hoping the states established west of the Rocky Mountains would be superior to those east of them, Burnett presumed that such pre-eminence could be achieved only by avoiding "the evils . . . of mixed races." This apprehension regarding the Negro was evident in Burnett's first speech to the legislature. Praising the constitution for prohibiting slavery and freeing California from a great social and political evil, he pointed out that the document lacked a provision excluding free Negroes and suggested that the legislature adopt one. Such a law could be justified on the ground that the constitution did not grant equal status to the race. To allow Negroes to live in California and, simultaneously, to refuse them social and civil equality would only force them into a more degraded position. If the legislature intended to continue the constitutional restrictions against free Negroes, then they should be excluded from the state. The commercial and mineral attractions of California "would bring swarms of [Negroes] to our shores,"

[20] U.S. Congress, House of Representatives, *House Miscellaneous Documents,* 31 Cong., 1 Sess., No. 44 (ser. no. 581), 13-14.

[21] Delilah L. Beasley, "Slavery in California," *JNH,* III (Jan., 1918), 44; Hubert Howe Bancroft, *History of California, 1848-1859* (Vol. XXIII, *The Works of Hubert Howe Bancroft,* San Francisco, 1888), 664.

Burnett insisted. Because the state already contained "a heterogeneous mass of human beings, of every language and of every hue," the legislature should prevent a further mixing of the races. Immediate action, warned the new governor, would avoid "the inevitable consequences of tomorrow." Burnett realized that some of the legislators might consider an exclusion law harsh, but he proposed it to produce the "greatest good for the greatest number" and to save the state from the evils of a mixed population.[22]

The political opponents of the Democratic governor announced publicly that the speech revealed his unlimited race prejudice. Denouncing Burnett's proposal as "unduly influenced by prejudice and behampered by fear and favor," Whig legislators agreed that Burnett had "many prejudices to overcome." Gilbert of the *Alta*, a staunch Whig, thought the entire speech was disappointing, and the remarks about Negro exclusion disturbed him. He questioned the advisability of reintroducing the exclusion issue because it had nearly wrecked the constitutional convention and it would again raise conflict. Although he did not favor racial equality, Gilbert opposed excluding Negroes and thus denying them the chance to improve themselves economically. Furthermore, he firmly believed that Negroes would not migrate to California in large enough numbers to produce a change in the racial make-up of the state.[23]

Despite the objections of the Whigs, the Democrats in the "legislature of a thousand drinks," as the first assembly was called, enacted Burnett's proposal. However, the bill was defeated by a thirteen to

---

[22] Peter Burnett, *Recollections and Opinions of an Old Pioneer* (New York, 1880), 220-221; State of California, *Senate Journal, 1850* (San Jose, 1850), 38; *Daily Alta California*, Dec. 31, 1849.

[23] *New York Tribune*, Feb. 9, 1850; *Daily Alta California*, Dec. 31, 1849. Burnett's attitude toward Negroes was again severely criticized in 1858 when, as a state supreme court justice, he read the opinion in the Archy case. Archy, the slave of Charles Stovell of Mississippi, was brought to California and sold to Robert Blakely. The slave fled from Blakely, who petitioned the U.S. Commissioner for California, George Johnston, for his return. Deciding that Archy was not an escaped slave under the meaning of the Fugitive Slave Act of 1850, Johnston refused to return him. A Sacramento County court upheld Johnston's decision. However, the state supreme court returned Archy to Blakely. Several newspapers maintained that Burnett's prejudice against Negroes influenced his decision. Helen Catterall (ed.), *Judicial Cases Concerning American Slavery and the Negro* (5 vols., Washington, D.C., 1937), V, 332-334; William E. Franklin, Jr., "The Political Career of Peter Hardeman Burnett" (unpublished Ph.D. dissertation, Stanford University, 1954), 187-192; *Daily Alta California*, Mar. 22, 1858.

twelve vote. The voting pattern revealed that the mining districts continued to be the principal strongholds for Negro exclusion. Representatives from the mining areas cast nine of the twelve votes in favor of the measure.[24] Whereas delegates from the mining districts had abstained from voting during the constitutional convention, now the representatives strongly supported exclusion.

Anti-Negro legislators introduced another exclusion measure in the house several months later, during the same session. Within one day they pushed the bill through its legislative steps and passed it. Its supporters in the senate attempted to rush the bill through before significant objections could be raised. Only the delaying tactics of David C. Broderick, a future United States Senator, provided time for the opposition to unite effectively and postpone the measure. The senate vote, unlike the house vote on the first exclusion bill, was not a contest between the mining and nonmining interests. Rather, it was influenced by the sectional backgrounds of the senators. Of the eight votes to postpone the bill, five were cast by men from the free states, one by a man from the slave states, and two by native Californians. All of the five votes against postponement were given by men from the slave states.

Despite the refusal to consent to exclusion, the liberal thinking of the senators was limited. Later in the session, the senate accepted a house bill which defined a Negro as any person having one-sixth "African blood" and which debarred him from testifying against a white person in the courts. Another act prohibited all marriages between Negroes, thus defined, and white people.[25]

The state census of 1852 revealed a rapid growth in the Negro population, from 692 in 1850 to 2,206.[26] As might be expected, the legis-

---

[24] The name, although not descriptive, was tagged on to the first legislature because Thomas Green, a senator, often invited members to his home at the end of the day, and Green's imbibing habits were well known. C. T. Ryland described the first legislature as a "fine body of men" and very capable of performing the duties required of them. Parish (ed.), "A Project for a California Slave Colony," 171; C. T. Ryland, "Connections with the History of California," MS (Bancroft Library), n.p.; State of California, *House Journal, 1850* (San Jose, 1850), 723, 729; Goodwin, *Establishment of Government in California,* 320.

[25] State of California, *House Journal, 1850,* 1223, 1225; *Senate Journal, 1850,* 337, 347; *The General Laws of the State of California, 1850-1864* (San Francisco, 1868), 4462; *New York Tribune,* July 10, 1850.

[26] State of California, *House Journal, 1852,* 71, 95; *Senate Journal, 1852* (San Francisco, 1852), 413; *Daily Alta California,* May 8, 1852; Josiah Royce, *California from the Conquest in 1846 to the Second Vigilance Committee in San Francisco* (Boston, 1886), 328.

lature again considered measures to prevent further increases. One measure, which remained in force until 1855, permitted a slaveholder to reclaim any Negro in the state whom he had held as a slave prior to the adoption of the state constitution. Apprehended Negroes were not allowed to testify on their own behalf. Moreover, any white person assisting former slaves in escaping arrest was liable to a $500 fine and a prison sentence.[27] A second bill, prohibiting the immigration of Negroes as defined by California law and requiring all Negroes in the state to leave, did not pass. Delayed in the lower house for two months, the bill was still in a senate committee at the close of the session.[28] These measures temporarily ended anxiety about Negro immigration because Californians now became more concerned about the Chinese.

The first Chinese immigrants arrived in California in 1849; by 1852 there were 17,000 in the state. When this fact was learned, through the state census, demands for Chinese exclusion became rampant. As before, the new agitation came primarily from the mining districts where the Orientals congregated. Usually they took over abandoned claims and by arduous labor, which the white miners would not perform, made these claims pay. The legislature was reluctant to proscribe a foreign group, but in 1853 it did consider a bill excluding the Chinese from the mines. The possible international complications which the bill might produce, however, caused its defeat.[29]

As their mining efforts became less profitable, the Orientals moved into the cities, especially San Francisco. Gilbert of the *Alta,* who had been unconcerned about Negro immigration, began an editorial campaign against the Chinese. Noting the passage of the Illinois black law of 1853, Gilbert hoped the legislature would not consider a similar measure for California because Negroes were not numerous enough to warrant one. Instead he suggested a Chinese exclusion law because, he thought, Orientals had more vices and fewer virtues than Negroes, and

[27] *New York Tribune,* May 20, 1852; Bancroft, *History of California,* 665. Later in the year the state supreme court upheld the law. Catterall (ed.), *Judicial Cases,* V, 331-332.

[28] State of California, *House Journal, 1852,* 703-704, 711; *Senate Journal, 1852,* 438; *Daily Alta California,* May 8, 1852.

[29] Rodman W. Paul, "The Origin of the Chinese Issue in California," *MVHR,* XXV (Sept., 1938), 182; Catterall (ed.), *Judicial Cases,* V, 332; John H. Kemble (ed.), "Andrew Wilson's Jottings on the Civil War in California," *CHSQ,* XXXII (Dec., 1953), 308-312.

they were too clannish and deceitful to serve a useful purpose in society.[30]

Most of the legislators presumed that a law excluding the Chinese would violate trade agreements between the United States and the Chinese governments; therefore, they refused to consider one for several years. Finally in 1855, without specifically mentioning the Chinese, the legislature passed an act restricting them by levying a $50 tax on shipowners for each incoming foreign national who had not previously lived in the United States and who was not eligible for American citizenship. Perhaps to the legislature's dismay, the state supreme court declared the bill unconstitutional almost immediately.[31]

The influx of Chinese continued during the fifties. Between 1852 and 1860 the Oriental population doubled, from 17,000 to 34,935. By contrast, there were only 4,086 Negroes in 1860, and of this number 2,062 were mulattoes. Orientals were also more dispersed throughout the state; only four counties did not contain a Chinese population, and 13 of the state's 44 counties contained over 1,000 Chinese. On the other hand, only four counties contained more than 100 Negroes or mulattoes. San Francisco had the greatest concentration of Negroes, slightly over 1,000. Considering the large number of mulattoes, however, the colored population was less noticeable than the 3,000 Chinese in the city.[32] No matter where they resided, the Orientals were more evident because their customs and dress, which they steadfastly retained, were markedly different.

Discrimination against Negroes increased following the failure to restrict Chinese immigration in 1855. In the main, the anti-Negro attitude perplexed former slaves. Some of them, at least, became antagonistic enough about discrimination to leave the state. A manumitted slave, formerly belonging to a Major Dalton of Galveston, Texas, requested his own return to his master, declaring that he preferred to live in slavery rather than with the restrictions placed on him in California. James Williams, a fugitive slave, migrated to Vancouver Island in 1857 to escape the prejudice against Negroes in California. Finding the British just as antagonistic and economic opportunity more limited,

---

[30] *Daily Alta California*, Jan. 13, June 14, Dec. 24, 1853, Feb. 21, 1855, Apr. 20, 1858.
[31] *Laws of the State of California, 1850-1864*, 574; Paul, "Chinese Issue," 195.
[32] *1860 Census, Population*, 28.

he returned to Sacramento and worked as an express wagon driver, one of the few jobs available to Negroes. The editor of the *Indiana Sentinel,* who frequently published uncomplimentary articles about free Negroes, encountered a former slave who had been liberated in California and who had returned to his master in Arkansas. Defending his action, the Negro declared: "In California I was free, but there was a wider difference between the white and the black man than in Arkansas. I labored hard, but I was a nigger and that was enough with the Yankees, and I preferred to be a slave with my old master, where I could be respected as such, than to be a free man among white men in a free State." Undoubtedly the most flagrant violation of Negro rights occurred in 1857 when James Estell, the state prison director, sent Negro inmates from the state prisons to New Orleans where they were sold into slavery.[33]

Although California Negroes unwillingly submitted to most restrictions, they hotly objected to the law which disqualified them from testifying against whites. In 1852, soon after the law was passed, the Negroes of San Francisco petitioned the legislature to repeal it. By an almost unanimous vote the legislators rejected the petition and agreed not to entertain further petitions from Negroes. By 1855 two court cases aroused such great indignation among Negroes that they held a protest convention in Sacramento. In the first instance a white man murdered a Negro and the only known witness was another Negro. It appeared as if the murderer would be acquitted until the testimony of an unknown white witness was produced. In spite of the conviction, the Negro community was chagrined because the murderer received only a light prison sentence. In the second case, a Negro was again the only witness to a murder. This time the jury acquitted the murderer because the Negro was not allowed to testify. In the protesting convention the Negroes claimed that their influence as citizens and their accumulated wealth, estimated at $2,375,000, entitled them to witness privileges. The lack of sympathy regarding the request caused the whites to question the Negroes' claims. Upon investigating, one editor said he was unable to find more than eight Negroes in the state

---

[33] *Chicago Journal,* Feb. 15, 1850; James Williams, *The Life and Adventures of James Williams, a Fugitive Slave* (San Francisco, 1874), 31-33; *Indiana State Sentinel,* Mar. 31, 1853; *San Francisco Bulletin,* n.d., in John D. Carter, "Thomas Sim King, Vigilante Editor," *CHSQ,* XXI (Mar., 1942), 33; Sue Bailey Thurman, *Pioneers of Negro Origin in California* (San Francisco, 1949), 56.

worth over $75,000 each. The convention was not successful; rather, it only strengthened the resistance against granting witness privileges. As late as 1861, Andrew Wilson, a member of the legislature, noted that a number of the lawmakers favored a bill permitting the admission of evidence from an Oriental, but they felt it would be difficult to justify allowing illiterate Chinese to testify while refusing the same right to an intelligent Negro — "and they will not allow the negro to testify."[34]

Negro exclusion again became a lively topic in the 1857 legislature. Even though the proposed measure failed to pass, the consternation it caused among Negroes resulted in the formation of an emigration society which encouraged California Negroes to settle on Vancouver Island. The Canadians refused to associate with the new immigrants and demanded their deportation.[35]

In 1858 an exclusion measure, similar to the 1853 law in Illinois, was introduced in the legislature. It required Negroes to register by October 1, 1858. Any Negro unable to produce proof of registration after that date was to be auctioned for six months' labor; the person purchasing the Negro's services was obligated to provide for his removal from the state after the service term. The bill passed the house by an overwhelming vote of 45 to 8. Fierce opposition in the senate was slowly overcome by amendments exempting present Negro residents from punishment. However, the lower house failed to act on the amendments before the end of the session, and the bill did not become law.[36]

Toward the end of the Civil War all restrictions against Negroes in California were removed from the statute books. This was no indication that all white Californians had assumed a new attitude on the Negro question. In 1865 a Union party convention in Yuba County, protesting the repeal of the restrictions, declared, "we still believe this to be

[34] State of California, *House Journal, 1852,* 395; Delilah L. Beasley, *The Negro Trail Blazers of California* (Los Angeles, 1919), 54; Dorothy H. Huggins (comp.), "The Annals of San Francisco," *CHSQ,* XVI (Dec., 1937), 339; *Shasta* (California) *Courier,* Dec. 1, 1855; Kemble, "Wilson's Jottings," 308.

[35] State of California, *House Journal, 1857* (Sacramento, 1857), 811, 823, 824; (Olympia, Washington) *Pioneer and Democrat,* Nov. 16, 1860.

[36] State of California, *House Journal, 1858* (Sacramento, 1858), 408, 417, 444-445; *Senate Journal, 1858* (Sacramento, 1858), 553, 661, 664; Carl Wheat (ed.), "California's Bantam Cock: The Journal of Charles E. DeLong, 1854-1863," *CHSQ,* IX (Sept., 1930), 256, 281; *Daily Alta California,* Apr. 9, 22, 27, 1858.

a white man's government and the extension of the natural rights to the negro is degrading, impolitic and unnatural." Democrats in 1864 advocated the necessity of electing their own party members because they believed the republic was a "White Man's Government as it had come from the hands of the founders," and they would uphold the white man's pre-eminence.[37]

The abolition of the anti-Negro restrictions was caused by the nature of the population, the inability to enforce the laws, and the fact that the Negro was not the dominant minority problem in California. The increase from 962 to 4,086 Negroes between 1850 and 1860 seemed trifling when compared to an influx of almost 35,000 Chinese during the same decade. It was even less significant because over half of the Negroes were either mulattoes, quadroons, or octoroons. Since there were also 50,000 Latin Americans in California in 1860, it must have been impossible to distinguish between a Latin American of mixed parentage and a person who was part Negro. Unlike other western regions, which were almost exclusively settled by Americans, the Americans in California in 1860 comprised only two-thirds of the total population. This racial and national mixture in Eldorado resulted from the gold rush; the quest for wealth destroyed Peter Burnett's dream of a white empire in California.[38] As early as 1851 an eastern newspaper correspondent correctly surmised the reason why racial restrictions would not last in California.[39] Any attempt to restrict a non-Oriental racial group could not succeed because, except for the Chinese, the population was too racially mixed. Native Californians before 1848 had intermarried with Negroes, and now they married Latin Americans and Europeans. Laws restricting an individual because of his color were simply unworkable in California; in a land with such a conglomerate population, the formal concept of racial discrimination was alien to too many people.

---

[37] Winfield J. Davis, *History of Political Conventions in California, 1849-1892* (Sacramento, 1893), 215; (Santa Rosa, California) *Sonoma Democrat*, Sept. 22, 1864.
[38] *1860 Census, Population*, 23, 28, 34.
[39] *New York Tribune*, Nov. 5, 1851.

Beyond the Cascades

The attitudes and reactions in the Pacific Northwest toward the slavery and the free Negro questions were strikingly similar to those found in the Old Northwest. Indeed, except for minor changes in detail, it seems as if the story were being repeated. Despite the prohibition of slavery by an act of the Oregon provisional government in 1844 and by the federal act which created the Oregon Territory in 1848, proslavery men openly advocated the adoption of the institution in the Far Northwest. Their actions, of course, led to the solidification of an antislavery bloc determined to prevent Negro servitude. Although the legalization of slavery was not the most pressing problem in the Oregon Territory during the early 1850's, it became an issue of utmost importance when Oregonians formed their state government in 1857. The exclusion of free Negroes, however, was an ever-present and explosive issue. The two became so inseparably linked that Oregon's political leaders, regardless of party, decided that only the people could settle the issues by voting on them in a separate referendum when the constitution was submitted for popular approval. Oregonians, like midwesterners, firmly rejected both slavery and free Negroes and, as in the Middle West, their action was "not [solely a protest against] human servitude but against the Negro himself. [Most] settlers had little sympathy with slavery but [many] had a greater aversion against free Negroes."[1]

The similarity regarding the Negro question occurred because the Middle West was the "crucible in which the population of the Pacific Northwest was molded."[2] According to the census of 1860, roughly

---

[1] Walter C. Woodward, "The Rise and Early History of Political Parties in Oregon," *OHQ*, XII (June, 1911), 146.

[2] Jesse S. Douglas, "Origins of the Population of Oregon in 1850," *PNQ*, XLI (Apr., 1950), 107-108. Several contemporaries wrote that the Middle West

23 per cent of the population in Oregon had been born in the Old Northwest. Missouri, Kentucky, and Tennessee contributed an additional 17 per cent of the population, 10 per cent of which came from Missouri.[3] Moreover, the vast majority of the people who had migrated to the Far Northwest from these three southern states were nonslaveholders. Like the southern yeomen who had previously moved into the Old Northwest, the former southerners in the Pacific Northwest left the South to escape the economic and social inequities of a slave society. One of them also remarked that he moved to Oregon "to get rid of Saucy free Negroes."[4] The hatred of many former southerners in the region for the Negro was openly acknowledged, and when it came into contact with the comparable antipathy of the people born in the Old Northwest, racial antagonism beyond the Cascades solidified.

The influence of the Middle West upon the Pacific Northwest, however, cannot be measured by nativity alone. Until they left the towns along the frontier, pioneers seldom traveled west in extensive moves; the movements were made at short intervals and it was not uncommon for a pioneering family to spend several years in one location before moving on. Martha Collins, an early settler in Oregon, recalled the numerous moves made in her family's travels westward and stated that until it reached the Pacific Northwest, her family considered itself a transient element of society.[5]

Information given by the delegates at the Oregon Constitutional Convention in 1857 about their places of birth and their last state of residence indicated that many of these Oregonians had lived in the Middle West. Although only 8 delegates had been born in the Old

---

was the region from which most people in the Far Northwest came. See Matthew P. Deady, "History and Progress of Oregon After 1845," MS (Bancroft Library; microfilm, University of Washington Library), 39; William Strong, "History of Oregon," MS (Bancroft Library; microfilm, University of Washington Library), 61; Delazon Smith in the (Salem) *Oregon Statesman,* Dec. 19, 1854.

[3] The slave states, other than those mentioned, contributed slightly less than 5 per cent of the population, New England a little over 4 per cent, and 8 per cent of the population in the Pacific Northwest came from the Middle Atlantic states. The remaining 43 per cent consisted of a small number of foreign born and those born in the Far West, most of whom were children in 1860. *1860 Census, Population,* 405.

[4] John Minto, "Antecedents of the Oregon Pioneers and the Lights These Throw on Their Motives," *OHQ,* V (Mar., 1904), 40; George B. Curry, "Address Before the Oregon Pioneer Association," *OPAT* (1887), 34.

[5] Fred Lockley (ed.), "Reminiscences of Mrs. Frank Collins, Nee Martha Elizabeth Gilliam," *OHQ,* XVII (Sept., 1916), 358.

Northwest and 4 in Missouri, 31 declared Ohio, Indiana, Illinois, Michigan, or Iowa as their former home state and sixteen named Missouri. Thus, 47 of the 60 members of the convention had definitely lived in the Middle West. Moreover, 34 of the 47 left the Middle West for Oregon between 1847 and 1853, years in which the Negro question was most prominent in the Old Northwest. Undoubtedly they were familiar with some of the discussion that had occurred in connection with the constitutional exclusion provisions in Illinois (1847) and Indiana (1851) and the exclusion laws in Iowa (1851) and Illinois (1853). Perhaps some of them had even voted in the Illinois and Indiana exclusion referenda.[6]

Even former southerners were not totally immune to the influence of the Old Northwest. Of the 25 men at the convention born in the slave states, 11 claimed one of the states in the Old Northwest as their last residence: seven from Illinois, three from Iowa, and one from Indiana. The Indianian and two of the Iowans arrived in Oregon after 1852; five of the seven Illinois men after 1847. Therefore, these eight men must have had some awareness of the anti-Negro discrimination in those states.[7]

The influence of the Middle West was evident from the very beginning of government in the Pacific Northwest and was made manifest in two laws passed by the Oregon provisional government in 1844. The first measure, in June, prohibited slavery and required slaveholders to remove their chattels within three years; all free Negroes and mulattoes were warned to leave the territory within two years, and the act, like the Illinois territorial law of 1813, subjected any Negro who remained to periodic floggings. Later, in the December session, the provisional council repealed the whipping clause and replaced it with a provision, similar to the one passed in Illinois in 1819, apprenticing the labor of free Negroes for a short period to a white man. The person accepting the Negro's service had to guarantee his removal from the territory after the service period ended.[8] Thus, an analysis of the laws indicates

---

[6] *Oregon Debates*, 68; (Portland) *Weekly Oregonian*, Aug. 29, 1857. The *Oregon Debates* were reprinted from the contemporary newspapers, mainly the *Statesman* and the *Oregonian*. For simplicity, only the pages in the debates are cited.

[7] *Ibid*.

[8] Fred Lockley (ed.), "Some Documentary Records of Slavery in Oregon," *OHQ*, XVII (Mar., 1916), 109-111; H. W. Scott, "The Formation and Administration of the Provisional Government of Oregon," *OHQ*, II (June, 1901), 110.

that there were both slaves and free Negroes in Oregon in 1844 and that their presence was a matter of public concern. Although the census of 1850 listed 207 Negroes, Jesse Douglas estimated that there were probably about 55.[9] However few the Negroes, bond or free, they were not wanted by the majority of the white settlers.

Peter Burnett, a former Missourian, a member of the provisional council, and, later, the first governor of California to recommend a Negro exclusion bill, initiated both laws of the provisional government. He defended his action by maintaining that each state had the right to determine whether or not a person born outside of it was entitled to citizenship. An individual born in one community was not, *"as a matter of right,"* Burnett thought, entitled to live in another community if residence were denied him. In his memoirs Burnett wrote that he proposed the laws because he had always opposed slavery. However, a letter, written in December, 1844, the same month that the provisional council passed the second law, suggested a less humanitarian consideration. Burnett wrote, "The object is to *keep* clear of that most troublesome class of population. We are in a new world, under most favorable circumstances, and we wish to avoid most of those evils that have so much afflicted the United States and other countries."[10]

The immediate impetus for the expulsion measure came from an affray involving a free Negro. In May, 1844, one month before the first law was passed, a free Negro under arrest, James D. Sauls, threatened to arouse the Indians against the white people. As Sauls was married to an Indian woman, the threat was not idle. Nevertheless, it was not carried out because Elihah White, the federal government's Indian

---

[9] Douglas pointed out that Joe Meek, the census taker in Clark, Clackamas, and Lewis counties, listed 114 Indians or half-breeds and 38 Hawaiians as Negroes. Douglas, "Origins of the Population in Oregon," 98-99; *1850 Census, Statistics,* 993.

[10] Jesse Applegate, "Views of Oregon History," MS (Bancroft Library; microfilm, University of Washington Library), 9, 39-40; "Oregon Provisional and Territorial Government Papers," Journal of the Legislative Committee, June 18-27, 1844, No. 1681, December 16-24, 1844, No. 1682 (microfilm, University of Oregon Library); LaFayette Grover (comp.), *The Oregon Archives, Including the Journals, Governors' Messages and Public Papers of Oregon* (Salem, 1853), 29; Burnett, *Recollections,* 218, 220-221; Burnett to an unknown correspondent, Dec. 25, 1844, reprinted in (Jefferson City, Missouri) *Jeffersonian Inquirer,* Oct. 23, 1845, and quoted in Franklin, "Political Career of Burnett," 65. Unfortunately, to date, no large collection of Burnett's papers has been found which might throw light on his anti-Negro attitude. Franklin suggested they were probably destroyed in the San Francisco earthquake.

agent, persuaded Sauls to leave the immediate area after his release from jail. At the same time, White wrote to Robert Moore, a justice of the peace, that Sauls and all other Negroes were a baneful influence on the Indians and should be removed from the territory, and that provisions should be enacted to prevent their further immigration. The legislative action in June, 1844, was, therefore, in response to White's letter.[11]

The ban against slavery did not discourage slaveholders from bringing their chattels to the Pacific Northwest; yet the number, although unknown, was small. Possibly because of the prohibition, Oregon census takers in 1850 conveniently listed all Negroes as free, or perhaps slaveholders declared them free in order to circumvent the ban. At any rate, George Williams, chief justice of the territorial supreme court, frustrated the further importation of slaves by his decision in the most famous slave case heard in the Pacific Northwest. The situation involved Nathaniel Ford of Missouri and the Robin Holmes family, whom Ford had brought with him as slaves when he crossed the plains to Oregon in 1844. After several years the parents fled with the youngest child while Ford continued to hold the other children. Holmes sought to regain his children and to secure legally his own liberty by suing for his freedom, but the courts refused to consider the suit. Finally in 1853, Williams, an Iowa Free Soil Democrat, placed the case at the head of his docket. Deciding against Ford and thereby freeing the Negroes, Williams declared that slavery could not exist in Oregon without specific legislation to protect it. Once slaves reached the territory they were automatically released from any further obligations toward their masters. Interestingly, Williams did not base his decision on the laws prohibiting slavery. The decision, understandably, was not favorably received by the proslavery settlers, but it set a precedent, and after 1853 no attempt was again made to retain slaves through court action.[12]

---

[11] U.S. Congress, House of Representatives, *House Executive Document,* 29 Cong., 1 Sess., I, No. 2 (ser. no. 480), 629; W. Sherman Savage, "The Negro in the History of the Pacific Northwest," *JNH,* XIII (July, 1928), 258; William Henry Gray, *A History of Oregon* (New York, 1870), 395-397.

[12] *1850 Census, Statistics,* 993; Fred Lockley, "The Case of Robin Holmes vs. Nathaniel Ford," *OHQ,* XXIII (June, 1922), 111-137; George Williams, "Political History of Oregon from 1853 to 1865," *OHQ,* II (Mar., 1901), 2, 5; George Williams, "Annual Address Before the Oregon Pioneer Association," *OPAT* (1885), 28; *Oregon Statesman,* July 26, 1853; R. P. Boise to T. W. Davenport, June 4, 1906, in T. W. Davenport, "The Slavery Question in

In 1849 the first territorial legislature re-enacted the provisional government's exclusion law by a decisive vote, and in one known instance it was enforced.[13] However, the legislature unintentionally repealed the measure in 1854.[14] Immediately the legislative council passed another exclusion bill which failed to pass the house; similar bills met defeat in the house during the 1855 and 1856 sessions. Because the measure was not voted on in 1854, the extent of opposition to it is indeterminable. In the 1855 and 1856 sessions, the house rejected the bill by votes of 24 to 4 and 23 to 3, respectively.[15]

Although the representatives voting for exclusion were in the minority, they were not hesitant about defending their positions. One member feared that unlimited Negro immigration would create serious problems with the Indians. Reminding the other representatives of the Sauls affair, he declared, "the cross between the Indian and the negro [produces] bad blood." Furthermore, he insisted that Negroes had "no right to a part of our inheritance" because they had not helped to colonize the territory.[16] Other members repeated phrases often heard in similar debates in the Middle West: "the United States is a government of white men"; "the declaration of independence [is] a declaration of the equality of free citizenship for white men"; and "the con-

Oregon," *OHQ*, IX (Sept., 1908), 196. In 1860 an Oregon slaveholder tried to secure the return of a slave who had escaped to Canada but this case was not within the jurisdiction of the state courts. See Robert W. Johannsen, *Frontier Politics and the Sectional Conflict: The Pacific Northwest on the Eve of the Civil War* (Seattle, 1955), 20-21.

[13] Theophilus Magruder filed a complaint in the Clackamas County court in 1851 against Jacob Vanderpool, a mulatto, requesting his removal from the territory. Vanderpool's lawyer argued that the 1849 law was not within the scope of the legislature's power and was illegal because it violated various amendments to the federal Constitution. Thomas Nelson, the judge who heard the case, disagreed with the argument and ordered Vanderpool to leave the territory within 30 days. Lauding the decision, the editor of the *Oregon Statesman* declared it "a re-affirmation of a well settled doctrine" and hoped other judges would follow Nelson's example. Territory of Oregon, *House Journal, 1849* (Oregon City, 1849), 36, 56; Territory of Oregon, *Council Journal, 1849* (Oregon City, 1849), 89, 95; *Theophilus Magruder* v. *Jacob Vanderpool*, MS Court Record (transcripts, Oregon Historical Society Library); *Oregon Statesman*, Sept. 3, 1851.

[14] The exclusion act was omitted from a list of bills which were not meant to be repealed and, as a result, it was repealed. *Oregon Statesman*, Jan. 13, 1857.

[15] Territory of Oregon, *House Journal, 1854* (Corvallis, 1855), 42-43; *Weekly Oregonian*, Jan. 7, 1857; *Oregon Statesman*, Jan. 20, 1857.

[16] *Ibid.*, Jan. 13, 1857.

struction of our revolution [refers only] to white men."[17] The most vituperative comment was made by N. V. Holmes:

niggers . . . should never be allowed to mingle with the whites. They would amalgamate and raise a most miserable race of human beings. If niggers are allowed to come among us and mingle with the whites, it will cause a perfect state of pollution. Niggers always retrograde, until they get back to that state of barbarity from whence they originated. . . . I don't see that we should equalize ourselves with them — and we do equalize ourselves with them by letting them come among us. They never *kin* live with the whites. The Almightly has put his mark on them, and they are a different race of human beings. Let any gentleman read the history of a physician that has dissected a nigger, and see what you will find: their very brain is tinctured with black.[18]

The humanitarianism of an unknown number of representatives dictated their feelings and votes against the exclusion bills, yet there were other reasons why the house rejected the measures. For one thing, such a measure was unnecessary because Negroes were not migrating to Oregon. Those who settled on the West Coast preferred California where economic opportunity was more varied. The possibility of locating gold strikes and the commercial activities, particularly of San Francisco, were a greater inducement for Negro settlement than the agricultural life of the Pacific Northwest. Delazon Smith, a Democratic politician, noting these facts, believed that the remoteness of Oregon would also discourage Negro immigration in the future. Smith disliked the Negro because "his heels stick out too far; his forehead retreats too much; his smell is too strong," but he thought that the consideration of exclusion bills was a waste of time.[19]

The house rejected the 1856 bill for two other reasons. A requirement that captains of ships using Oregon's ports must post a $500 bond for each Negro crew member distressed the commercially minded members of the legislature. Even though the money was to be refunded if

[17] *Ibid.*, Jan. 13, 20, 1857.
[18] *Weekly Oregonian*, Jan. 6, 1855. The exclusion issue caused an intermittent battle between Thomas Dryer, editor of the *Oregonian*, and Asahel Bush, editor of the *Statesman*, who was joined by the editors of the *Oregon Weekly Times* and the *Democratic Standard*, both of Portland. Dryer referred to all three editors as "knaves, liars, villains and swindlers," but he saved his special brand of sarcasm for Bush, to whom he gave the added epithet: "Animal of the Oregon Statesman." Negro exclusion, according to Dryer, was the creed of the Democratic party which in Oregon had become subservient to the wishes "of one A. Bush." Following accusations that Dryer sought Negro equality and racial miscegenation, Dryer called a halt to the whole affair. *Weekly Oregonian*, Apr. 26, May 10, 1856, Oct. 24, 1857; *Oregon Statesman*, May 6, 1856.
[19] *Weekly Oregonian*, Dec. 30, 1854, Jan. 6, 1855.

the Negro left with the ship, these representatives felt that the provision would be detrimental to trade: ships' captains employing Negroes would consider the stipulation offensive and, therefore, bypass Oregon's ports. By 1856, moreover, Democrats began to realize the political consequences of passing an exclusion bill. Because they controlled the legislature, their opponents would make political capital out of an exclusion measure.[20] Pointing this out to his fellow Democrats, one member declared, "You go home, after passing this bill and you will find that the abolitionists are saying, 'oh, yes!' the democracy of Oregon . . . without motive [and] without cause, must condemn the blackman. . . .They are determined to pass laws that are onerous [and] unchristian . . . when there is no motive, no occasion."[21] The failure of the legislature to enact a Negro exclusion bill was not an indication of the public attitude in Oregon. When Oregonians were faced with making a decision regarding the residence of free Negroes, they repudiated their legislature's stand.

The free Negro and slavery questions became all-absorbing issues when Oregonians formed their state government in 1857. Whereas Congress had required the prohibition of slavery in Illinois in 1818 because of the Northwest Ordinance, Oregonians now presumed that the popular sovereignty principle, which had been engrafted into the Kansas-Nebraska Act, gave them the right to decide the matter of slavery. Popular sovereignty, wrote Delazon Smith, gave to the people of Oregon the privilege of deciding "for ourselves what we will adopt [and] what we will not adopt, in the government of our local affairs." Smith doubted that Oregonians would approve of slavery because the climate and the soil could not support a slave economy. "In my humble judgement there is about as much danger [of establishing slavery in Oregon] as there is of . . . going to the moon," Smith insisted, because 95 per cent of the people opposed the institution. Asahel Bush, editor of the *Oregon Statesman,* also believed that slavery would be rejected, but he warned that the greatest advantage of the proslavery element would be the fanatical opposition of the abolitionists. The

---

[20] Although attempts had been made in 1856, the Republican party was not firmly established in Oregon until mid-1857. Even at that late date, some Whigs and Free Soilers refused to join the new party. Johannsen, *Frontier Politics,* 32, 37.

[21] *Weekly Oregonian,* Jan. 24, 1857; (Oregon City) *Oregon Argus,* Jan. 31, 1857.

antislavery agitation of "fanatics and nigger-struck dames" would sway the uncommitted people in the territory to vote for slavery in order to register their opposition to rabid abolitionism.[22]

A referendum for a constitutional convention had been held on three previous occasions before 1857 but it had failed each time. The opposition vote gradually declined in each referendum, and in 1856 a convention proposition was defeated by only 249 votes. Encouraged by the growing sentiment for statehood, the legislature provided for another referendum in June, 1857; delegates to the convention were to be elected at the same time. Whereas Thomas Dryer, a Whig and the editor of the *Oregonian*, had previously opposed a convention, he now announced his approval. His conversion was due to James Buchanan's success in the election of 1856 and the prospect of four more years of Democratic rule on a platform permitting the extension of slavery into the territories. Dryer hated slavery but he insisted that "if we are to have slavery forced upon us, let it be by the people here and not by the slavery propagandists at Washington City." If the people of Oregon adopted slavery, Dryer would accept their decision but, he thought, the matter should be settled locally.[23]

As the date of the election grew nearer and as the slavery question became more intensely discussed, both Dryer and the other antislavery sympathizers publicly announced that the Democrats were attempting to force slavery upon the future state. Dryer predicted that the Democratic leaders, office holders, and office seekers would be "whipped into line" and that the average voter would be swayed by branding the antislavery people as "Abolitionists or Black Republicans." The antislavery forces became concerned enough about the Democratic party's alleged control over the minds of the electorate to unite and organize a "Free State Republican party." Meeting at Eugene in April, 1857, they drafted an address reviewing the whole slavery question and resolved to confine their efforts "to the sole and single object of making Oregon a free State, as the best and only means of securing it to the white race." The *Oregon Argus*, which had been established earlier, became the new party's organ and immediately introduced the race issue by writing that *"out of love for the poor nigger"* the Democrats wanted to extend slavery into Oregon, while the Republicans were in favor of preserving

---

[22] *Oregon Statesman*, July 14, 21, 1855, Mar. 31, 1857; Johannsen, *Frontier Politics*, 24-26.
[23] *Weekly Oregonian*, Nov. 1, 8, 1856.

Oregon "to free labor, out of love for the teeming millions of poor white laborers." Both Dryer and Bush scoffed at these budding Republican efforts. Still clinging to the Whig party and refusing to admit that it was dead, Dryer declared that the Republicans acted as if antislavery sentiment had been originated by them. On the other hand, Bush announced that the Republicans exaggerated the slavery issue, and he warned the electorate not "to leave the old Democratic flag" to join "this National Wool party — this Eugene Negro equality movement."[24]

Democrats held a series of county conventions to counteract the antislavery propaganda. Stoutly denying that theirs was a proslavery party, they objected to making slavery an issue and followed the lead of the Lane County Convention which demanded a referendum on the question. The Polk County Convention also demanded a public vote on "a clause prohibiting the emigration [sic] and residence, among us of *free negroes and mulattoes.*"[25] Democratic leaders immediately supported the referendum suggestions. In fact, some Democrats became so committed to the idea that they advocated electing only those candidates to the constitutional convention who favored a referendum. When Matthew P. Deady, a prominent Democrat, announced himself as a proslavery candidate and declared he would "regret [seeing] the party split in trying to establish slavery," Addison Gibbs, the future war governor of Oregon, expressed surprise. Writing to Deady, Gibbs main-

---

[24] *Ibid.*, Feb 7, Mar. 21, Apr. 11, 1857; *Oregon Argus,* Feb. 21, Apr. 11, 1857; *Oregon Statesman,* Mar. 11, 1857. The first political party in the Pacific Northwest devoted exclusively to halting the expansion of slavery was organized in the Washington Territory, created in 1853. One of the first acts of the territorial legislature of Washington limited the franchise to white men even though there were less than 30 Negroes in the territory. In August, 1854, a group of men, mainly from Thurston County, organized a Free Soil party movement which was as vehemently anti-Negro as antislavery. The leader, Samuel James, feared that slavery in the Pacific Northwest would result in a large, free Negro population. "If your efforts prevail," he asked the proslavery advocates in the Far Northwest, "and slavery [is eventually abolished] what is to be done [with] this black-colored, degraded African race? Surely, you would not want to let them loose among us [and destroy] the superior qualities and endowments of the Anglo-Saxon race?" James advocated confining American Negroes to their own territory to prevent miscegenation. Washington Free Soilers, as a group, embraced the idea that the United States was a country for the Anglo-Saxon race and that the people who migrated west to escape the presence of the Negro should not be forced to contend with slavery in the territories. *Pioneer and Democrat,* Mar. 11, Sept. 1, 1854, Aug. 31, 1855; *1860 Census, Population,* 582.
[25] *Oregon Statesman,* Apr. 14, 21, 1857; Johannsen, *Frontier Politics,* 42-43.

tained that if he assumed a proslavery stand, he would not receive 30 votes in Umpqua County where he lived. Gibbs doubted that it had even 15 proslavery men.[26]

The excitement over the slavery issue caused numerous letters to be written to the newspapers in the territory. Bush opened the columns of the *Statesman* to both sides of the argument, but he asked his contributors to concern themselves only with the economic value of the institution.[27] Various writers quickly took up their pens. Believing that slavery would be unprofitable, Thomas Norris insisted that slaveowners in Oregon, surrounded by free territory, would be unable to prevent their slaves from escaping to Canada or California. Another writer agreed, adding that the introduction of slavery would bring in eastern fanatics to "steal, without remorse," thousands of slaves annually.[28] Proslavery advocates argued that slavery would economically enhance the Pacific Northwest and lessen the labor hardships of individual Negroes because slaves could not be expected to plow or work in the fields throughout the whole year in Oregon. As a result, they "would only have to do one half of the labor . . . that [they] would in any of the States east of the mountains."[29]

The *Oregon Argus* had published antislavery letters as early as 1855. Therefore, in 1857 the free state element concentrated its efforts in that newspaper. Besides believing that slavery would create a social caste and deplete the soil, the majority of the writers contended that it would also discourage the white people of the northern states and Europe from settling in the Pacific Northwest. Thus, Oregon would lose the "habits and industry [and] thrift so characteristic among that element of the population." While "a *free white* population" more than anything else was necessary for Oregon to develop her resources, slavery would drive away this productive element of the population. Soon conditions in the state would be similar to those found in the less well-

---

[26] *Oregon Statesman,* May 19, Aug. 4, 1857; *Weekly Oregonian,* May 23, 1857; Gibbs to Deady, Feb. 3, June 23, 1857, Addison C. Gibbs Papers (Oregon Historical Society Library).

[27] Bush also solicited arguments. In March, 1857, he wrote to Deady asking for promised letters in favor of slavery and urged Deady to send them as quickly as possible. Bush to Deady, Mar. 19, 1857, in Florence Walls, "The Letters of Asahel Bush to Matthew P. Deady, 1851-1863" (unpublished B.A. thesis, Reed College, 1941), 35.

[28] *Oregon Statesman,* Mar. 31, July 21, Aug. 4, 1857.

[29] *Ibid.,* Aug. 4, 18, 1857.

developed regions of the South. Just before the election, "X. Y.," in a lengthy letter, repeated all the antislavery arguments. Yet, he was apprehensive about the people's final decision on slavery. He presumed that the attitude of many Oregonians toward statehood was similar to an experience he once had with three boys: "I had a pet squirrel which I said I would give to one of the three boys, if they would best answer this question: 'Are you a Whig or a Democrat?' The first said I am a Whig, sir. The second said I am a Democrat. The third said, 'Sir, I am just anything you want me to be for that squirrel!' "[30]

Matthew P. Deady was the only proslavery candidate elected as a delegate to the convention. His opinion on slavery was expressed in a letter to Benjamin Simpson following the election and just prior to the convention. Deady insisted that by legal definition Negroes were "just as much *property* as horses, cattle or land." Even though the federal government did not compel any man to buy such property, it could not prevent a man from owning slaves and taking them throughout the country. To Deady any argument about the economic value of Negro labor was "begging the question or rather dodging it." Whether or not slavery was profitable was a question for each individual to decide for himself and not the business of the community to decide for him. New England fanaticism over the slavery question was without foundation, Deady maintained, for, in the long run, the agricultural society necessary for the slave system would improve the New Englanders' conditions and prevent them from "swarming into overgrown cities, living by their wits, and becoming sharpers, thieves, rowdys, bullies and vagabonds."[31]

The constitutional convention, meeting on August 17, 1857, in Salem, quickly approved of articles restricting Negroes from militia service and from voting.[32] However, all attempts to prohibit slavery and the residence of free Negroes failed. A special committee had been appointed to deal with these problems and the delegates, with dogged determination, refused to discuss them until the committee reported. The report provided for separate articles on slavery and the exclusion of free Negroes to be submitted to the people.

Only one delegate, William Watkins, opposed the report of the spe-

---

[30] *Oregon Argus,* Dec. 1, 1855, Dec. 1, 1856, Jan. 3, 31, Mar. 14, 21, May 16, June 6, 1857.
[31] *Weekly Oregonian,* July 4, 1857; Deady to Simpson, July 28, 1857, Matthew P. Deady Papers (Oregon Historical Society Library).
[32] *Oregon Debates,* 224, 317-324.

cial committee and the exclusion of free Negroes. Believing that Oregon would soon cease to be an agricultural area and would become a commercial region, Watkins thought that the exclusion of free Negroes would prevent the growth of commerce. Many Negroes served on vessels, and without protection for members of their crews, captains would not come into Oregon's ports. Although Watkins disliked Negroes, he recognized that their backgrounds were the same as most white Americans and that their futures were linked with those of the white people. Therefore, he asked how white Americans could talk of freedom and, simultaneously, not attempt to ameliorate the conditions of a group of their own citizens? Rather than placing severe restrictions upon the Negro, Americans were under an obligation to improve the Negro's status because "his destiny and ours are so eternally linked." Amazingly, Watkins demanded the exclusion of the Chinese. Other delegates also favored Chinese exclusion, but they were unable to muster enough support to pass a Chinese exclusion article.[33]

From the adjournment of the convention in September until the election in November, the agitation over the slavery and free Negro issues continued. Proslavery interests made a special effort by stressing the economic value of slavery and by employing Biblical justification to sway the voters. Even outsiders took an interest in the proceedings. Charles E. Pickett of San Francisco forwarded a proslavery address to Deady, asking that it be printed. Lamenting the presence of numerous racial groups in California, Pickett warned that every foreign racial element would immigrate to Oregon if the state remained free. The only positive method of keeping every color and race from settling in Oregon was to adopt slavery. The opposite point of view was presented by the correspondent of the *Sacramento Union*. Characterizing the proslavery advocates as indolent, he wrote that the only people desiring slavery in Oregon were those who owned one or two slaves or those who had secured large land grants under the congressional donation act and were too lazy to cultivate it. The more recent settlers in Oregon, with their small holdings, were not in favor of slavery, he continued, and they would decide the issue and prohibit the institution.[34]

---

[33] *Ibid.*, 361-362, 384-385.
[34] (Corvallis, Oregon) *Occidental Messenger,* Sept. 26, Oct. 17, 1857; *Sacramento* (California) *Union,* n.d., in *Oregon Argus,* Sept. 12, 1857; Pickett to Deady, Sept. 1, 1857, Deady Papers.

The *Oregon Argus,* with less frequency than it had before the convention, continued to publish antislavery letters. Generally the *Argus'* antislavery following was pleased about the short lapse of time between the convention and the referendum date. It did not give proslavery adherents enough time to swarm into the territory and achieve the legalization of slavery. Only Leander Holmes, a prominent Republican, argued at length against slavery, and then solely on racial grounds. "We prefer the society of white people," he wrote. The claims of the proslavery element that the Republicans desired to uplift Negroes, Holmes insisted, were induced only to play on the prejudices of their followers. The Republicans did not want the Negro "as [a] bosom companion, but the proslavery element [was] attempting to force racial association upon them." Holmes regretted that the members of the constitutional convention had decided to submit the free Negro exclusion proposition to a public vote. If the exclusion policy was not approved, Negroes in the East would be encouraged to flock to Oregon and the state would be overrun with them.[35]

The most notable, and probably the most influential antislavery argument was George Williams' "Free State Letter," which was similar to Morris Birkbeck's letter written to the people of Illinois some 30-odd years before.[36] Williams began by informing his readers that his antislavery sentiment for Oregon did not extend to the whole country. Slavery was a local institution and he would never reproach the slaveholders of the South. In fact, he "consider[ed] them as high minded, honorable, and humane a class of men as [could] be found in the world, and throughout the slavery agitation [were] more sinned against than sinning." Tracing the early efforts in the Indiana Territory to secure the establishment of slavery, Williams noted that Indianians had based their request on the need for labor. Oregon was in a similar situation

[35] *Oregon Argus,* Oct. 14, 17, 1857. Holmes was nominated as the Republican candidate for secretary of state in 1858 but was defeated. In 1860 he was elected to serve at the Chicago Republican Convention. Hubert Howe Bancroft, *History of Oregon, 1848-1888* (Vol. XXX, *The Works of Hubert Howe Bancroft, San Francisco,* 1888), 431, 446.

[36] The reader may wonder whether or not Williams was aware of Birkbeck's "Appeal." Williams was born in New York in 1823, the year the "Appeal" was written, and moved to Iowa as a young man. Williams never mentioned the "Appeal" in articles or speeches in which he recalled his own letter. George H. Williams, "The 'Free State Letter' of Judge George H. Williams (Reprinted from the Oregon Statesman of July 28, 1857)," *OHQ,* IX (Sept., 1908), 254-273.

because the labor shortage was common to all the territories in their early years of development. The natural increase of population would soon rectify the situation, he thought. If the people really wanted to insure themselves of a labor supply, they should reject slavery because the institution stifled the population growth rather than increased it. To prove his point, Williams noted that Iowa and Missouri had equal populations even though the latter state had been created 25 years earlier.[37]

The primary thrust of the argument dealt with the economic value of slavery, which Williams insisted was an economic burden rather than a blessing. Slaves had no ambition and they cared little about the future, whereas the enterprising "free white man" was anxious to establish a comfortable home, to educate his children, and to provide for his old age; therefore, he had a strong inducement to "be diligent and faithful in his work." In addition, few Oregonians would be able to buy slaves because once they were transported to the Pacific Northwest, Negroes would be sold at much higher prices than in the East. Those slaves transported, moreover, would be of the worst type because few slaveholders sold valuable servants but only disposed of their troublesome Negroes. Even if Oregonians willingly paid the higher price for slaves, what assurance would they have that the slaves would work for them? Escape from Oregon through the forest and mountain ranges of Washington or to California, where the Negro community and the antislavery element would protect them, was too easy not to be attempted. Worse still, a slave might flee to the Indians and no white man would attempt to aid in his recapture.[38] Economically, the Oregon farmer would profit by using hired labor because a salary would only have to be paid for the working period. A slave, however, became a member of the household and all of his expenses, for the entire year, had to be assumed by his master. In return the slave could only work during the planting and harvesting seasons. "What could a negro fitted by nature for the blazing sun of Africa, do in an Oregon winter?" Williams asked. Throughout his economic argument Williams hinted that slave labor would prove so unprofitable for those who owned slaves that they would be forced to liberate them, thus inflicting a free Negro population upon the state.[39]

---

[37] *Ibid.*, 256-257, 265.
[38] *Ibid.*, 260-261.
[39] *Ibid.*, 267-268.

Finally Williams assumed a strong anti-Negro bias, claiming that Negroes were degraded and ignorant; if they lived among white men even as slaves, they would corrupt the morals of those whites who associated with them. The status of the Negro might improve but that of the white would be lowered, for society "like water, seeks a common level." Eventually both the Negroes and the whites would resemble each other in the habits, tastes, and activities of their lives. In the convention Williams also advocated the exclusion of the Chinese, stating that he wished to "consecrate Oregon to the use of the white man, and exclude the negro, Chinaman, and every race of that character. He believed the interests of Oregon would be promoted by such a course."[40]

The people of Oregon voted on three propositions when they went to the polls on November 9, 1857: the acceptance of the constitution, the acceptance of slavery, and the exclusion of the free Negro. They approved the constitution by a 4,000 majority and rejected slavery by a majority of 5,082 votes. The institution was favored by 2,645 people and rejected by 7,727. When Deady learned of the vote on slavery he declared, "I must console myself with the fact of being found with 'the honest minority.' " Least surprising, Oregonians approved of Negro exclusion by an overwhelming majority of 7,559. The electorate wanted none of the Negro race and they said so by a vote of 8,640 to 1,081.[41] Compared to the amount of agitation that had taken place, the vote made the whole affair seem like a tempest in a teapot.

The secretary of the American Antislavery Society in his annual report commented that the vote on the free Negro proposition proved that Oregonians were antislavery because of selfish policy rather than moral principle. In saying this he failed to realize that the Oregon vote simply reflected further the anti-Negro bias of the Middle West. The average western farmer, on the small plot of land which he tilled to meet his economic needs, could not see himself as a slaveholder. Nor did he wish the evils of the slave economy to follow him. By prohibiting the institution he hoped to prevent economic competition with slave labor. Many western farmers, whether they lived in Illinois or Oregon, equated the Negro with slavery, and if slavery was to be prohibited

---

[40] *Ibid.,* 268-269; *Oregon Debates,* 362.
[41] Deady to J. W. Nesmith, Nov. 14, 1857, Deady Papers; Charles Henry Carey, *A General History of Oregon Prior to 1861* (2 vols., Portland, 1935), II, 511-512; Matthew P. Deady (comp.), *The Organic and Other General Laws of Oregon, 1845-1864* (Portland, 1866), 129. Carey gave a county-by-county breakdown of the vote.

then the Negro was also to be excluded. In this respect the contention of Charles Stevens, that uniting the slavery and Negro questions on the same ballot determined the outcome in Oregon, is correct. Slavery and the Negro, to the average farmer, were one and the same. As the editor of the *Oregon Weekly Times* wrote when he noted the exclusion vote: "Oregon is a land for the white man, refusing the toleration of negroes in our midst as slaves, we rightly and for yet stronger reasons, prohibit them from coming among us as free negro vagabonds." John McBride, a member of the convention, later recalled that Oregonians had "no relish for the 'peculiar institution,' " but they desired less to mingle with the Negro race because "we were building a new state on virgin ground; its people believed it should encourage only the best elements to come to us, and discourage others."[42]

The policy of Negro exclusion was unsuccessful in most of the states where it was initiated. Despite the exclusion or restriction laws in the Mississippi Valley, the Negro population, except for Indiana, increased fairly rapidly. Oregon, however, witnessed only a slight increase in its Negro population between 1850 and 1860. If Jesse Douglas' figure of 55 Negroes is accepted as the number in 1850, the Negro population expanded by only 73, totaling only 128 by 1860. In the same decade California's Negro population grew by 3,924. However, the failure of Negroes from the East to migrate to Oregon cannot be fully explained in terms of race prejudice. The territory was in reality too distant to encourage Negro migration or serve as a refuge for fugitive slaves. Few escaping slaves would chance a trip across the plains and the mountains when Canada was a more accessible and much safer destination. Oregon failed to attract Negroes because it was principally an agricultural region. Negroes preferred to migrate to urban centers because the economic opportunities were more attractive and because the majority of them did not have the capital to establish themselves as farmers. It might be noted that prejudice in Oregon played some part in preventing other Negroes on the West Coast from settling in the territory. In 1857, when a large group of Negroes fled California, they chose Vancouver Island, and undoubtedly the anti-Negro attitude of the Ore-

---

[42] *Annual Report of the American Anti-Slavery Society, 1857-58* (New York, 1859), 115-116; Stevens to his brother, Dec. 26, 1857, in Ruth E. Rockwood (ed.), "Letters of Charles Stevens," *OHQ*, XXXVIII (June, 1937), 184; *Oregon Weekly Times*, Nov. 14, 1857; John McBride, "Annual Address Before the Oregon Pioneer Association," *OPAT* (1897), 42.

gonians, which was a popular topic in California newspapers, influenced their choice.[43]

Oregonians considered their settlement of the slavery and free Negro problems a triumph for the principles of the Kansas-Nebraska Act but their confidence proved premature. When their constitution came before Congress, it was connected with the ever-present slavery struggle. For a time the Oregon and Kansas statehood measures were linked. Republicans refused to vote for the admission of Oregon unless Kansas were also admitted. Southern politicians were reluctant to admit either territory and increase the free state balance in the Senate. The exclusion of the free Negro from Oregon caused several antislavery senators to oppose the constitution. However, other antislavery senators, notably Lyman Trumbull of Illinois, defended the exclusion measure, declaring that his antislavery principles did not require that Negroes "be placed on an equal footing in the States with white citizens." Reviewing all the objections raised, Dryer concluded that "the chances of our admission are extremely doubtful."[44] Finally in February, 1859, the statehood bill was passed by the narrowest of margins and Oregon entered the Union. Moreover, Oregon was the only free state with a Negro exclusion provision in its original constitution that Congress ever admitted.

Proslavery interests tried to secure slave property already in the territory during the interval in which Congress debated the admission of Oregon. Barely a month after the November decision, William Allen asked the legislature to appoint a committee to formulate a bill for the purpose but his proposal was defeated. The next month he made the same proposal and presented a formal bill. Dryer reported that a "bill to protect slave holders in their property (meaning negroes), has kicked up quite a stir among the harmonious democracy." But after the "stir" was over the bill was lost. In the following session, W. W. Chapman and William T'Vault presented a series of petitions and were successful in securing a judiciary committee consideration of a slavery protection bill. However, it received the same treatment as the previous one. The defeat of the last measure, coming just before the achievement of state-

---

[43] See note 9, this chapter. *1850 Census, Statistics*, 993; *1860 Census, Population*, 582.
[44] *Congressional Globe*, 35 Cong., 1 Sess., 1964-66, 2204, 2207; *Weekly Oregonian*, Apr. 10, 1858.

hood, ended any further attempts to secure slave property. The slavery protection element realized that their designs were of a "now or never" character and had to be achieved before Oregon became a state. With statehood all discussion about protecting slaves ceased.[45]

The anti-Negro attitude in the Pacific Northwest remained strong. As the Civil War engulfed the nation, one Oregonian remarked: "I am for the union but against free negroes on this continent. But save the union if we have to cut the damned Negroes head off and give his Boddy [sic] to the dogs for I have no love for them." Following the war, during the discussion about the adoption of the Fourteenth Amendment, an Oregon lawyer noted the opposition and declared that the middlewestern background of many Oregonians influenced their attitudes toward the possibility of Negro franchise. "There are [sic] a large class of former Northwesterners afraid of the nigger," he wrote. "Negro equality is their dread — If [the Negro] is enfranchised, they are perfectly certain they will have to sleep with him. You might as well bay at the moon as to reason with such men."[46]

In summary, the racial prejudice of the Oregonian was one factor among several that led to the exclusion of all Negroes, bond or free, from the territory. This was evident from the passage of the expulsion law of 1844 and remained prevalent during the 1850's. The people had no desire to furnish a refuge for the Negro in any condition. In this respect, the pioneers in the Pacific Northwest and the people in the Middle West held strikingly similar attitudes. For at the same time that the people in both regions reacted against the extension of slavery, they restricted the civil status of free Negroes and made it increasingly difficult for them to remain within their borders even as second-class citizens.

---

[45] Territory of Oregon, *House Journal, 1857* (Salem, 1858), 51-53, 270; Territory of Oregon, *House Journal, 1858* (Salem, 1859), 111-112, 118, 129; *Weekly Oregonian,* Dec. 26, 1857, Jan. 23, 1858, Jan. 15, 1859; Johannsen, *Frontier Politics,* 48-50.

[46] J. S. Miller to Henry Cummings, Sept. 30, 1862, in Johannsen, *Frontier Politics,* 204; O. Jacobs to Benjamin F. Dowell, Oct. 23, 1867, Benjamin F. Dowell Papers (Oregon Historical Society Library).

On the High Plains

The exact nature and extent of the slavery controversy in Kansas is complex and vague and perhaps it will never be completely known. The simple fact that antislavery groups in other sections of the nation equated every quarrel among the settlers in the territory with the slavery expansion issue threw the slavery question in Kansas out of proportion to its actual local importance. Their exaggerations caused "Bleeding Kansas [to become] more important in American life than in Kansas."[1] Moreover, antislavery Kansans, who had lived in the territory during the 1850's, later presented similar views in their reminiscences which they so willingly wrote to glorify the pioneering spirit. While recalling events in the territory from 1854 to 1860, members of the once active Topeka Movement ignored other issues, stressing the struggle over slavery and describing their efforts as a valiant attempt to prevent the fastening of Negro servitude on the territory. Although such descriptions were in part accurate, they failed to reveal the entire story. The Topeka Movement secured support for other than antislavery reasons. Some adherents joined it to acquire political prominence which they felt could not be achieved within the ranks of the more firmly united proslavery element. A considerable number of the early followers, especially those from the Old Northwest, supported the movement because they believed that the proslavery or "bogus" legislature had assumed too much authority and had deprived them of the right to choose local officials.

The attitudes within the Topeka Movement regarding slavery and the free Negro were dissimilar. Members of the Free State party, as the Topeka Movement was commonly called, who had previously lived in New England or New York and who had migrated to Kansas under

---

[1] Avery Craven, *The Coming of the Civil War* (2d ed., Chicago, 1966), 361.

the auspices of the New England Emigrant Aid Company, regarded slavery as a moral evil and endorsed the policy of equal rights for all individuals regardless of race. The vast majority, settlers from the Old Northwest and nonslaveholders from the border slave states, was generally unconcerned about the moral correctness of slavery. Moreover, many of them saw in the movement the chance to exclude all Negroes from Kansas. Anti-Negro midwesterners presumed that slavery was the prerequisite for a large free Negro population; therefore, one means of preventing the residence of free Negroes was to prohibit slavery. Although both eastern and midwestern factions usually agreed on their opposition to the "bogus" legislature, they were seldom in accord on other matters. Furthermore, the movement remained on the verge of complete disruption until the two groups compromised their divergent views on the major problem, namely the residence of free Negroes.

From the beginning of the Topeka Movement, the midwestern exclusion sentiment prevailed because midwesterners were the most numerous element of the antislavery population in Kansas. According to the territorial census of 1855, 83 per cent of the settlers in Kansas had previously lived in the Old Northwest, Iowa, Kentucky, or Missouri.[2] Antislavery agitators in the East sometimes ignored this fact. Although Charles Branscomb, a propagandist for the Aid Company, charmed his audiences in New England with exaggerations about the number of New Englanders in Kansas and about their importance in territorial affairs, a Boston editor refuted Branscomb's claims, noting that only "a tenth of the population" in Kansas was from New England and New York. Amos A. Lawrence, the capitalist sponsor of the Aid Company, recognizing the lack of enthusiasm among the people on the Atlantic seaboard toward migrating west, informed the resident agent of the company in Kansas to secure antislavery support from among the settlers who had previously lived in the Old Northwest. "We are too far off," he wrote, "we can pay some money and we can hurrah; but we can't send you men."[3]

Many of the first settlers from the Northeast lost interest in pioneer-

[2] U.S. Congress, House of Representatives, *Report of the Special Committee Appointed to Investigate the Troubles in Kansas,* 34 Cong., 1 Sess., No. 200 (ser. no. 869), 72 (hereafter, *Howard Report*).

[3] *Boston Daily Advertiser,* Nov. 19, 1855, in "Thomas H. Webb Scrapbooks" (17 vols., Kansas State Historical Society Library), VI, 233; Lawrence to Charles Robinson, Feb. 12, 1856, in James C. Malin, *John Brown and the Legend of Fifty-Six* (Vol. XVII, *Memoirs of the American Philosophical Society,* Philadelphia, 1942), 511.

ing once they arrived in the territory; the Kansas pictured by the Aid Company propagandists did not exist. Instead of fertile land with numerous streams and a mild climate, easterners found a waterless, timberless plain which they soon described as "the most dismal place possible." They also discovered that very little land was actually available for settlement. On the day that Congress officially opened the territory, May 30, 1854, not a single acre of land had been ceded by the Indians. Five months later only small portions in the northeastern part of the territory could be legally claimed by pioneers.[4] Nor did New Englanders find the facilities they anticipated. Restaurants were almost nonexistent, and hotel rooms, extremely primitive by eastern standards, had to be shared with strangers. Those men who had been merchants and who hoped to continue their trade soon realized that commercial enterprise in Kansas was too limited to be profitable. Therefore, many of these "fancy emigrants," as they were called by one Kansas editor, returned home after their initial introduction to pioneering.[5]

In contrast to the easterners' lack of interest, Missourians surged into the territory during the first several years of settlement. Their movement was stimulated by recent crop failures in Missouri and by the impression that New Englanders were migrating to Kansas in large numbers and were laying claim to the better land. Like all frontiersmen, the Missourians regarded the territory nearest them as rightfully theirs when it was opened to settlement. Although most of the Missourians pushed westward to acquire land, antislavery easterners presumed they were attempting to secure the territory for slavery. Eastern newspaper correspondents contradicted this idea, reporting that the Missourians in Kansas were primarily interested in land speculation, but antislavery agitators insisted that the quarrels over land claims were really arguments over slavery.[6] Moreover, they minimized the fact that lawlessness was common on the frontier and that easterners in Kansas usually were not involved in quarrels over land claims. The *St. Louis*

[4] Paul Wallace Gates, *Fifty Million Acres: Conflict over Kansas Land Policy, 1854-1890* (Ithaca, New York, 1954), 19.

[5] *New York Tribune,* Aug. 14, 1854; *New York Times,* Aug. 4, Nov. 24, 1854; *Ohio State Journal,* Aug. 10, 17, 1854; (Lawrence, Kansas) *Herald of Freedom,* Aug. 18, 1855; Malin, *John Brown,* 511.

[6] *New York Times,* Aug. 18, Nov. 11, 1854; Elmer LeRoy Craik, "Southern Interest in Territorial Kansas, 1854-1856," *KSHSC,* XV (1919-22), 348; David S. Sparks, "The Birth of the Republican Party in Iowa, 1854-1856," *IJH,* LIV (Jan., 1956), 30.

Democrat, probably more aware of the Kansas situation because of its proximity, reported that Missourians did "most of the fighting. . . . The people from the North come [but] do not get into trouble."[7]

Some Missourians in Kansas, of course, desired to make the territory a slave state, but the majority of the settlers from Missouri were nonslaveholders who favored establishing a free state. They suspected, however, that the members of the Aid Company planned to create an "abolitionized" Kansas which would serve as a haven for fugitive slaves and encourage the settlement of free Negroes. While openly proclaiming their free state sentiment, these nonslaveholding Missourians announced that they would never consent to a free Kansas unless provisions were enacted to keep out fugitives and free Negroes.[8]

At a slower but steadier pace, settlers arrived from the Old Northwest, mainly Ohio, Indiana, and Illinois. Their migration was spasmodic and part of a general movement westward from the Ohio Valley. Very few northwesterners moved to Kansas in 1854, but reports of agricultural conditions encouraged their settlement from 1855 to 1857. Thereafter, until 1860, emigration from the Old Northwest declined because of drought and economic depression in Kansas, due to the Panic of 1857. While a considerable number of northwesterners settled in Kansas during the 1850's, more people from the Old Northwest moved to adjacent midwestern states. Whereas 30,930 people from Ohio, Indiana, and Illinois pushed westward to Kansas between 1850 and 1860, 152,778 people from those states settled in Iowa during the decade.[9] And even though the westward movement from the Old Northwest was not directed specifically at Kansas, northwesterners comprised 50 per cent of the population in the territory by 1856. Six years after Kansas had been opened for settlement, the states of the Old Northwest and Iowa had furnished slightly less than 39 per cent of the Kansas population, 37,425 out of 96,217 people.[10]

---

[7] *St. Louis Democrat,* n.d., in *New York Tribune,* Oct. 23, 1854.

[8] *New York Times,* Aug. 3, 16, 1854; *New York Tribune,* Jan. 29, 1856; Craik, "Southern Interest in Territorial Kansas," 390; Samuel Wood, "Address of Col. Samuel Wood," *KSHST,* III (1883-85), 428.

[9] *1860 Census, Population,* 104, 156, 301; William O. Lynch, *Population Movements in Relation to the Struggle for Kansas* (Vol. XII, *Indiana University Studies,* Bloomington, 1925), 387, 402-403; William O. Lynch, "Popular Sovereignty and the Colonization of Kansas from 1854 to 1860," *MVHAP,* IX (1917-18), 380-392.

[10] *1860 Census, Population,* 166; (Lawrence) *Kansas Free State,* Mar. 3, 1856; Daniel Wilder, "The Story of Kansas," *KSHST,* VI (1897-1900), 337.

The majority of the settlers from the Old Northwest, like the anti-slavery Missourians, disapproved of slavery, but they were more interested in settling the land than becoming involved in the slavery question. The midwesterners were also disturbed by the New Englanders' advocacy of equal privileges for Negroes. A New Englander in Osawatomie, an area populated by northwesterners, wrote that there was an almost universal sentiment among them against admitting Negroes, slave or free, and against granting free Negroes equal civil rights. This anti-Negro prejudice of the northwesterners was strengthened by the similar attitude of the settlers from the border slave states. Thus, in territorial Kansas a large group of settlers was more anti-Negro than antislavery. Their principal objection to slavery was motivated by the realization that it would increase the Negro population, a population they did not want living in the territory. Concluding that this racial antipathy was the salient factor in guiding the antislavery sentiment of the midwesterners, a Kansas historian wrote: "The western settlers did not talk about the sinfulness of slavery; they despised the negro."[11]

The Topeka Movement began as a protest against the fraudulent elections held in the territory in 1854 and 1855 and against the subsequent acts of the proslavery or "bogus" legislature. Before the first territorial election in November, 1854, which resulted in the selection of a proslavery delegate to Congress, most of the midwestern settlers were only passively interested in politics. Many of them, in fact, did not vote in the election because of their lack of interest or because they thought the distance from their homes to the polling places was too tedious a journey. Following the election, however, the midwesterners and other antislavery groups grumbled about the interference in Kansas politics by proslavery Missourians who had swarmed into the territory on election day and who had cast fraudulent ballots. When the proslavery legislature was elected in March, 1855, by similar tactics on the part of Missourians, the discontent among midwesterners caused them to unite with the New Englanders and the antislavery southerners as an opposition group to the election procedure.[12]

---

[11] John Everett to his father, Jan. 25, 1856, in "Letters of John and Sarah Everett, 1854-1864," *KHQ*, VIII (Feb., 1939), 25-26; Wilder, "Story of Kansas," 337.
[12] *New York Times*, Jan. 8, Apr. 12, May 11, 1855; *New York Tribune*, Dec. 12, 1854; *Howard Report*, 73.

Despite its disapproval of the election results, the opposition force did not at first overtly resist the legislature. Rather, it waited to see what action the newly elected lawmakers would take. Meeting in July, 1855, the legislature played directly into the hands of the opposition by enacting a slave code and a law which empowered the solons to choose county officials. To the midwesterners especially, this latter law seemed a direct contradiction to their concept of popular sovereignty. Since county officials were elected throughout the Middle West, they resented the imposition of local officials upon them. Furthermore, county officials selected by the legislature would certainly enforce the slave code.

The legislature also refused to seat a number of antislavery men who had been elected in special elections called by Governor Andrew Reeder in those districts where fraud in the March election had been too evident to be denied. As a result, these men and the one antislavery representative elected in March, Martin Conway, returned to their districts, announcing that the legislature was a tyrannical body determined to force its rule on the people regardless of their wishes and encouraging open opposition to frustrate the legislators' laws and plans. In the words of one Kansas editor, the law regarding county officials and the refusal to seat the men chosen in the special elections did more to arouse "the long slumbering moral sense of the people" than the abolitionists "could have done in five years of incessant labor."[13]

Charles Robinson, the resident agent of the Aid Company, assumed the initial leadership of the Topeka Movement. Although Robinson succeeded in forming a military company, he was unable to unite effectively the New Englanders with the northwesterners and the antislavery southerners because he attempted to incorporate all three groups into the Lawrence Association, a local governmental organization established by him soon after Lawrence was founded. This was a mistake inasmuch as the settlers from the Old Northwest thought that the association was undemocratic. It had previously refused to grant nonmembers access to the timber and water resources in the area around Lawrence and would not allow them to vote at the association meetings although they could attend. Moreover, the extreme pro-Negro stand of some association members and their opposition to Negro exclusion caused the midwesterners to question the motives of the Lawrence Association. Some of them even spread the rumor that Robinson and his

---

[13] *New York Times,* May 29, July 20, 1855; (Topeka) *Kansas Freeman,* Oct. 30, 1855; Charles Robinson, "Topeka and Her Constitution," *KSHST,* VI (1897-1900), 293.

followers were working toward miscegenation. First they planned to encourage Indian and Negro marriages, hoping that the white people, after a time, would intermarry with the quasi-mulatto children of the Negro-Indian couples. Robinson denied the whole scheme, declaring that the racial mixture which resulted from slavery was "a very strong argument against the institution," but the rumor had its effect.[14] Believing that Robinson and the members of the Lawrence Association would be just as inconsiderate of their wishes as the "bogus" legislature had been, the midwesterners sneered at the Lawrence group, referred to them as abolitionists and Yankees, and openly declared that no midwesterner agreed with their Negrophile sentiment. The semblance of unity between the groups began to disintegrate almost as soon as it was established. Some of the midwesterners, who feared that the Topeka Movement would result in unlimited free Negro immigration into the territory, even transferred their allegiance to the proslavery forces.[15]

In order for the movement to become effective, it was necessary for the midwesterners to find a leader whom they could follow, who expressed their attitudes, and who could cooperate with the Yankee faction. James H. Lane supplied this leadership when he became a member of the Topeka Movement. Lane, a native southern Indianian, served as the lieutenant governor of that state from 1849 to 1852, years in which Article XIII of the revised Indiana Constitution was framed. In 1853 he became a member of the House of Representatives, where his wavering and irrational attitude toward the Kansas-Nebraska Act and other measures favored by the Democratic party caused him to fall into disfavor. After his congressional term expired in 1855, Lane went to Kansas; there he soon acquired the nickname of the "Grim Chieftain."[16]

---

[14] *Kansas Free State,* Aug. 20, 1855; James C. Malin, "The Topeka Statehood Movement Reconsidered: Origins," *Territorial Kansas Studies Commemorating the Centennial (University of Kansas Social Science Studies,* No. 4, Lawrence, 1954), 34-38; *Howard Report,* 658, 858, 898-899; William Phillips, *The Conquest of Kansas by Missouri and Her Allies* (Boston, 1856), 139. Frank Blackmar, *The Life of Charles Robinson* (Topeka, 1902), is a dated and favorable but informative biography. See especially pp. 43-87.

[15] *Herald of Freedom,* Aug. 18, 1855; *Kansas Free State,* Aug. 20, 27, 1855; *New York Tribune,* Feb. 15, 1855; Charles Robinson, *The Kansas Conflict* (New York, 1892), 83, 174; John Speer, *The Life of General James H. Lane* (Garden City, Kansas, 1897), 42.

[16] *Indiana State Sentinel,* Mar. 24, 1854; Wendell Holmes Stephenson, *The Political Career of General James H. Lane* (Vol. III, *KSHSP,* Topeka, 1930), 37-39; Jay Monaghan, *Civil War on the Western Border, 1854-1865* (Boston, 1955), 34.

Lane's contemporaries presumed that he settled in Kansas to recoup his political fortune. The "Grim Chieftain" continually denied the fact, insisting that because of his personal popularity, Indiana Democrats wanted him to stand for re-election in 1854.[17] The editor of the *Kansas Tribune* wrote that Lane "cares less for our interest . . . than for personal aggrandizement in the eyes of the world. Give him fame and he would — in our opinion — leave Kansas to her fate." But the editor also acknowledged that the "Grim Chieftain's" activities were responsible for the unity of the Topeka Movement. Although disagreeing with Lane's anti-Negro attitude, the editor considered it "just to Col. Lane, to say that we believe he is doing yeoman's service in the great Free-State cause."[18]

Upon his arrival, Lane was unsure of the political situation in Kansas and did not immediately join the movement. James R. McClure, recalling that Lane had spent several of his first days in the territory at his home, concluded that Lane favored the proslavery element but was willing to join the antislavery faction if membership in that group would be more advantageous to his political aspirations. By June 8, 1855, Lane cast his lot with the Topeka Movement. Speaking in Lawrence on that day, he criticized the fraudulent elections and the "bogus" legislature and supported the admission of Kansas into the Union as a free state.[19]

Lane succeeded in bringing the Yankees and the midwesterners together again by August. Meeting in Lawrence, both groups agreed on resolutions denouncing the election of the previous March as a great outrage, denying the legality of the "bogus" legislature, and pledging resistance to its authority. They split, however, on the course of action which the movement should take. Lane and his followers simply wanted to form a strong opposition party, but the Yankees insisted on creating a state government.[20] The major obstacle to immediate agree-

---

[17] Lane's claim is disputed by Stephenson. Considering the vindictive attitude on the part of the Democratic delegation in the House of Representatives toward Lane when he tried to persuade them to vote for the Topeka Constitution in 1856, his statements seem totally unfounded. See Stephenson, *Lane,* 87 *et passim.*

[18] (Topeka) *Kansas Tribune,* Dec. 21, 1855, Oct. 19, 1859.

[19] James R. McClure, "Taking the Census and Other Incidents in 1855," *KSHST,* VIII (1903-4), 242; Malin, "Topeka Statehood Movement," 63; *Herald of Freedom,* Aug. 18, 1855 (contains Lane's June 8 speech).

[20] *New York Tribune,* Aug. 25, 1855; *New York Times,* Aug. 24, 1855; *Herald of Freedom,* Aug. 18, 1855; Richard Cordley, "The Convention Epoch in

ment developed over what attitude the proposed government would assume on Negro exclusion. Lane declared that the midwesterners would only consent to a free state constitution which contained a Negro exclusion clause. Furthermore, he added that if an exclusion policy were not adopted, he and his followers might side with the proslavery element. Disturbed by Lane's threat to withdraw from the movement but still unwilling to consent to Negro exclusion, the Yankees proposed another meeting at Big Springs to discuss the matter further.[21]

The difference over Negro exclusion was resolved before the Big Springs meeting. Privately Lane and Robinson agreed to submit a Negro exclusion referendum when a state constitution was presented for popular approval. Undoubtedly this was Lane's suggestion; at least it cannot be denied that he was familiar with the policy of exclusion referenda. Moreover, Lane realized that such a provision would be approved because of the overwhelming number of midwesterners in Kansas. Robinson was probably aware of that fact too; yet, he had little choice but to accept Lane's solution if he wanted the support of the midwesterners for a statehood movement.[22]

The testimony of Andrew J. Francis before the Howard Committee, a congressional group sent to Kansas to investigate the situation in the territory, indicated that Lane and Robinson worked together closely after they resolved the Negro exclusion question. When Francis was

---

Kansas History," *KSHST*, V (1891-96), 42-43; Isaac T. Goodnow, "Personal Reminiscences and the Kansas Emigration, 1855," *KSHST*, IV (1886-90), 252; *Howard Report*, 85.

[21] Robinson, "Topeka and Her Constitution," 294. Lane's attitude regarding the Negro underwent several changes. During the Leavenworth Constitutional Convention he opposed exclusion. As a United States Senator from Kansas, Lane advocated the deportation of Negroes to Haiti or Central or South America. "Our prejudices against them," he said, "are unconquerable. I, myself, certainly entertain these prejudices, in common with others." Lane also promoted a plan to colonize free Negroes in western Texas. In the longest speech he delivered in the Senate, Lane suggested that an area in southwestern Texas be set aside as a country for free Negroes and former slaves. At no time did the "Grim Chieftain" approve of immediate Negro suffrage. Rather, he felt that Negroes should be educated before the franchise was given in order to prevent corrupt politicians from using the Negro's voting power. A year after Lane's death, 1866, his wife, Mary, an advocate of women's suffrage in Kansas, received a letter from a fellow advocate, suggesting that suffragists unite with Negro suffrage advocates to secure both reforms. Phillips, *Conquest of Kansas*, 139; *Congressional Globe*, 38 Cong., 1 Sess., 145, 672; Raymond G. Gaeddert, *The Birth of Kansas* (Topeka, 1940), 7-8; Thomas Moonlight to Mary E. Lane, Nov. 8, 1867, James H. Lane Papers (University of Kansas Library).

[22] Speer, *Lane*, 43-44.

initiated into the movement, Robinson explained its purpose and Lane administered a secret oath of membership. "The substance of [Robinson's] explanation was that Kansas was a beautiful country and well adapted to freedom, and the best territory in the world for the friends of freedom to operate on, more especially for those who were engaged in the free-white State cause." By the oath Francis promised to do all in his power to make Kansas a "free-white State." This account of Robinson's remarks reveals that he publicly acceded to the anti-Negro bias of the midwesterners. In addition, the *Leavenworth Herald* reported that the major aim of the Topeka Movement, after Lane successfully united the midwesterners and the Yankees, was to run all the Negroes out of the territory.[23]

The unification of the numerous groups comprising the Topeka Movement did not produce harmony; the abolitionists, antislavery southerners, Democrats, former Whigs, Republicans, and members of the Know Nothing party who joined the movement found it difficult to agree on anything except their opposition to the "bogus" legislature and the extension of slavery. And even with those common goals, the movement was "not an Abolition affair, nor a Republican affair, in any proper sense," wrote one newspaper editor.[24] Rather, most of the members thought of themselves as oppressed and abused by an illegally elected legislature. Noting the diverse membership, a Missouri editor concluded that the anti-Negro, midwestern faction would dominate the movement because it was the only one large enough to oppose successfully the "bogus" legislature. Nor were the midwesterners rabidly antislavery, the editor added: "The majority of them adopt the cry of 'leave Slavery alone where it already exists;' but 'no more slave States.' "[25] A Kansan more accurately described the antislavery attitude of the Topeka Movement:

First, then be not deceived in the character of the anti-Slavery feeling [of the movement]. Many who are known as Free-State men are not anti-Slavery in our Northern acceptation of the word. They are more properly negro haters, who vote Free-State to keep negroes out, free or slave; one half of them would go for Slavery if negroes were to be allowed here at all. The inherent sinfulness of Slavery is not once thought of by them. One-third of the Free-State

---

[23] *Howard Report,* 192-193; *Leavenworth Herald,* n.d., in *Herald of Freedom,* Aug. 26, 1855.

[24] (Springfield) *Missouri Republican,* n.d., in *New York Tribune,* Feb. 20, 1856.

[25] *Herald of Freedom,* June 2, 1855; *St. Louis Democrat,* July 24, 1855, in *New York Times,* Aug. 3, 1855.

party is made up of men who act from convictions of conscience — the remaining two thirds are Free-State men from conviction that the profits of Freedom, derivable in the shape of customers, would be greater than if Slavery existed.[26]

The reports of the deliberations at Big Springs, on September 5, 1855, were somewhat garbled and confused, but they all revealed that the major decision reached initiated the Topeka Constitution and that the major topic was Negro exclusion.[27] In fact, a resolution in the platform report, demanding the exclusion of all Negroes and stringent laws to enforce the provison, caused a seven-hour discussion. Most of the Yankees and a few Pennsylvanians opposed the resolution, but the midwestern element threatened to disrupt the meeting if it was not included in the report. Therefore, all but one of the delegates accepted the platform report.[28] Charles Stearns, dissenting solely because of the exclusion provision, wrote: "All sterling anti-slavery men, here and elsewhere, cannot keep from spitting on it, and all pro-slavery people must, in their hearts, perfectly despise the base sycophants who originated and adopted it."[29]

Several of Lane's contemporaries later remarked that Negro exclusion was the "Grim Chieftain's" idea and that he alone achieved its incorporation in the platform report. Writing on this period of Kansas history, eastern historians stressed the importance of the slavery question while ignoring the issue of the place of the Negro in the territorial society. They also presumed that Lane, whom they pictured as a diabolical Negro-hater imposing his will upon the majority, was solely responsible for the Negro exclusion provision. Such conclusions fail to

---

[26] *New York Tribune*, July 12, 1855.

[27] The three major free state newspapers in the territory which reported the proceedings contained different accounts about the order of business. George W. Brown, editor of the *Herald of Freedom*, went to the convention intending to take down a verbatim account but was prevented from doing so by an arm injury. Brown's version, however, was accepted by the New York newspapers and reprinted almost as it appeared in the *Herald. Herald of Freedom*, Sept. 8, 15, 1855; *New York Times*, Sept. 22, 1855; *New York Tribune*, Sept. 21, 1855; *Kansas Free State*, Sept. 10, 1855; *Kansas Tribune*, Sept. 15, 1855. For an account of other matters discussed at Big Springs see R. G. Elliott, "Proceedings of the Territorial Delegate Convention Held at Big Springs on the 5th and 6th of September, 1855," *KSHST*, VIII (1903-4), 372.

[28] *Herald of Freedom*, Sept. 8, 1855; *Kansas Tribune*, May 12, 1856; *New York Tribune*, Sept. 21, 1855, Apr. 19, 1856; *New York Times*, Sept. 22, 1855; Daniel W. Wilder, *The Annals of Kansas* (Topeka, 1875), 60-61.

[29] *Kansas Free State*, Sept. 24, 1855.

take into consideration the dominant midwestern sentiment on Negro exclusion. The majority of the people in Kansas were from the Old Northwest, and they reflected the patterns of their former place of residence. Lane's influence on the exclusion provision was exerted as that of a midwesterner expressing a midwestern attitude. It seems doubtful that he could have secured the adoption of the resolution without support. Moreover, activities prior to the meeting suggest the existence of support. At six district meetings to elect delegates to the Big Springs convention, the voters specifically instructed the delegates to secure a Negro exclusion provision. Except for the districts along the Kansas River in the vicinity of Lawrence, anti-Negro sentiment was overwhelming among the antislavery settlers. Lane thus found backing for the exclusion resolution from most of the delegates at the Big Springs meeting. Opposition existed but as R. G. Elliott later recalled, the majority of the delegates at Big Springs felt that "if we are to have the negro (pronounced nigger), we want to be masters of them."[30]

Despite the resolution adopted at Big Springs, the conflicting opinions regarding Negro exclusion continued to cause dissension in the movement. Settlers outside of the Lawrence area, demanding a more definite assurance of a "free-white state," hinted that they would not vote for delegates to the proposed constitutional convention at Topeka unless a firmer guarantee were given. Therefore, the members of the movement's executive committee, meeting in the latter part of September, 1855, to implement the convention, offered an inducement to encourage voting. Thomas W. Higginson, a member of the committee, mentioned such an inducement without specifically stating what it was. It might have been the decision to debar Negroes from voting in the election for delegates to the constitutional convention, or perhaps it was a promise to submit the Negro exclusion question to a popular referendum. The "Record of the Executive Committee" reveals that the committee adopted the restrictive franchise at the September meeting. During the constitutional convention, the committee on miscellaneous business reported that previous action of the executive committee obligated the convention to submit the Negro question to a popular vote. Whatever the inducement it was effective, for the election occurred without incident.[31]

---

[30] *Ibid.*, Sept. 3, 1855; *Herald of Freedom,* Sept. 1, 1855; Malin, "Topeka Statehood Movement," 46; Elliott, "Big Springs Convention," 373.

[31] [Joel K. Goodwin], "Record of the Executive Committee of the Kansas Territory, from August 15, 1855 to February 11, 1856," MS (Kansas State Historical

The Topeka Constitutional Convention split into three political factions upon meeting on October 23, 1855: the Yankees and two Democratic groups. Members of the one Democratic group, composed primarily of the younger men, hoped to make their political fortunes at the convention, while members of the other presumed the convention might help them regain the political fortunes they had lost. The Democrats, having interests in common, united on controversial issues. Moreover, Democrats could easily be detected because, as one of them recalled, "they carried constitutions of Indiany and Pennsylvany to guide them in their work."[32]

The first item of business, of course, was the election of officers; only the presidency was seriously contested. The candidates were John A. Wakefield, described as a "free-soiler, up to the hub — hub and all," William Y. Roberts, a young Democrat, and Lane, who was elected.[33] The *New York Times* correspondent at the convention wrote that Lane was not popular and was not even considered for the presidency before the convention met, but that "the honest squatters" did not possess the "wily cunning of a trained politician" to combat his campaign. On the other hand, a Democratic editor, in New York state thought that the Negro question influenced Lane's election. His strong championship of the exclusion policy adopted at Big Springs won for him the votes of the midwestern element because "the Western States have peculiar notions about that matter." This latter interpretation seems more accurate than the somewhat biased opinion of the *Times* reporter. At least Lane emphasized the exclusion question in his opening address. "The perplexing question will be the Negroes, and I think the people will be

---

Society Library), n.p.; Higginson to H. B. Hurd, n.d., Thomas Wentworth Higginson Papers (Kansas State Historical Society Library); *Howard Report*, 47; *New York Tribune*, Nov. 14, 1855.

[32] Robinson, "Topeka and Her Constitution," 295; Phillips, *Conquest of Kansas*, 129-131.

[33] Samuel Smith, "Journal of the Topeka Convention," MS (Kansas State Historical Society Library), n.p.; *Herald of Freedom*, Nov. 6, 1855; *New York Times*, Nov. 10, 1855; Phillips, *Conquest of Kansas*, 44. Lane said he wanted to be elected president of the convention to vindicate himself from and to end gossip about a rape scandal in which he was involved. If this was the true reason, it did not succeed. During the convention the scandal continued, and Lane challenged G. P. Lowrey to a duel because of uncomplimentary remarks. Robinson intervened, explaining to Lane that a duel would do more damage than good for the movement. The New Englander persuaded Lane not to fight; however, the challenge was not withdrawn. Robinson, "Topeka and Her Constitution," 296; *New York Times*, Nov. 10, 1855.

called upon to vote directly on the issue of allowing *free blacks* to reside in the State," he said, "and there is no doubt that on the grounds of expediency, a decided majority will favor such exclusion."[34]

Although there is no published record of the Topeka convention, newspaper accounts and a rather sketchy "Journal" reveal the major problems — a resolution endorsing the principles of the Kansas-Nebraska Act, and, naturally, the Negro question. The younger element of the Democratic faction proposed and supported the Kansas-Nebraska resolution, but opposition from the Yankees and midwestern Republicans caused its defeat.[35]

The Negro question was discussed in five aspects: suffrage, office holding, militia service, slavery, and exclusion. Suffrage, office holding, and militia service were quickly limited to white men and Indian males who would give up their tribal membership. Robinson caused a sharp but unreported debate by proposing to remove the word "white" from the militia article, but the motion was overwhelmingly rejected. Although slavery was prohibited, it was given temporary recognition by a provision allowing slaveholders two years to remove their chattels from the territory. Lane and his followers demanded a "fair and reasonable" attitude and announced that they would never consent to the prohibition of slavery if it inflicted a financial loss on any resident in the territory. Possibly Lane gained added support for the motion by stressing that the two-year provision insured the removal of slaves who might otherwise remain if they were freed in Kansas.[36]

As soon as Negro exclusion was raised, Lane proposed the formation of a special committee to write an exclusion article for submission to a popular referendum. The vote was not recorded but Lane's proposal and the committee's article were adopted. However, before the measure was approved several men expressed their opinions of Negroes. Lane, while offering his proposal, declared that the Negro was the connecting link between man and the orangutan. Rev. J. M. Tuton, a man of many professions and "generally down on everything . . . he

---

[34] *New York Times,* Nov. 5, 10, 1855; *New York Tribune,* Nov. 14, 1855; *Rochester* (New York) *Daily Democrat,* Nov. 7, 1855, in "Webb's Scrapbooks," VI, 158, 167.

[35] *New York Tribune,* Nov. 26, 1855; *New York Times,* Nov. 20, 1855; Smith, "Journal of the Topeka Convention," n.p.

[36] *Topeka Constitution, 1855,* Art. I, Secs. 6, 21; Art. II, Sec. 1; Art. X, Sec. 1, in *Kansas Freeman,* Nov. 28, 1855; Smith, "Journal of the Topeka Convention," n.p.; "Webb's Scrapbooks," VI, 226; *New York Tribune,* Nov. 26, 1855.

considered 'abolitioner,' " made the most scathing remarks. A native Tennessean and a former resident of Missouri, Tuton professed to be a minister, farmer, and former slave trader. Although his vilifying remarks were not fully recorded, he concluded with, "I kem to Kansas to live in a free-state, an' I don't want niggers a' trampin' over my grave." G. A. Cutler approved of Negro exclusion because he had "a holy horror of 'niggers' and abolitionists."[37]

The reaction among the antislavery settlers to the exclusion referendum was slight. Generally the midwesterners in Kansas approved the policy because, in the words of a *New York Times* correspondent, "they are terribly frightened at the idea of being overrun by negroes. They hold to the idea that negroes are dangerous to the State and a nuisance, and measures have to be taken to prevent them from migrating to the territory." Only one Kansas editor, to the author's knowledge, commented on the exclusion referendum and he favored it, insisting that the Negro question had to be settled and withdrawn from territorial politics at the earliest possible date. It had already been discussed too long, he wrote, and had caused too much dissension in the Topeka Movement. Although making no prediction of the outcome, he concluded that the votes of the people would permanently decide the matter.[38]

Following the adjournment of the convention, Lane, in accordance with a constitutional provision, called for a referendum in December to approve or disapprove the constitution and the Negro exclusion provision. Since the proslavery faction would ignore the referendum and only the antislavery element would vote, it was not necessary for either side to engage in a mass propaganda effort to sway the electorate. However, pro-exclusion men campaigned in Lawrence, and there were outbursts between them and the Yankees but these were neither extreme nor violent. The *Kansas Free State* reprinted articles about crimes committed by Negroes in Missouri, a policy which may have been simply a matter of reporting news or an attempt to influence the vote. The returns indicated that not much persuasion was necessary. Antislavery Kansans approved the constitution by a vote of 1,731 to 46. Of the 1,778 votes cast on the Negro provision, 1,287 favored

---

[37] Smith, "Journal of the Topeka Convention," n.p.; *New York Tribune*, Nov. 26, 1855; Phillips, *Conquest of Kansas*, 134-137.
[38] *New York Times*, Nov. 26, 1855; *Kansas Freeman*, Nov. 1, 1855; Webb's Scrapbooks," VI, 224.

and 453 opposed it; 38 people did not vote on the proposition. The *Howard Report,* probably the most reliable source on the vote, gave conflicting figures. The majority report recorded 453 votes against the provision, while appendaged material placed the opposition vote at 429. Regardless of the discrepancy, three out of every four people who voted approved Negro exclusion. Only the precincts of Lawrence, Manhattan, and Wabaunsee rejected the provision and their total combined opposition vote was only 103.[39]

The result of the referendum was easily predicted. R. J. Hinton, a newspaper correspondent, reported that "large numbers [of Kansans] believe in the Black Laws that disgrace some Western States." A settler in Osawatomie admitted that the majority of the members of the Topeka Movement favored exclusion.[40] This attitude prevailed because the people from the Old Northwest and the border slave states who opposed slavery were just as adamant, if not more so, in their opposition to the residence of free Negroes. Antislavery settlers from the border slave states, unjustly considered the Negro, and not the slavery system, responsible for the conditions from which they had fled. The people from the Old Northwest were still under the influence of the race prejudice expressed in that area. But in whichever section they had previously lived, the midwestern concept of society held no place for free Negroes.

The Topeka Movement underwent a final factional struggle in the election of state officers; again the Negro exclusion question played the major role. In December, 1855, after the constitution had been approved, a caucus drew up a slate of officers, naming Robinson for governor and William Y. Roberts for lieutenant governor. The slate displeased a group of aspiring political hopefuls who felt they deserved more recognition and who feared that Robinson would not encourage Negro exclusion. Therefore, they bolted and formed a "Free-State Anti-Abolition Ticket," nominating Roberts for the governorship and other midwesterners for the lesser offices. Neither Lane nor Roberts

---

[39] [Goodwin], "Record of the Executive Committee," n.p.; *Howard Report,* 54, 713-757; *Kansas Freeman,* Dec. 19, 1855; *Herald of Freedom,* Dec. 15, 1855; *Kansas Free State,* Oct. 29, Nov. 12, 1855; "Charles Robinson Scrapbooks" (2 vols., University of Kansas Library), II, n.p. The *Howard Report* indicates that one more vote was cast on the Negro provision than on the Topeka Constitution.

[40] "Webb's Scrapbooks," IX, 12, 66-67, 127; Malin, *John Brown,* 516.

supported the bolting group. Roberts publicly announced that he would not run on this "loaves and fishes" ticket.[41]

The bolters denounced the Robinson ticket members as abolitionists. To one Lawrence resident, Henry P. Waters, the accusation was absurd. He knew of very few "*true* friends to the cause of freedom" in the territory, and Charles Robinson and the men on his ticket were not among them. Rather, the Robinson ticket had been selected to draw support from the diverse groups in the free state element, and the bolting ticket was composed of rigid Negrophobes who based their campaign solely on prejudice against Negroes, hoping to secure the votes of the people who had supported the exclusion provision. Nevertheless, the bolting ticket was overwhelmingly defeated in the election held in January, 1856. Despite the victory for the Robinson slate, the unity of the Topeka Movement was still doubtful. One free-stater wrote that unity would be achieved only after the newly elected government passed prohibitory laws against Negro immigration.[42]

There were five meetings of the free state legislature but nothing was accomplished to implement the Negro exclusion provision. Robinson mentioned the provision in his opening address to the legislature in March, 1856, saying: "Also, the people, by a separate and direct vote, have instructed the assembly to provide for the exclusion of free negroes." This was the last official mention of the subject in the Topeka Movement. The first legislature elected Lane and Andrew Reeder as senators, memorialized Congress for admission, and adjourned.[43] The

[41] The slate of both groups was printed in the *New York Times,* Jan. 21, 1856. Wilder, *Annals,* 73; *New York Tribune,* Jan. 7, 8, 19, 28, 1856; *New York Times,* Jan. 9, 21, 1856; *Howard Report,* 604.

[42] *New York Times,* Jan. 9, 21, 1856; *New York Tribune,* Jan. 19, 28, 1856; Henry P. Waters to Charles Sumner, Jan. 21, 1856, Edward L. Pierce Papers (Kansas State Historical Society Library); *Howard Report,* 56, 650; "Webb's Scrapbooks," IX, 127.

[43] The exclusion provision caused a quarrel between Stephen A. Douglas and Lane, and it was responsible for Lane's final withdrawal from the Democratic party. Early in 1856, when Lane took the Topeka Constitution to Washington, he persuaded Lewis Cass to present it to the Committee on Territories. Douglas, the chairman, objected to the document, insisting that the Negro exclusion provision was part of the constitution and had been deliberately suppressed. According to Douglas, approval by the people automatically engrafted the provision into the constitution; yet, he could find no evidence of it. The Democrats were generally vindictive toward Lane for his role in the Topeka Movement. On his return to Kansas, Lane spoke at Chicago, May 31, 1856, vehemently lashing out against those Democrats who referred to members of the Topeka Movement as "nigger worshippers." Pointing to the acts of the "bogus" legisla-

"bogus" legislature dispersed the second and third meetings. At the fourth meeting, in June, 1857, several laws were passed, none of them dealing with free Negroes. After the free state element won control of the recognized territorial legislature in October, 1857, the Topeka Movement disintegrated.[44]

Briefly, it can be concluded that the race issue was all-important in the Topeka Movement and could have caused its disruption. Only the stronger opposition to the "bogus" legislature encouraged the various antislavery elements to compromise their differences on the race problem. In doing so, however, the referendum policy commonly relied on in the Old Northwest was adopted. The midwesterners had little doubt that exclusion would be approved because they were the numerical strength of the movement. On the other hand, the Yankees had no choice but to accept a referendum. Although they did not agree with the anti-Negro sentiment of the midwestern element, they had to acquiesce in order to secure an antislavery constitution. Looking back at the Topeka Movement one could easily criticize the midwesterners for not being concerned with freedom for all men.[45] Essentially their antislavery sentiment was selfish and unhumanitarian. Yet, it must be remembered that the anti-Negro attitudes expressed in

ture, which provided for a six-month jail sentence for kidnapping a white child and the death penalty for secreting slaves out of the territory, Lane asked, "Who worships 'niggers,' and slave 'nigger' babies, at that?" Charles Robinson, "Origins of the Topeka Movement" (MS copy of an article in Charles Robinson Papers, University of Kansas Library), n.p.; *New York Tribune,* Apr. 19, 1856.

[44] *Organization of the Free State Government in Kansas with the Inaugural Speech and Message of Governor Robinson* (Washington, D.C., 1856), 6; "Journal of the Topeka House of Representatives," MS (Kansas State Historical Society Library), 27; Franklin G. Adams, "The Capitals of Kansas," *KSHST,* VIII (1903-4), 346-347; Timothy Dwight Thacher, "The Rejected Constitutions," *KSHST,* III (1883-85), 438. Robinson declared that the purpose of the Topeka Movement was simply to hold together the various forces opposed to the "bogus" legislature and that few of the movement's leaders believed Kansas would be admitted under the Topeka Constitution. Timothy Dwight Thacher, agreeing with Robinson, insisted that even for this purpose the Topeka Movement was necessary. There were so many divergent groups in the territory that without unity they would have drifted, become demoralized, and probably been beaten. By August, 1856, five months after the Topeka government had been put into operation, antislavery Kansans assumed that the movement would not succeed, but they wanted the government to continue in order to serve as a barrier against the enforcement of the laws of the "bogus" legislature. Robinson, *Kansas Conflict,* 169; Thacher, "Rejected Constitutions," 438; Green B. Raum to John A. Logan, Aug. 7, 1856, Logan Family Papers.

[45] See Alice Nichols, *Bleeding Kansas* (New York, 1954), 251 *et passim.*

the Topeka Movement and the racial attitudes expressed in the older Middle West were identical. Actually, the majority of the settlers in Kansas were from the Old Northwest and Missouri, and they brought to Kansas their ideas and ideals developed east of and just beyond the Mississippi River. It is hardly to be expected that the pioneers from the Ohio Valley who had settled in the Kansas Territory would vault to the moral leadership of the whole country by granting equal social and political status to free Negroes. Their faults were obvious but they were no worse than those of the people they had left behind them.

The Negro exclusion and slavery questions became less important in Kansas and in the other western territories during the latter part of the 1850's. Negro exclusion was discussed but, for all practical purposes, such discussions were concerned with a nonexistent problem. The slavery expansion issue, on the other hand, shifted almost completely into national politics and the actual threat of slavery in the territories, without positive legislation to protect it, was hypothetical. After the free state element in Kansas gained control of the territorial legislature in the October elections of 1857, the slavery issue in the territory began to wane. The failure of the proslavery element to secure statehood for Kansas under the Lecompton Constitution, which incidently prohibited the residence of free Negroes, was the death knell for slavery in the territory. This fact was so evident to the small number of slaveholders in Kansas that they removed their chattels. Of the 55 slaves reported to be in the territory in 1856, only 2 remained by 1860.[46]

After 1857 the liberal element in the free state faction also effectively suppressed attempts to place restrictions on free Negroes. During the meetings at which the Leavenworth Constitution was framed, in March and April, 1858, restricted suffrage and Negro exclusion motions were introduced but quickly and quietly dropped. The document which emerged, in the words of a Kansas editor, contained no "blots [or] dark doctrines of hate or malice." Even James H. Lane, who had so ardently demanded exclusion in 1855, championed equal rights and pleaded with the anti-Negro faction at the convention "to become educated [on the Negro question] as I have."[47]

---

[46] Monaghan, *War on the Western Border,* 40-44; *Kansas Free State,* Mar. 3, 1856; *1860 Census, Population,* 166.

[47] Leverett Spring, *Kansas: The Prelude to the War for the Union* (Boston, 1885), 259-260; Robinson, "Origins of the Topeka Movement," n.p.

The people of Kansas rejected the Leavenworth document but not because of its generosity to the Negro. On the whole, the electorate had lost interest in constitutions and constitutional referenda. Besides the public vote on the Topeka Constitution in December, 1855, Kansans had since been called upon to vote twice on the Lecompton Constitution, first by the proslavery forces in December, 1857, and again in January, 1858, by the free state legislature elected the previous October. As a result, only 4,000 voters, out of an electorate totaling about 14,000 or 15,000, bothered to cast their ballots on the Leavenworth document. William Phillips undoubtedly stated the sentiments of most Kansans by writing that after 1857 "constitution making, like the grasshopper had become a burden."[48]

When Kansans framed the Wyandotte Constitution in July, 1859, the civil rights question was heatedly debated. In fact, one delegate commented that the Negro "is of such an important personage that whenever you find [convention delegates] talking together, Mr. Sambo must be introduced and his cause duly attended. It is in the convention, outside the bar, in the streets and hotels, boarding houses and even in the fashionable parlours of our Wyandotte friends."[49] Although the majority of the delegates unhesitatingly adopted articles debarring Negroes from voting and providing for the establishment of a segregated school system, they steadfastly refused to consider Negro exclusion.[50] Undoubtedly their decision was prompted by the desire to secure statehood for Kansas. During the previous session of Congress the opposition of several Republican senators to the exclusion provision in the Oregon Constitution caused extensive debate. For a time it appeared as if the provision would prevent congressional approval of the Oregon document. With this knowledge still fresh in their minds and aware that their constitution would have to secure every Republican vote in order to insure the admission of Kansas, the delegates at

---

[48] Robinson, *Kansas Conflict*, 383; Spring, *Kansas*, 261; John A. Martin, "The Address of Gov. John A. Martin," *KSHST*, III (1883-85), 387; Gaeddert, *Birth of Kansas*, 36.

[49] Statement dated July 18, 1859, James Hanway Papers (Kansas State Historical Society Library).

[50] *Kansas Constitutional Convention: A Reprint of the Proceedings and Debates of the Convention Which Framed the Constitution of Kansas at Wyandotte in July, 1859* (Topeka, 1920), 56, 77, 121, 172, 180, 182, 193, 324-325, 465; Benjamin Simpson, "The Wyandotte Constitutional Convention: A Recollection," *KSHST*, I (1881), 236.

Wyandotte did not wish to risk the possibility of having their constitution rejected.

A number of the Democratic delegates, however, refused to accept the decision of the convention. They repudiated the constitution, declaring that it failed to comply with popular sentiment on exclusion. Pointing to the overwhelming approval which exclusion had received in the referendum of December, 1855, these Democrats insisted that feelings on the subject could not have been completely reversed in four years.[51]

Democratic editors promptly warned the people about the dire consequences of permitting the unlimited immigration of free Negroes. The editor of the *Kansas Herald* announced that the "future state [would become] a sort of Botany Bay [for] all the lazy, worthless, vagabond Free negroes of the other States." Or worse still, Kansas would become a haven and a home for Missouri's runaway slaves.[52]

Republican editors denied such predictions. Moreover, they agreed that Negro exclusion was a "stale and threadbare" question raised by the Democrats only to offset their disappointment resulting from their inability to control territorial politics. The editor of the *Emporia News* realistically stated that the time had come in Kansas for politicians to stop inserting the cry of "Nigger, nigger, nigger" into every issue in territorial politics and to stop relying on the nonexistent slavery and free Negro questions to secure political advantage.[53] The ever-cantankerous editor of the *Herald of Freedom,* George W. Brown, took the occasion to criticize Democrats for their anti-Negro stand and Republicans for not granting Negroes the right to vote and for establishing segregated schools. According to Brown, Republicans were "miserable hypocrites" who flaunted their devotion to the Negro but would not grant him equal rights.[54]

Despite the lack of an exclusion provision, the Kansas electorate approved the Wyandotte Constitution on October 4, 1859.[55] After a

---

[51] Democrats also opposed the boundaries of Kansas and the failure of the constitution to limit the powers of the legislature. See Gaeddert, *Birth of Kansas,* 57, 73.

[52] (Leavenworth) *Kansas Weekly Herald,* Aug. 6, 17, 1859. Other statements can be found in the *Kansas Tribune,* Aug. 4, 1859, and the (Wyandotte, Kansas) *Western Argus,* May 21, 1859.

[53] *Lawrence* (Kansas) *Republican,* Sept. 22, 1859; *Emporia* (Kansas) *News,* Aug. 13, 17, Sept. 19, 24, 1859.

[54] *Herald of Freedom,* Aug. 13, 1859.

[55] Spring, *Kansas,* 164.

fourteen-month delay, Congress finally admitted Kansas in January, 1861. Robinson became the first governor and Lane one of the first senators. Thus, after many constitutional conventions and much waiting, the leaders of the Topeka Movement finally controlled the political affairs of Kansas.

Restrictions against free Negroes in Utah, Colorado, New Mexico, and Nebraska varied, but they were similar to the restrictions found in the Ohio Valley. All of the territories debarred Negroes from voting and from testifying against a white person. New Mexico and Colorado also prohibited marriage between Negroes and whites. Only the constitution of Deseret in Utah restricted Negroes from the militia.[56]

Insofar as slavery was concerned, the Mormons adopted a noncommittal attitude; their laws neither sanctioned nor prohibited the institution. Although Brigham Young personally disapproved of slavery, he welcomed religious followers who owned slaves. Basically, Young attempted to avoid involving the Mormons in the national slavery controversy, and he presumed that his attitude would prevent pro- and antislavery Mormons in Utah from involving themselves in the problem locally. Yet, when Congress prohibited slavery in the territories in 1862, Young accepted the decision, demanding that his slaveholding followers release their chattels. The Mormons also considered the Negro inferior to the white man and even presumed that this inferiority continued to exist "in the next world," but they were unwilling to prohibit Negro immigration on the ground that such action was unnecessary. The argument was certainly valid; in 1860 there were only 59 Negroes in Utah, and half of these were slaves. Since 1850 the Negro population had increased by only nine. In all likelihood these were children, and perhaps no Negroes had migrated to the territory during the decade.[57]

---

[56] *Laws of the Territory of New Mexico, 1856-1857* (Santa Fe, 1857), 48; *Constitution of Deseret,* Art. VI, Sec. 1; Art. V, Sec. 1, in *Laws and Ordinances of the State of Deseret* (Salt Lake City, 1919), n.p.; Territory of Nebraska, *Council Journal, 1855,* (Omaha City, 1855), 136; *Provisional Laws and Joint Resolutions of the General Assembly of Jefferson Territory* (Omaha, 1860), Chap. II. The Jefferson territorial government, not approved by Congress, existed in the Colorado region before the Colorado Territory was created.

[57] *New York Tribune,* Feb. 13, 1857; Jack Beller, "Negro Slaves in Utah," *UHQ,* II (Oct., 1929), 124, 126; *1860 Census, Population,* 993.

The abortive Jefferson Territory, in the Colorado region, also failed to pass an exclusion measure; the 46 Negroes in the territory in 1860 could hardly have caused attention. Unlike California, the Colorado mines did not attract free Negroes to any extent. Nor was the legalization of slavery likely. The Colorado rush of 1858-59 served as an escape valve for midwesterners who were hard pressed by the Panic of 1857. The miners in Colorado came principally from the Ohio and Mississippi valleys and their interests were almost exclusively directed toward prospecting for gold. Even newspapers in the region ignored national problems. Only one editor mentioned to any extent the struggle in the East which was disrupting the nation, and he placed the entire blame on the "almighty Negro."[58]

The opinions of the New Mexican legislatures toward slavery and the free Negro questions vacillated. During the early 1850's numerous resolutions requesting the prohibition of slavery were passed or forwarded to Congress. While racial antipathy was not mentioned as a reason for the requests, the passage of an exclusion law in 1856, similar to those in the Middle West, gave evidence that racial enmity existed in New Mexico. The law forbade the further immigration of free Negroes and required those living in the territory to post a $200 bond to insure their good behavior and self-support.[59]

Completely reversing its antislavery position in 1859, the New Mexican legislature passed a slave code. However, it seems doubtful that the members of the legislature were fully aware of the true meaning of the act. The bill was probably the work of the proslavery interests in the territory. This was evidenced by the fact that the report issued by the committee considering the bill declared the lack of a slave code discriminatory against slaveholders in the territory and contrary to the Dred Scott decision. In addition, the five members of the committee who signed the report were of Spanish origin, could not read English (the language in which the report was written), and if they spoke the language, it was with difficulty. After the Civil War

---

[58] N. T. Bond, "Early History of Colorado, Montana, and Idaho," MS (Bancroft Library; microfilm, University of Washington Library), 4-5; (Denver, Colorado) *Rocky Mountain Herald*, Aug. 1, 1860; *1860 Census, Population*, 574; Paul, *Mining Frontiers*, 41.

[59] *New York Tribune*, Oct. 13, 1851; Hubert Howe Bancroft, *History of Arizona and New Mexico, 1530-1888* (Vol. XVII, *The Works of Hubert Howe Bancroft*, San Francisco, 1889), 442-443; *Laws of New Mexico, 1856-1857*, 48.

began, moreover, the legislature was easily persuaded by the Republican governor, Henry Connelly, to repeal the code.[60]

Nebraskans, at times, seemed unduly concerned about free Negroes; there were only 67 in the territory in 1860.[61] On the whole, the activities of Nebraska's lawmakers regarding the Negro question were influenced by events in Kansas.[62] The referendum on the Negro exclusion proposition in the Topeka Constitution caused the first Nebraska territorial legislature, meeting in December, 1855, to consider an exclusion measure. Following the postponement of the bill, the Negro question in Nebraska, as in Kansas, faded into the background for the next several years.[63]

Negro exclusion again became a public issue in 1859 after the Republicans gained control of the territorial legislature. Possibly the issue was revived by the arguments in Kansas over the lack of a Negro exclusion provision in the Wyandotte Constitution and by the charge of Nebraska Democrats that the Republican victory would result in equal rights for Negroes. At any rate, Republicans in the legislature introduced a series of bills and resolutions prohibiting free Negroes and slavery. Although the free Negro exclusion measure failed to pass, Democrats seemed stunned by the support it received from some Republicans. Aside from the fact that the bill was unnecessary, both parties decided to drop the measure in order to "steer clear of the negro worshipper, the negro enslaver and the negro persecutor."[64]

The Nebraska legislature passed slavery prohibition bills in 1859 and 1860 but the territorial governor, Samuel Black, vetoed them, declaring that the terms of the Louisiana Purchase treaty and the Dred Scott

[60] Loomis M. Ganaway, "New Mexico and the Sectional Controversy, 1846-1861,"*NMHR,* XVIII (July, 1943), 211, 213, 220, 243-244; Territory of New Mexico, *House Journal, 1858-1859* (Santa Fe, 1859), 79, 91; *Laws of New Mexico, 1858-59* (Santa Fe, 1859), 64-80.

[61] *1860 Census, Population,* 555.

[62] The population movement into Nebraska was similar to that of Kansas. Approximately 41 per cent, 9,206 out of 22,475 people in the territory in 1860 were born in the Old Northwest. Ohio led with 3,116 persons, furnishing more inhabitants by 1860 than any other state. Missourians did not settle in Nebraska in great numbers. At least in 1860 only 1,523 people listed their birthplace as Missouri. *Ibid.,* 560.

[63] Territory of Nebraska, *Council Journal, 1855,* 125, 136; Addison E. Sheldon, *Nebraska: The Land and the People* (3 vols., Chicago, 1931), I, 132-133.

[64] Territory of Nebraska, *House Journal, 1859* (Nebraska City, 1860), 124-126, 128-129; *Council Journal, 1859* (Nebraska City, 1860), 39, 43, 48, 53-54.

decision prevented any definite prohibition of Negro servitude until Nebraska became a state.[65] However, when that time arrived in 1866, it was no longer necessary for Nebraskans to make such a decision.

The slavery expansion issue created less excitement in the territories after 1857 because the pioneers realized that without legislation to protect the institution, large numbers of slaveholders would not migrate into the territories. This had been true in Indiana, Illinois, and California and was again proved in Kansas. Even though the "bogus" legislature protected slavery in Kansas, most slaveholders were still wary about settling in the territory. Possibly many of them agreed with a Virginia slaveholder who ventured to Kansas in 1854 and decided that the predominance of people from the free states automatically guaranteed the doom of Negro servitude in the territory if the decision were made strictly on a popular sovereignty basis.[66] In any territory where the populations of the free and the slave states were pitted against each other for control and where the people from the free states were interested in settling, they had the upper hand. The people in the free states, especially those in the Old Northwest, were eager to push westward from the Ohio Valley, and they were joined by the nonslaveholders from the border slave states. Because both of these groups far outnumbered slaveholders and their sympathizers, the political control of the territories would eventually fall into their hands. Their desire to exclude slavery from the areas in which they lived would almost certainly produce measures prohibiting the institution. All things considered, the knowledge of these facts quieted the territorial situation after 1857 and, at the same time, made popular sovereignty more unpalatable to the South.

The free Negro problem also diminished in the territories after 1857. The exclusion proposals presented at Wyandotte were, in reality, carryovers of past fears. The introduction of the Negro exclusion bill in Nebraska in 1859 was, in part, a Republican attempt to counter Democratic propaganda. Because pioneers presumed that slavery was responsible for a large, free Negro population, their concern about free Negroes lessened when it became evident that slavery would not be successfully established. Moreover, they believed that free Negroes did

---

[65] Territory of Nebraska, *House Journal, 1859,* 161-166; *Nebraska City News,* Jan. 14, 1860.
[66] *New York Tribune,* Aug. 14, 1854.

not have the financial means to establish themselves as farmers and, therefore, would not settle in sufficient numbers to cause concern. Certainly statistics would support such a contention. By 1860 the vast region between California and Missouri, except for the slave states, contained less than 600 Negroes, and 359 of them were in Kansas.[67] Of course, it must be realized that a larger influx of Negroes may have produced exclusion policies, but as of 1860 there were too few Negroes on the high plains to cause concern.

Immediately following the Civil War, any attempts to enact legal restrictions against Negroes in the territories were stymied by the newly acquired, liberal attitude of Congress. As late as 1866, Nebraskans attempted to incorporate a restrictive franchise provision in their state constitution but Congress forced them to remove it.[68] Whereas the lax attitude of Congress regarding legal restrictions because of color had permitted the enactment of black laws in the free states and territories before 1860, the opposition of leading radical Republicans to such policies immediately following the war and the later inconsistency of such measures with the Fourteenth and Fifteenth amendments, adopted in 1868 and 1870, prevented legal restrictions. Henceforth, Negroes encountered prejudice in the Old Northwest and beyond, but they were no longer limited by statute provisions. Slowly legislators removed the black laws from the books. Although ignored and unenforced, the Oregon exclusion provision was not officially repealed until 1927. Indiana, one of the first western states to adopt a black law, held out the longest; the legislature did not remove the word "white" from the militia article in the state constitution until 1926.

---

[67] *1860 Census, Population,* 166, 547, 555, 568.
[68] Sheldon, *Nebraska,* I, 167.

Western Politicians and the Negro Question

Congressmen and senators, especially those from the Middle West, reflected the race prejudice of their constituencies on the national level. They restated much of the anti-Negro sentiment expressed in the constitutional debates and newspaper columns while either defending the black laws of their states or, as the election of 1860 approached, explaining the principles of the Republican party regarding racial equality and slavery extension. Prejudicial statements expounded by the most radical and by the most conservative Republicans clearly indicated that adherence to antislavery or anti-extension of slavery doctrines did not denote a lenient attitude toward free Negroes. The more politically astute Republicans, sensing the importance of the accusation of Negro equality which the Democrats circulated against them, attempted to allay the public apprehension that their party would drastically alter the existing status of the Negro, free or slave. Shortly after the election of 1856, Henry Wilson, the abolitionist senator from Massachusetts, declared that he could never believe in the mental or intellectual equality of the Negro "with this proud and domineering white race of ours," and he warned Republicans "to close their mouths against" the system of slavery and concentrate on nonextension. William H. Seward's more radical expressions declined in severity and by 1860 he described the Negro as a "foreign and feeble element, like the Indian, incapable of assimilation [and] unwisely and unnecessarily transplanted to our fields."[1]

Southern representatives took a special pleasure in baiting their colleagues from those states where black laws were on the statute

---

[1] *Congressional Globe,* 35 Cong., 1 Sess., 1967; 36 Cong., 1 Sess., 1684; George Baker (ed.), *The Works of William H. Seward* (5 vols., Boston, 1884), IV, 317.

books. This aroused ire among the northern representatives and forced them to defend their states' laws. Augustus Caesar Dodge, a Democratic senator from Iowa, declared that the 1851 exclusion law of his state was prompted by the fear of racial equality and miscegenation, two ideas he personally considered "wicked and disgraceful." As long as the two races lived side by side in the same country, he continued, the white race should remain superior and take all steps necessary to discourage Negroes from seeking any degree of equality.[2]

The Illinois senators, Lyman Trumbull and Stephen A. Douglas, were always in the front ranks when a defense of black laws was required. Trumbull, a Republican, expressed his attitude quite clearly during the debate over the Negro exclusion provision in the Oregon Constitution. Reprimanding William Pitt Fessenden of Maine and Seward for using the provision as an argument to reject the constitution, Trumbull declared, "I by no means assent to the doctrine that negroes are required by the Constitution of the United States to be placed on an equal footing in the States with white citizens." His opposition to the extension of slavery, Trumbull pointed out, did not indicate that he favored giving Negroes equal privileges because, "that is a doctrine I do not advocate."[3]

During his years in the House of Representatives and the Senate, Douglas persistently defended black laws and the right of a state to enact them. In respect to this defense, as with most of Douglas' policies, he never wavered. Upholding the free Negro exclusion provision in the Florida Constitution of 1845, the "Little Giant" argued that the only stipulation required for a territory's admission as a state was a republican form of government and this the Florida document provided. Douglas informed congressmen that the people of each state were entitled to form their constitution and laws in accordance with their views and needs as long as these did not violate the United States Constitution. Later in the Senate, in reference to the Illinois exclusion law, the "Little Giant" declared, "We believe that we have a right to pass all those laws that we deem necessary to the quiet and peace of our community." Because Illinois bordered on two slave states which required emancipated slaves to leave, the law was necessary to prevent the state from becoming "an asylum for the old and decrepit and broken-down negroes that may emigrate or be sent to it." Douglas also staunchly defended the Oregon exclusion provision, insisting that the

---

[2] *Congressional Globe,* 32 Cong., 1 Sess., Appendix, 118-119.
[3] *Ibid.,* 35 Cong., 1 Sess., 1964-66.

inchoate state, like Illinois, had the right to prevent the immigration of free Negroes if she chose. This, he maintained, was a question for Oregon to decide for herself, "and not for any other State to interfere with."[4]

When antislavery Kansans submitted the Topeka Constitution, Douglas raised strong objections but only because the exclusion provision was not included in the document. The failure to inform Congress specifically of a vital clause in the future state's fundamental law was reprehensible, he said, and he demanded that the document not be considered until the exclusion provision was incorporated into it. During the 1860 campaign one Illinois Republican remembered Douglas' position and suggested that Trumbull use it to argue that Douglas opposed Negro exclusion and favored racial equality. The Republican senator, however, ignored the suggestion of his somewhat naive correspondent.[5] Furthermore, on this issue both senators were in complete agreement.

Anti-Negro prejudice became more pronounced as the extension of slavery became a more dominant issue. It found its major expression among the peoples in the western free states who by their exclusion laws hoped to restrict the Negro to his then present location, and who feared that the territories might be inundated by the Negro race if slavery were allowed to expand. Early opposition to slavery extension centered in the Free Soil party, and some of the members adhering to its principle did so more out of "repugnance to the presence of the Negro" than to the moral revulsion of slavery. But abolitionist support and the tinge of Negro equality which abolitionism conveyed prevented most antislavery midwesterners from accepting the party; they remained within their own political groups and opposed the extension of slavery.[6] David Wilmot, the Pennsylvania Democrat, did not introduce the now historic proviso because he felt sympathy for the Negro as a slave. "I plead the cause and the rights of white freemen [and] I would preserve to free white labor a fair country, a rich inheritance, where the sons of toil, of my own race and own color, can live without the disgrace which association with negro slavery brings upon free

---

[4] *Ibid.*, 30 Cong., 1 Sess., Appendix, 44; 31 Cong., 1 Sess., Appendix, 1664; 35 Cong., 1 Sess., 1965.

[5] *Ibid.*, 34 Cong., 1 Sess., Appendix, 228; W. McCormick to Trumbull, Feb. 18, 1860, Lyman Trumbull Papers (Manuscript Division, Library of Congress).

[6] Louis Filler, *The Crusade Against Slavery, 1830-1860* (New York, 1960), 142, 187.

labor," he told his colleagues in the House. Privately he expressed his prejudice more explicitly, saying: "By God, sir, men born and nursed of white women are not going to be ruled by men who were brought up on the milk of some damn Negro wench!"[7] Such statements made it evident that in introducing the proviso, Wilmot really wished to preserve the western territory exclusively for the white race.

Race prejudice also influenced a number of the proviso's supporters. Jacob Brinkerhoff, an Ohio Democrat, who in later life claimed that he suggested the idea to Wilmot, strongly opposed any measure to improve the Negro's status while, at the same time, he attacked the extension of slavery. "I have selfishness enough greatly to prefer the welfare of my own race to that of any other," he declared, "and vindictiveness enough to wish . . . to keep [in] the South the burden which they themselves created." Or the remark of John Fairfield, a Maine Democrat and a staunch advocate of the proviso, might be noted. He preferred to receive dinner invitations from foreign ministers rather than from his colleagues in Congress because the diplomatic corps did not employ Negroes or use slaves, and there were no "black odoriferous niggers" present.[8] When a southern senator, as late as 1854, insisted that racial antipathy prompted Free Soil doctrine, Augustus Dodge was surprised at the remark. He had always been under the impression that opposition to the expansion of slavery existed in order to insure a white population in the West and could not remember anyone who had ever demanded the nonextension of slavery "for the benefit of the Negro."[9]

---

[7] *Congressional Globe,* 29 Cong., 2 Sess., Appendix, 317; Charles Buxton Going, *David Wilmot Free-Soiler: A Biography of the Great Advocate of the Wilmot Proviso* (New York, 1924), 174-175; Litwack, *North of Slavery,* 46-47.

[8] Brinkerhoff to Chase, Nov. 22, 1847, in Thomas Stirton, "Party Disruption and the Rise of the Slavery Extension Controversy, 1840-1846" (unpublished Ph.D. dissertation, University of Chicago, 1957), 312; Fairfield to his wife, Dec. 29, 1844, in Arthur G. Staples (ed.), *The Letters of John Fairfield* (Lewiston, Maine, 1922), 349.

[9] *Congressional Globe,* 33 Cong., 1 Sess., Appendix, 377-378. Race prejudice also produced support for the annexation of Texas. In 1843 a writer, signing himself "Veto," concluded that Texas would be valuable because it would drain the Negro population from the Altantic seaboard states, thus removing "this loathsome nuisance." Even earlier, 1838, a Michigan resident suggested that Texas, as a slave state, would draw off Negroes from the border areas and hinted that eventually the Negro population could be moved into Mexico. (Washington, D.C.) *Madisonian,* Dec. 22, 1843; *Detroit Daily Advertiser,* Jan. 27, 1838, in Kooker, "Antislavery Movement in Michigan," 257.

Anti-Negro sentiment at home forced midwestern congressmen to refrain from expressions which could be construed as favoring racial equality. Prior to the Indiana Constitutional Convention of 1850, as prejudice mounted in the state, Caleb Blood Smith was warned to guard his remarks about abolishing slavery in the District of Columbia so that they would not imply favoritism toward the Negro. Few anti-slavery leaders exceeded Joshua Giddings' blunt attacks on slaveholders, but even he admitted that the "black man [was not] the equal of the white man." When a colleague, whom Giddings had been baiting, asked him outright if he favored Negro suffrage in Ohio, Giddings refused to answer. Another Ohio antislavery representative insisted that he sympathized with Negroes, slave or free, but he would never consent to their living among the white people and would "vote against any measure that [prolonged] their . . . residence."[10]

The abolitionism of Benjamin Franklin Wade of Ohio was based on his dislike of Negroes and even after he became a radical Republican, he strongly advocated colonization to prevent the North from being flooded with Negroes. When Wade first arrived in Washington in 1851, he was impressed by the great number of Negroes in the capital, and he described the city as "a mean God forsaken Nigger ridden place." Although Wade professed to like the Negro better than the southern white man, he wrote that he could not abide their odor and bemoaned the fact that the food was "all cooked by niggers until I can smell and taste the nigger." As late as 1873 Wade was annoyed about the lack of available white housekeepers in Washington. He had tried in vain to find one because he was "sick and tired of niggers."

The Ohio senator's attitude was known among his followers because he admitted that his abolitionism in Washington did not carry over at home. As a result, one follower wished Wade continued good health "to fight the white man's battle." Moreover, conservative Republicans in Ohio favored Wade over Salmon P. Chase as a favorite son nominee during the Republican convention of 1860. They felt that Wade, a former Whig and a conservative on the Negro question, would gain more support from the uncommitted electorate than Chase, a former

---

[10] John Defrees to Caleb Blood Smith, Sept. 5, 1849, Caleb Blood Smith Papers (Manuscript Division, Library of Congress). *Congressional Globe,* 33 Cong., 1 Sess., 1057-58, 1071-73; 35 Cong., 2 Sess., 346; Filler, *Crusade Against Slavery,* 145.

Democrat who had acquired political eminence by defending fugitive slaves.[11]

During the attempt by Seward and Fessenden to deny Oregon admission, Wade refused to condemn the Negro exclusion provision. Rather, he based his opposition to the constitution on the provision debarring the Chinese from voting because he considered it the first step to the disfranchisement of all foreign groups. This was undoubtedly a much safer political stand and it might secure support from the foreign element in his state.[12]

The growth of the Republican party, more than any other factor, brought the race issue to the surface because Democratic editors and leaders fastened the doctrine of Negro equality to it. Republicans were portrayed as favoring miscegenation and full social and political equality. Democrats warned that the "Black Republican" party would appoint Negroes to governmental offices and elect them as state and federal legislators. "Negro equality," insisted one Indiana Democrat, "is the necessary logical and inevitable consequence of [Republican] principles."[13] By 1856, even before the name Republican had been accepted by a number of anti-extension state groups, Francis P. Blair, Jr., decided that the rise of the party had made the issue of race all important in the slavery extension controversy.[14]

Labels conveying racial equality were attached early to the Republican party, and Democratic editors continued to use them during the Civil War. Such epithets as "Abolitionists," "Amalgamationists," "Miscegenationists," "Freedom Shirkers," "Nigger Worshippers," and "Woolies" were common. An Iowa editor warned that the new party in his state was intent on glorifying the Negro at the expense of the white man and that its members would go to any extremes to follow

---

[11] Wade to his wife, Dec. 29, 1851, Mar. 9, 1873, in Hans L. Trefousse, *Benjamin Franklin Wade: Radical Republican from Ohio* (New York, 1963), 311-312; J. S. Cole to Wade, Feb. 4, 1860, Benjamin Franklin Wade Papers (Manuscript Division, Library of Congress); James Elliot to Chase, May 21, 1860, Salmon Portland Chase Papers (Manuscript Division, Library of Congress); Filler, *Crusade Against Slavery*, 224-225.

[12] *Congressional Globe*, 35 Cong., 1 Sess., 1966, 2204, 2207.

[13] *Ibid.*, 36 Cong., 1 Sess., Appendix, 238-239, 282; Litwack, *North of Slavery*, 268.

[14] Francis P. Blair, Jr., to Montgomery Blair, Sept. 21, 1856, in Helen Marie Cavanagh, "Antislavery Sentiment and Politics in the Old Northwest, 1844-1860" (unpublished Ph.D. dissertation, University of Chicago, 1938), 130.

the tenets of "Seward niggerology."[15] An editor in Ohio reprinted selected quotations from speeches of the more radical Republican anti-slavery proponents, labeled them the "Congo Creed," and used them to prove his charges of equal suffrage and miscegenation.[16] Democrats even revised the old abolition alphabet against the new party. Some of the selections included: "A is for argument — we've only one,/The almighty Nigger and then we are done; N is for Nigger, we fondly adore,/Without him we know that our party's no more; U is for Union, the patriot's pride,/But negro equality, or 'let her slide.' "[17]

In Illinois Charles Lanphier, editor of the *State Register,* printed stories of Negroes marching in Republican parades in the East and argued that this indicated the Republican desire for racial equality. Playing on the fear of Negro immigration, Lanphier pointed out that the abolition sentiment of the party would encourage masses of "a degraded and inferior race" to flock to the North. "Our jails and almshouses would be filled to overflowing [and] outrages too monstrous to be named would be of daily occurrence. Had we not better let well enough alone?" he asked.[18] Indiana Democratic editors emphasized white supremacy and vitriolicly attacked Negroes and the Republican party during the 1860 campaign. Mainly they charged Lincoln with favoring Negro equality and declared that Republican policies would lead to an influx of Negroes into Indiana. Republicans were planning to enfranchise the Negro, wrote one editor, and worse yet, amalgamate the races.[19]

Republicans, in answering the Democratic charges against them, were almost frantic to disclaim any intention of improving the Negro's

---

[15] Herriott, "Iowa and the First Nomination of Lincoln," VIII, 194-195; (Burlington) *Iowa State Gazette,* Jan. 16, Feb. 26, Sept. 16, Oct. 18, 1856, in Joel H. Silbey, "Proslavery Sentiment in Iowa, 1838-1861," *IJH,* LV (Oct., 1957), 312.

[16] Roseboom, *The Civil War Era,* 327-328.

[17] (Farmington, Maine) *Patriot,* n.d., in "John A. Logan Scrapbooks, 1859-1860" (2 vols., Logan Family Papers), I, n.p. The abolitionist alphabet, for example, included: "A is an abolitionist,/A man who wants to free the wretched slave; D is for Driver, cold and stern, who follows whip in hand,/To punish those who dare rest, Or disobey command; Z is a Zealous man, sincere, Faithful, and just, and true,/An earnest pleader for the slave — Will you not be one too?" Craven, *Coming of the Civil War,* 143-144.

[18] *Illinois State Register,* June 16, Sept. 28, Oct. 14, 1860.

[19] *Indiana State Sentinel,* May 5, June 21, Aug. 17, Sept. 1, Oct. 10, 30, 1860; Emma Lou Thornbrough, "The Race Issue in Indiana Politics During the Civil War," *IMH,* XLVII (June, 1951), 167, 168.

status and made it abundantly clear that their party had little or no humanitarian interest in Negro welfare. One Ohioan wrote that "the 'negro question,' as we understand it . . . is a white man's question, the question of the right of free white laborers to the soil of the territories." He further warned the Democrats to stop "shouting 'Sambo' at us. We have no Sambo in our platform. . . . We object to Sambo. We don't want him about. We insist that he shall not be forced upon us." For him the Republican party was created to improve and enhance the status of the white and not the Negro race.[20]

Republicans continually stressed nonextension as their major antislavery principle and declared it was impossible to interfere with slavery in the states where it existed because the institution was local and protected by the federal Constitution. In addition, they maintained that their nonextension policy would prevent the spread of the Negro westward. Negroes would not migrate to the territories unless they were taken by slaveholders; by prohibiting the extension of slavery, Negroes would be kept out.[21] Possibly Horace Greeley expressed the Republican party's stand most succinctly by writing that "all the unoccupied territory . . . shall be reserved for the benefit of the white Caucasian race — a thing which cannot be except by the exclusion of slavery."[22] Julian M. Sturtevant, the president of Illinois College, long considered a hotbed of abolitionism by former southerners living in west-central Illinois, noted the changing effect that the nonextension argument was having on individuals who had previously opposed the Republicans. Moreover, Sturtevant did not "regard the Republican party as less worthy of confidence and honor because it guarded against attacking 'the peculiar institution' in the slave states. Without that limitation it could not have been organized at all in this region."[23]

Besides defending themselves against accusations of racial equality and abolitionism, Republicans frequently turned the Democratic charges back on the accusers. Incorrectly asserting that Richard M.

---

[20] Earl W. Wiley, " 'Governor' John Greiner and Chase's Bid for the Presidency in 1860," *OSAHQ,* LVIII (July, 1949), 261-262.

[21] *Illinois State Journal,* June 20, 1860; (Indianapolis) *Daily Journal,* June 22, Oct. 6, 1860, in Thornbrough, "Race Issue in Indiana Politics," 168.

[22] *New York Tribune,* Dec. 17, 1860; Robert F. Durden, "Ambiguities in the Antislavery Crusade of the Republican Party," in Martin Duberman (ed.), *The Antislavery Vanguard: New Essays on the Abolitionists* (Princeton, 1965), 365.

[23] Sturtevant to Theron Baldwin, June 1, 1860, Julian M. Sturtevant Papers (Illinois College Library); J. M. Sturtevant, Jr. (ed.), *Julian M. Sturtevant: An Autobiography* (New York, 1896), 284.

Johnson, Vice President during the Van Buren administration, had a Negro wife, they insisted that miscegenation was more prevalent in the South where the Republican party was virtually nonexistent.[24] They also pointed out that Negro suffrage had been granted in Maine, Massachusetts, and New York during Democratic administrations and claimed that Democrats wanted slavery in the territories so that "capital should own labor" there in order to perpetuate the only practical "nigger equality in the nation."[25] While reversing racial equality indictments, Republican editors became just as emotional as their Democratic counterparts. One declared that the opposition party should be referred to as the "Mulatto Democracy," because its main efforts were directed toward "bleaching the darkies . . . the best blood of the Democracy [ran] in the veins of the 'peculiar property.'" Editors from Oregon to Ohio and beyond used the term "Black Democracy" and condemned the principles of the party as upholding the "divine right of niggerism." In Iowa the campaign slogan, "WE ARE FOR LAND FOR THE LANDLESS, NOT NIGGERS FOR THE NIGGERLESS" became increasingly popular.[26] One Iowan wrote to an editor in the Pacific Northwest that the charge of equality against either party was absurd, since it could only be achieved by sinking the white race into a partial state of barbarism to reach the present level of the Negro and to this no white man would ever consent.[27]

Republican leaders, despite their expressed opposition to charges of racial equality, felt something had to be done to indicate more clearly their position on the race question. In 1858 Francis P. Blair, Jr., his brother Montgomery, James Doolittle, and Edward Bates found the solution in a Republican supported colonization project in Central America. Montgomery Blair wrote, "It would do more than a thousand speeches [to allay the fears of the people] that the Republicans wish to set negroes free among them to be their equals."[28] Francis Blair, Jr.,

---

[24] This was an exaggeration; Johnson had two children by a mulatto slave, Julia Chinn, but he never married her. Leland Meyer, *The Life and Times of Colonel Richard M. Johnson of Kentucky* (New York, 1932), 317-325.

[25] *Illinois State Journal*, Aug. 14, Oct. 1, 1860.

[26] *Ibid.*, Oct. 8, 1860; (Eugene, Oregon) *The People's Press*, Jan. 15, 1860; *Rocky Mountain Herald*, Nov. 10, 1860; *Cincinnati Daily Commercial*, Mar. 16, 1861, in Perkins, *Northern Editorials*, I, 461; Luella M. Wright, "Henry A. and George D. Perkins in the Campaign of 1860," *IJHP*, XLII (Apr., 1944), 182.

[27] *People's Press*, Feb. 25, 1860.

[28] Litwack, *North of Slavery*, 272; Reinhard Luthin, *The First Lincoln Campaign* (Cambridge, Massachusetts, 1944), 66.

and Doolittle introduced resolutions to promote the plan in the House and Senate respectively. Blair declared that only by colonization could Negroes improve themselves and achieve happiness. Careful not to offend the more liberal adherents to his party, Blair described colonization as a principle of the founding fathers and used their statements to reveal the advantages it would offer to both races.[29]

Numerous Republican leaders quickly supported the new colonization plan. Trumbull wished any measure to remove the Negro "Godspeed." Giddings gave his blessing but insisted that colonization should be voluntary. Even the outspoken critic of the American Colonization Society, Gerrit Smith, declared the plan gratified him. Bates's approval remained so strong that he continued to stress colonization although Congress failed to take action on the resolutions.[30] Republican editors also gave the Central American project avid support. One in Oregon proclaimed colonization as a Republican standard and the only solution to the increasing threats presented by the presence of the Negro race.[31]

As the election of 1860 approached, Republican leaders, especially from Illinois, Indiana, and Ohio, made a concerted effort to disprove the charges that Republicans favored complete emancipation and Negro equality. Declarations that the Republican party was the "white man's party" became almost daily utterances in Congress during April and May, 1860. James Harlan, an Iowa senator, answered his question, "Shall the Territories be Africanized?" by concluding that Republican policy would prevent this and preserve the vast domain for the white race.[32] Albert G. Porter of Indiana, defending Article XIII of his state's constitution, insisted that the Republican party existed for the same reason that the article was adopted: to keep Negro labor from coming into competition with white labor. Neither he nor his party, Porter stated, ever accepted the doctrine of social and political equality because to support such ideas in Indiana would mean political annihilation. An Ohio representative maintained that not one Republican in

---

[29] *Congressional Globe,* 35 Cong., 1 Sess., 193, 3034; Francis P. Blair (comp.), *Collection of Pamphlets on the Slavery Question,* n.d., n.p. (Francis P. Blair, Jr., "Colonization Speech Before the Young Men's Mercantile Library Association of Cincinnati, Ohio, Nov. 29, 1859," 7-8).

[30] Litwack, *North of Slavery,* 273; Howard K. Beale (ed.), *The Diary of Edward Bates, 1859-1866* (Vol. IV, *AHAAR, 1930,* Washington, D.C., 1933), 192.

[31] (Corvallis) *Oregon Weekly Union,* Apr. 3, 1860; (Philadelphia) *Daily News,* Nov. 22, 1860, in Perkins, *Northern Editorials,* I, 425-426.

[32] Blair (comp.), *Collection of Pamphlets* ("Shall the Territories Be Africanized?" delivered in the United States Senate, Jan. 4, 1860, 4-5).

a thousand in his state favored extending equality, to any degree, to Negroes.[33] During the campaign the conservative element depended upon Thomas Corwin, an old Whig, to dispel radical notions. He stumped southern Ohio and southern Indiana declaring, "I am for the white man."[34] From the conservative viewpoint, the party had more to gain from the "wishy-washy" element of the Tom Corwin school than from the more extreme group. At the same time, Chase was urged to keep the extremists quiet because "they are losing the conservative vote . . . in southern Ohio and southern Indiana and that element will go over to the Democratic party if it is not stopped."[35]

Some of the radical antislavery Republicans also began to speak more softly about abolition and Negro rights. Giddings has been mentioned. Owen Lovejoy, brother of the martyred abolitionist, Elijah Lovejoy, and a congressman from Illinois, was another example. Representing the "most abolitionized district" in the state, Lovejoy's acid comments on the "peculiar institution" were well known. However, even as early as 1856 he assumed a more conservative position, and by 1860 he repudiated the abolitionists in his hometown, Princeton, Illinois. William Lloyd Garrison was saddened to find that Lovejoy had sunk to proclaiming Negro inequality and to declaring that the government of the United States belonged only to the white man.[36]

No individual did more to assure the Negrophobes about the principles of the Republican party than Lyman Trumbull. Soon after Congress organized in 1859, he declared, "We, the Republican party, are the white man's party. We are for the free white man, and for making white labor acceptable and honorable, which it can never be when negro slave labor is brought into competition with it." The "Omnipotence himself," Trumbull insisted, had created a distinction between the races which never could be erased, and he would never consent to Negro equality on any terms. Turning to the Democrats, Trumbull asked them what they hoped to gain by declaring that the

[33] *Congressional Globe,* 34 Cong., 3 Sess., 91; 35 Cong., 2 Sess., 981; 36 Cong., 1 Sess., 1910.

[34] Daryl Pendergraft, "Thomas Corwin and the Conservative Republican Reaction, 1858-1861," *OSAHQ,* LVII (Jan., 1948), 6.

[35] W. S. Mills to Chase, Nov. 25, 1859; J. H. Barrett to Chase, Mar. 3, 1860, Chase Papers.

[36] J. O. Cunningham, "The Bloomington Convention of 1856 and Those Who Participated in It," *ISHST* (1905), 106-107; *The Liberator,* Nov. 9, 1860; Harold Preston James, "Lincoln's Own State in the Election of 1860" (unpublished Ph.D. dissertation, University of Illinois, 1943), 130.

Republican party sought racial equality and that every Republican was willing to lead the Negroes of the South in insurrection against their white masters. By their charges the Democrats were inciting apprehension among the people. "Treat us fairly, take our platform as it is," he continued. "When we say that all men are created equal, we do not mean that every man in organized society has the same rights. We don't tolerate that in Illinois." The senator concluded by stating that colonization was the only answer to the race question.[37]

The effect of Trumbull's remarks was immediately apparent. One correspondent declared that the senator's colonization suggestion was lauded throughout Illinois; another wrote that the "black man" must be deported to prevent miscegenation. Numerous letters assured the senator that his remarks were producing startling results in southern Illinois and disproving the "slander on the race question" leveled by the Democrats. A letter indicating that Trumbull's speech secured votes for the Republicans in 1860 was written by A. N. Ballinger. Stating that he and his friends had previously voted Democratic because they feared a Republican victory would result in Negro suffrage and social equality, Ballinger concluded, "that noble stand you have taken has made a telling effect amongst my immediate acquaintances. My relatives [who] especially loathe the idea of Negro amalgimation [sic] and have refused heretofore to vote the Republican ticket, now fully endorse your views."[38]

Throughout the campaign Republicans made no pretense of being concerned with the fate of the Negro and insisted that theirs was a party of white labor. By introducing a note of white supremacy, they hoped to win the votes of the Negrophobes and the anti-abolitionists who were opposed to the extension of slavery. For example, one party

---

[37] *Congressional Globe,* 36 Cong., 1 Sess., 39-40, 58-59, 61, 102.

[38] Ira McKibbon to Trumbull, Dec. 24, 1859; [no first name] Whithill to Trumbull, Jan. 1, 1860; James Wheatly to Trumbull, Jan. 7, 1860; H. Wing to Trumbull, May 4, 1860; H. S. Thomas to Trumbull, Feb. 26, 1860; E. B. Olmaten to Trumbull, Jan 3, 1860; A. N. Ballinger to Trumbull, Feb. 16, 1860, Trumbull Papers. One person, to the author's knowledge, disagreed with Trumbull's remarks, surmising that an educated Negro was a better citizen than a foreigner. William B. Doge to Elihu Washburne, Jan. 13, 1860, Elihu B. Washburne Papers (Manuscript Division, Library of Congress). During the campaign of 1860, Trumbull continued to stress his conservative attitude and returned home to stump his state. While he considered Illinois safe for Lincoln, he hoped his conservative viewpoint would help elect a Republican legislature. Trumbull to Zachariah Chandler, Aug. 27, Sept. 3, 1860, Zachariah Chandler Papers (Manuscript Division, Library of Congress).

leader said at the national convention, "It is not so much in reference to the rights of the negro that we are here, but it is for the protection of the rights of the laboring whites, for the protection of ourselves and our liberties." Or as one party newspaper expressed it: the Republican party's anti-extension views were contrived because Republicans liked white men better than Negroes, they believed the Caucasian superior, and saw the limitation of slavery as the one means to preserve the country from *"the pestilential presence of the black man."*[39]

Radical abolitionists, such as Garrison, and some Negroes were displeased with the Republican line. Garrison lamented the fact that Wade, Chase, and "even Father Giddings" took little interest in the Negro "since [they] found the liberties of the white man so seriously endangered." In Chicago, H. Ford Douglas, an Illinois Negro, told an audience that "both parties [were] barren and unfruitful . . . and unwilling to extend to [the Negro] the rights of a free man." If Negro parents dared to send their children to the schools of Illinois, Douglas charged, "Abraham Lincoln would kick them out in the name of Republicanism and anti-slavery!"[40]

The early positions assumed on the slavery question and Negro status by the more prominent contenders for the Republican presidential nomination affected their acceptability as possible candidates. As the May, 1860, convention approached, conservatives warned Republican leaders that the nomination of a conservative man was necessary. Trumbull was informed that "the great Bug Bear 'Nigger' [was] fast disappearing" as a detriment to the party but the selection of the wrong candidate might raise it again. James Sherman of New Jersey attempted to persuade the state committeemen in Wisconsin to discard their support for Seward because his nomination would "render [the] election hopeless."[41] In fact, Iowa, Illinois, Indiana, Ohio, Pennsylvania, and New Jersey were violently opposed to Seward's "Higher-law-ism" or anything that hinted at Negro equality. Even in New York, noted Charles Robinson while on a visit, Seward's early radical statements impeded his chances with the conservatives.[42] This same early

[39] Bernard Mandel, *Labor: Free and Slave* (New York, 1955), 149.
[40] *The Liberator,* Sept. 3, 1858, July 13, 1860.
[41] Alexander Morean to Trumbull, Jan. 23, 1860, Trumbull Papers; Sherman to J. H. Tweedy, May 5, 1860, John H. Tweedy Papers (Wisconsin State Historical Society Library).
[42] Robinson to Chase, Feb. 3, 1860, Chase Papers; F. I. Herriott, "The Conference in the Deutsches Haus, Chicago, May 14-15, 1860," *ISHST* (1928), 124.

radicalism lessened the possibility of Chase's nomination, and because of it "Salmon P. Chase . . . never had a chance." Conservative Ohioans preferred Wade because they considered his stand on the free Negro question a greater asset in gaining votes.[43] Edward Bates was an acceptable candidate insofar as the Negro question was concerned, but as a former Know Nothing he could not get votes from the German community, whose support the Republican party considered essential.[44]

The apprehension about Negro equality, the dislike of extreme abolitionism, and the necessity of securing votes in the southern counties of those states bordering on the slave states, where the Negro question was most pronounced, made Lincoln a logical choice for the Republican party. His view on the Negro was especially acceptable to the anti-extensionists in the abolition-hating counties of southern Indiana. "Indeed," wrote Giddings, "Lincoln was selected . . . because he was supposed to be able to carry [Illinois] and Indiana and [was] acceptable to Pennsylvania[,] and his anti-slavery sentiment had been less prominent" than that of the other possible candidates.[45]

Lincoln revealed his position in 1854, and he expressed it more clearly as Douglas threw the Negro equality charge at him in the senatorial campaign of 1858. To a Peoria audience in 1854 Lincoln declared, "Let it not be said I am contending for . . . political and social equality between the whites and blacks. . . . I am . . . arguing against the EXTENSION of a bad thing, which where it already exists, we must of necessity, manage as we best can. . . . Free [Negroes], and make them politically and socially our equals?" he asked. "My own feelings will not admit to this, and if mine would, we well know that those of the great mass of the white people will not." At Ottawa, four years later, Lincoln told his listeners that the physical differences between the two races prevented equality. One race must necessarily be supreme and, "I am in favor of the race to which I belong, having the superior position." The next month at Clinton the senatorial candidate reprimanded Douglas for his constant remarks about Republicans favoring racial equality. Such charges were made simply to gain votes, Lincoln

---

[43] Don E. Fehrenbacher, "The Republican Decision at Chicago," in Norman A. Graebner (ed.), *Politics and the Crisis of 1860* (Urbana, Illinois, 1960), 55; F. W. Wright to Chase, May 21, 1860, Chase Papers.

[44] Herriott, "Conference in the Deutsches Haus," 109.

[45] Reinhard, Luthin, "Indiana and Lincoln's Rise to the Presidency," *IMH*, XXXVIII (Dec., 1942), 389; Giddings to Julian, May 21, 1860, Julian-Giddings Correspondence (Manuscript Division, Library of Congress).

insisted, for "he knows that we advocate no such doctrines as those." The race question was prominent enough by the time the two men met at Charleston for Lincoln to begin his speech with the statement that he was not and never had been "in favor of making voters or jurors of negroes, nor of qualifying them to hold office, nor to intermarry with white people."[46] If the Republican party needed a man of conservative expression to win the uncommitted vote, Abraham Lincoln was their answer because he was politician enough to sense the regards of the people who opposed Negro equality and to express them in terms of his background and section.

Republicans were politically astute to demand the limitation of slavery and, at the same time, to refuse political equality to free Negroes. Beginning in the 1840's and definitely after 1854, the terms "abolitionism" and "antislavery" had different connotations for most westerners. Abolitionism as defined by a Negro writer in 1854 had a "deeper significance and a wider scope" than freedom for slaves; it also included the "collateral issues connected with human enfranchisement, independent of race [or] complexion."[47] On the other hand, antislavery meant opposition to the extension of the "peculiar institution." Furthermore, this was a concept which most westerners could accept because it coincided with what they considered their best interests. Since they believed the Negro inferior to the white man, westerners refused to accept them as equals on a political or social level. Understanding this attitude, Republican leaders, especially from the Middle West, made it sufficiently clear that they had no intention of uplifting the Negro or equalizing his place in society.[48] For some Republicans such statements were merely political propaganda, for others they were true expressions of their own attitudes. Whichever they were, they helped the Republican party to acquire the electoral votes of the Middle West and to place their candidate in the White House.

---

[46] Basler, *Collected Works of Abraham Lincoln*, II, 256, 266, 405; III, 16, 83, 145-146. The best statement of Lincoln's position on slavery and the Negro in the 1850's is Don E. Fehrenbacher, *Prelude to Greatness: Lincoln in the 1850's* (New York, 1964) — see especially pp. 96-121.

[47] Larry Gara, "Who Was an Abolitionist?" in Duberman (ed.), *Antislavery Vanguard*, 40-41.

[48] It should be pointed out, however, that other aspects of the Republican platform, mainly the demand for a transcontinental railroad and free homesteads in the West, were helpful in securing support in the Middle West.

Epilogue

Just before Lincoln's inauguration an Ohio newspaper reported that a group of free Negroes from Virginia had arrived in the state, and the editor complained bitterly that Ohio was again, as it had been in the 1820's and 1830's, becoming a general depot for southern Negroes.[1] Earlier James S. Pike, in an essay published in the *New York Tribune,* stated that the object of the "battles of Freedom against slavery" was to prevent the "white laboring classes" from coming into competition with Negro labor, whether free or slave. Because the Negro "stood in [the] way" of the white man's dreams and hopes, white Americans were perfectly justified to "hem him in [or] coop him up [and to] preserve just so much of North America as [was] possible to the white man, and to free institutions."[2]

During the war years, the anti-Negro sentiment in the Middle West did not diminish. In fact, it became more acute among the small farmers of southern origin and the foreign-born laboring class.[3] A mass meeting of working men in Quincy, Illinois, expressed the feelings of their fellow workers by passing a series of resolutions, declaring "that we hereby give notice to those engaged in this business of attempting to . . . crush . . . the free white workingmen of Illinois, by thus seeking to bring free negro labor into competition with white labor, that we cannot and will not tolerate it."[4]

---

[1] *Columbus* (Ohio) *Crisis,* Feb. 3, 1816, in Perkins, *Northern Editorials,* I, 444.
[2] *New York Tribune,* Mar. 13, 1860. For a more extensive treatment of Pike's essay see Durden, "Ambiguities in the Antislavery Crusade," in Duberman (ed.), *Antislavery Vanguard,* 373 *et passim.*
[3] See Jacque Voegeli, "The Northwest and the Race Issue, 1861-1862," *MVHR,* L (Sept., 1963), 235-251.
[4] Wood Gray, *The Hidden Civil War: The Story of the Copperheads* (New York, 1942), 100. To allay the fears of competition from Negroes, Julian M. Sturtevant wrote an amazing piece of sophistry, claiming that freedom for

Such statements only confirmed further that the people in the western free states wished to confine the Negro to the South, and that they objected to Negroes as residents. The idea was expressed early by the white settlers who fled the slave system. Their objections to the Negro were based on the fear of miscegenation, economic competition, and the lower class position of nonslaveholders in a slave society. The status of the Negro as a slave and the general belief that the Negro race was docile only lessened his acceptance as a free man where slavery was forbidden. Easterners also accepted the idea of racial inferiority and held prejudices against the Negro. As these settlers or their descendants and other pioneers, influenced by the prevalent ideas of the Old Northwest, moved beyond the Mississippi River, they carried the force of the pronouncements against the Negro with them. Whether a miner in California or a farmer of the plains, the white American was appalled by the thought of the Negro's presence. Not desiring the residence of free Negroes, the white people, through their legislatures, attempted to prevent it legally. Security and exclusion laws were initiated to discourage Negro immigration and when these failed, colonization was devised as a means of reducing the Negro population. Negrophobes could argue the advantages which colonization would offer to the Negro and thereby gain the support of those people whose attitudes were more liberal.

As the question of slavery expansion became more significant after 1854, the racial prejudice of many westerners caused them to support the nonextension of slavery. Not wishing the free Negro in their area, they did not want the Negro as a slave on the land they had previously considered reserved for themselves. The early nonextension groups

---

Negroes would lead to the eventual annihilation of the race. The only reward which the Negro could reap from competition with free white labor was "a grave" because Negroes, like Indians, were innately inferior to Caucasians. Possibly with tongue in cheek, Sturtevant maintained that slavery had been responsible for the survival of the Negro race on the American continent. Pampered and provided for by his master, the slave had no responsibilities other than doing his daily work. But, wrote Sturtevant, when "he is brought into direct competition with the white man . . . and he finds his place in [the] lower stratum [and] cannot support a family . . . the consequence is inevitable. He will either never marry, or he will in the attempt to support a family, struggle in vain against the laws of nature, and his children, many of them at least, [will] die in infancy. Like his brother, the Indian of the forest, he must melt away and disappear forever from the midst of us." Julian M. Sturtevant, "The Destiny of the African Race in the United States," *Continental Monthly*, III (May, 1863), 610.

failed to achieve success partly because of abolitionist support, which to most westerners smacked of racial equality and interference with slavery where it already existed. These were two ideas they refused to accept or consider. To quell the growth of the new Republican party, the Democrats attempted to transfer the tinge of abolitionism and Negro equality to the Republicans. It was this attempt and the refutation of the accusations which indicated the importance of the race question.

The exact extent of racial prejudice as a factor encouraging the limitation of slavery is indeterminable. The average man, in all ages, does not record his thoughts for posterity and is even less likely to do so on such thorny problems as race relations. Yet, if 79.5 per cent of the people of Illinois, Indiana, Oregon, and Kansas voted to exclude the free Negro simply because of their prejudice, surely this antipathy influenced their decisions to support the nonextension of slavery.[5] Also, the Republican party in 1860 was too diverse in its make-up to attempt a suggestion of the precise amount of support it received from Negrophobes. Its diversity helped it to offer something to every group from which it hoped to gain political support. In a phrase, it was a party "of all things to all men," and this included men whose racial enmity prompted their antislavery or anti-extension feelings. William Seward declared that "the motive of those who protested against the extension of slavery" had "always really been concern for the welfare of the white man" and not an "unnatural sympathy for the negro."[6] George W. Julian, the well-known militant abolitionist, was more concise about his opinion regarding some advocates of a free West. At a Fourth of July celebration in the small hamlet of Raysville, Indiana, in 1857, he described the antislavery expressions of some of the people as "superficial and sickly" because they were based on "a perfect, if not supreme hatred" of the Negro.[7] Three years later a northern editor bemoaned secession and declared it occurred only because of the *"everlasting negro"* question.[8] But in expressing his views, he acknowledged racial

[5] The votes cast in each of the states for and against exclusion were: Illinois, 50,261 to 21,297; Indiana, 113,628 to 21,873; Oregon, 8,640 to 1,081; Kansas, 1,287 to 453. The total number of votes in all these states were 218,520; votes favoring exclusion: 173,816; against: 44,704.

[6] James M. McPherson, *The Struggle for Equality: Abolitionists and the Negro in the Civil War and Reconstruction* (Princeton, 1964), 24.

[7] George W. Julian, *Speeches on Political Questions* (New York, 1872), 127.

[8] (Providence, Rhode Island) *Daily Post,* Feb. 2, 1861, in Perkins, *Northern Editorials,* I, 443.

prejudice as a factor in the slavery extension controversy; moreover, it had been present ever since the citizens of Harrison County in territorial Indiana had declared, "We are opposed to the introduction of Slaves or free negroes in any shape."

Note
on the Sources

Although I have included a traditional
bibliography, it seems appropriate to comment of some of the bibliographical materials. The most recent and most stim-
ulating work on anti-Negro prejudice in
the free states is Leon F. Litwack, *North
of Slavery*. Studies on the state level are
sadly lacking or out of date. Frank Quil-
lin, *The Color Line in Ohio*, and Charles Hickock, *The Negro in
Ohio*, need revising in light of new data which has been found since
their dates of publication. Delilah Beasley, *The Negro Trail Blazers
of California*, and Sue Bailey Thurman, *Pioneers of Negro Origin in
California*, are somewhat limited in their approach. To my knowledge, no comprehensive or recent studies of Negroes or anti-Negro discrimination are available for the ante-bellum period in Michigan, Oregon, Kansas, or Illinois. Norman Harris, *History of Negro Servitude
in Illinois*, is badly outdated and extremely biased. Harris, in the latter
portion of the book, was more concerned with placing the blame on
southern Illinoisans for the conditions of Negroes within the state
rather than with attempting to understand the issues involved. The
ante-bellum Negro in Indiana is admirably considered by Emma Lou
Thornbrough, *The Negro in Indiana*. The following articles make significant contributions on certain aspects of the Negro question: Delilah
Beasley, "Slavery in California"; Jack Beller, "Negro Slaves in Utah";
John Dancy, "The Negro People in Michigan"; Leslie Fishel, Jr., "Wis-
consin and Negro Suffrage"; D. G. Hill, "The Negro as a Political and
Social Issue in the Oregon Country"; Louis Pelzer, "The Negro and
Slavery in Early Iowa"; Sherman Savage, "The Negro on the Mining
Frontier"; and Charles Wilson, "The Negro in Early Ohio."

The racial attitudes of white abolitionists toward Negroes have been
widely researched. In this respect one should definitely check James

McPherson, *The Struggle for Equality,* and the essays by Robert Durden, Leon Litwack, Larry Gara, and James McPherson in Martin Duberman (ed.), *The Antislavery Vanguard.* The most revealing source materials describing the sentiments of white abolitionists toward Negroes and the Negroes' own conception of their role in the antislavery movement are Gilbert Hobbs Barnes and Dwight Dumond (eds.), *The Weld-Grimké Correspondence,* and Carter G. Woodson (ed.), *The Mind of the Negro.*

The papers of abolitionists or people with strong antislavery convictions who worked on the local level contain some pertinent statements about the role of the Negro in a white society, especially those at the Indiana State Historical Society Library. On the whole, however, the value of personal papers on the Negro question is spotty. The most important manuscripts of a national figure are those of Lyman Trumbull. A firm believer in racial inequality before 1860, Trumbull received numerous letters supporting his anti-Negro stand; these disclose the bias of average citizens on the subject. Although they contain less material on the Negro question, the Logan Family papers, and the papers of Benjamin Wade and Salmon P. Chase, are of value. In the state repositories the most illuminating collections are those of Allen Hamilton, James Hanway, Hazen Merrill, and Joseph Wright. Florence Walls, "The Letters of Asahel Bush to Matthew P. Deady, 1851-1863," is an invaluable timesaver because Miss Walls admirably deciphered Bush's illegible handwriting. The James H. Lane papers are rather skimpy, and one can only conclude that Lane corresponded little or did not save his correspondence. Much of the material in the Charles Robinson papers is dated in the 1890's. The passing of 40-odd years colored his views on the events in Kansas between 1854 and 1860. The same is true of the various statements made at a later date by the pioneers in California and Oregon.

Newspapers are a fruitful source for the Negro question. Editorials and letters to the editors were contemporary and they were, at times, brutally candid. Although I quoted at length from newspapers, much relevant material was deleted while revising. For the earlier period in Illinois see the *Western Intelligencer* (renamed the *Illinois Intelligencer* in 1818) and the *Edwardsville Spectator.* The *Western Sun* is the best newspaper source for early Indiana. The files of the free state newspapers in Kansas for 1855 and 1856, although usually incomplete, are useful for the Topeka Movement. On the free Negro question their importance is limited because, except for the *Herald of Freedom,* free state editors seemed reluctant to talk about the race issue. However, after 1857, as Democrats and Republicans in Kansas debated the Negro question, Kansas editors were more open in their remarks. New York newspapers are excellent for the ante-bellum Kansas period, but it must be remembered that the numerous reporters were biased. The *Oregonian* and the *Oregon Statesman* are extremely valuable. Thomas Dryer and Asahel Bush differed politically as well as in their views on the free Negro and slavery; consequently, they used the columns of their respective journals to attack each other. The willingness of Oregon editors to publish correspondence on the slavery and free Negro issues in 1857 only increases the value of Oregon newspapers for that year. As the election of 1860 approached its climax, Republican and Democratic editors throughout the nation eagerly commented on the race issue, revealing the various shades of opinion. Outstanding examples are the Democratic *State Register* and the Republican *State Journal* of Springfield, Illinois. The fact that both Lincoln and Douglas were candidates for the presidency caused the editors to attack the opposite party scathingly.

The proceedings of the constitutional conventions held in the various states are a wealth of information not only on the Negro question but on other matters of importance during the period. Except for territorial Kansas, they are complete. The major drawback of most of the volumes is their lack of or inaccurate indexes. Still, much can be gained by reading them even though the task is tedious. Other contemporary accounts, such as journals or reports made by travelers, should not be overlooked; see especially E. S. Abdy, *Journal of a Residence and Tour;* Harlow Lindley, *Indiana as Seen by Early Travelers;* and, naturally, the section entitled "The Present and Probable Future Condition of the Three Races That Inhabit the Territory of the United States," in Alexis de Tocqueville, *Democracy in America.*

I have read numerous theses and dissertations in the course of my research. While many of them are of doubtful value, several proved enlightening. Space does not permit me to mention the merits of every one from which I have quoted, but I feel that the doctoral dissertations by Merton L. Dillon, "The Anti-Slavery Movement in Illinois"; Harold P. James, "Lincoln's Own State in the Election of 1860"; Arthur Kooker, "The Antislavery Movement in Michigan"; and Thomas Stirton, "Party Disruption and the Rise of the Slavery Extension Controversy," should be cited here. On the less distinguished but no less valuable level, Helen Poulton's "The Attitude of Oregon Toward Slavery and Secession, 1843-1865" is a good introduction to the question in the Pacific Northwest.

There remains much work to be done on the role of anti-Negro prejudice in the ante-bellum period. Separate studies for the Liberty and Free Soil parties and the election of 1860 need to be undertaken. As I have indicated, there has been a general lack of interest on the part of historians to look at anti-Negro prejudice in the individual states. Although recent biographies of national antislavery leaders, such as Mark M. Krug's *Lyman Trumbull* and Hans Trefousse's *Benjamin Wade,* are welcome additions, the lives of antislavery leaders, or depending upon the individual, anti-Negro leaders, including Edward Coles, Morris Birkbeck, Charles Robinson, James H. Lane, George Williams, and Peter Burnett, should be reinvestigated or looked at for the first time.

Bibliography

MANUSCRIPT SOURCES

Collections and Papers

Sidney Breese Papers, Illinois State Historical Society Library, Springfield.

Peter Hardeman Burnett Papers, Bancroft Library, University of California, Berkeley.

Zachariah Chandler Papers, Manuscript Division, Library of Congress.

Salmon Portland Chase Papers, Manuscript Division, Library of Congress.

Matthew P. Deady Papers, Oregon Historical Society Library, Portland.

Benjamin Franklin Dowell Papers, Oregon Historical Society Library.

James Eastman Papers, Indiana State Historical Society Library, Indianapolis.

Elisha Embree Papers, Indiana State Library, Indianapolis.

William H. English Collection, Indiana State Historical Society Library.

Gershom Flagg Papers, Illinois Historical Survey, University of Illinois, Urbana (transcripts).

Addison C. Gibbs Papers, Oregon Historical Society Library.

Allen Hamilton Papers, Indiana State Library.

James Hanway Papers, Kansas State Historical Society Library, Topeka.

Thomas Wentworth Higginson Papers, Kansas State Historical Society Library.

William F. Jones Papers, Indiana State Library.

Julian-Giddings Correspondence, Manuscript Division, Library of Congress.

John Kirk Letter Books, Chicago Historical Society.

Henry S. Lane Papers, Indiana State Historical Society Library.

James H. Lane Papers, University of Kansas Library, Lawrence.

John A. Logan Family Papers, Manuscript Division, Library of Congress.

William D. Marmaduke Papers, California Historical Society Library, San Francisco (typewritten).

Hazen Merrill Papers, Indiana State Historical Society Library.

Meg W. Moore Papers, Indiana State Library.

Edward L. Pierce Papers, Kansas State Historical Society Library.

Charles Robinson Papers, University of Kansas Library.

Caleb Blood Smith Papers, Manuscript Division, Library of Congress.

William Henry Smith Collection, Indiana State Historical Society Library.

George L. Stearns Papers, Kansas State Historical Society Library.

Julian M. Sturtevant Papers, Illinois College Library, Jacksonville.

Lyman Trumbull Papers, Manuscript Division, Library of Congress.

John H. Tweedy Papers, Wisconsin State Historical Society Library, Madison.

Benjamin Franklin Wade Papers, Manuscript Division, Library of Congress.

Elihu B. Washburne Papers, Manuscript Division, Library of Congress.

William A. White Papers, Indiana State Library.

Joseph A. Wright Papers, Indiana State Library.

Statements and Journals

Applegate, Jesse. "Views of Oregon History," Bancroft Library (microfilm, University of Washington Library, Seattle).

Barnes, G. A. "Oregon and California in 1849," Bancroft Library (microfilm, University of Washington Library).

Bond, N. T. "Early History of Colorado, Montana, and Idaho," Bancroft Library (microfilm, University of Washington Library).

Churchill, George. "Annotations on Lippincott's Early Days," Illinois Historical Survey (transcripts).

Cosad, David. "Journal of a Trip to California by the Overland Route and Life in the Gold Diggings During 1849-1850," California Historical Society Library.

Deady, Matthew P. "History and Progress of Oregón After 1845," Bancroft Library (microfilm, University of Washington Library).

Gibbs, Addison C. "Notes on the History of Oregon," Bancroft Library (microfilm, University of Washington Library).

McBride, John. "Narrative of the Journey in 1846," Oregon Historical Society Library (typewritten).

Moore, M. J. "Essay on Slavery, 1847-1848," M. J. Moore Papers, Indiana State Library.

Robinson, Charles. "Origins of the Topeka Movement," Charles Robinson Papers, University of Kansas Library.

Ryland, C. T. "California Pioneers," Bancroft Library.

————. "Connections with the History of California," Bancroft Library.

Strong, William. "History of Oregon," Bancroft Library (microfilm, University of Washington Library).

Willey, Samuel H. "Personal Memorandum," Bancroft Library.

Wilson, Benjamin David. "Observations of Early Days in California and New Mexico," Bancroft Library.

Official Manuscripts

[Goodwin, Joel K.]. "Record of the Executive Committee of the Kansas Territory from August 15, 1855 to February 11, 1856," Kansas State Historical Society Library.

"Journal of the Topeka House of Representatives," Kansas State Historical Society Library.

"Oregon Provisional and Territorial Government Papers," Oregon State Archives (microfilm, University of Oregon Library, Eugene).

Smith, Samuel. "Journal of the Topeka Convention," Kansas State Historical Society Library.

Theophilus Magruder v. *Jacob Vanderpool,* MS Court Records, Oregon Historical Society Library (transcripts).

NEWSPAPERS

California

Los Angeles Star.
San Francisco *Daily Alta California.*
San Francisco *Californian.*
San Francisco *California Star.*
Santa Rosa *Sonoma Democrat.*
Shasta Courier.

Colorado

Denver *Rocky Mountain Herald.*

Illinois

Alton Daily Morning Courier.
Alton Telegraph and Democratic Review.
Bloomington Intelligencer.
Chicago Journal.
Daily Alton Telegraph.
Edwardsville Spectator.
Kaskaskia *Illinois Intelligencer.*
Kaskaskia Republican.
Kaskaskia *Western Intelligencer.*
Peoria Weekly Democratic Press.
Peoria Weekly Republican.
Quincy Whig.
Shawneetown *Illinois Gazette.*
Springfield *Illinois State Journal.*
Springfield *Illinois State Register.*
Springfield *Sangamo Journal.*

Vandalia *Illinois Advocate.*
Vandalia *Illinois Intelligencer.*

Indiana

Centerville *Indiana True Democrat.*
Corydon *Indiana Gazette.*
Indianapolis *Indiana Journal.*
Indianapolis *Indiana State Journal.*
Indianapolis *Indiana State Sentinel.*
Indianapolis *Indiana Statesman.*
Indianapolis Recorder.
New Albany Daily Ledger.
Newport *Free Labor Advocate.*
Vincennes *Western Sun.*

Iowa

Wisconsin Territorial Gazette and Burlington Advertiser.
Dubuque Weekly Times.

Kansas

Emporia News.
Lawrence *Herald of Freedom.*
Lawrence *Kansas Free State.*
Lawrence Republican.
Leavenworth *Kansas Weekly Herald.*
Leavenworth *Republican Union.*
Topeka *Kansas Freeman.*
Topeka *Kansas Tribune.*
Wyandotte *Western Argus.*

Massachusetts

Boston *The Liberator.*

Michigan

Detroit Daily Advertiser.
Detroit *Democratic Free Press and Michigan Intelligencer.*
Detroit Free Press.
Detroit Gazette.

150

Nebraska

Nebraska City News.

New York

New York Times.
New York Tribune.

Ohio

Chillicothe *Scioto Gazette.*
Chillicothe *Supporter.*
Cincinnati Advertiser and Ohio Phoenix.
Cincinnati *Cist's Weekly Advertiser.*
Cincinnati Enquirer.
Cincinnati *Liberty Hall and Cincinnati Gazette.*
Cleveland Plain Dealer.
Columbus *Ohio State Journal.*

Oregon

Corvallis *Occidental Messenger.*
Corvallis *Oregon Weekly Union.*
Eugene *The People's Press.*
Oregon City *Oregon Argus.*
Oregon City *Oregon Spectator.*
Portland *Democratic Standard.*
Portland *Oregon Weekly Times.*
Portland *Weekly Oregonian.*
Salem *Oregon Statesman.*

Utah

Salt Lake City *Deseret News.*

Washington

Olympia *Pioneer and Democrat.*

Washington, D.C.

Madisonian.
National Era.

Wisconsin

Madison *Argus and Democrat.*
Madison Express.
Madison *Weekly Wisconsin Patriot.*
Madison *Wisconsin State Journal.*
Milwaukee *Sentinel and Gazette.*

SCRAPBOOKS

John A. Logan Scrapbooks. 2 vols. Logan Family Papers, Manuscript Division, Library of Congress.
Charles Robinson Scrapbooks. 2 vols. University of Kansas Library.
Thomas H. Webb Scrapbooks. 17 vols. Kansas State Historical Society Library.

PUBLISHED SOURCES AND DOCUMENTS

Abdy, Edward S. *Journal of a Residence and Tour in the United States of North America, from April, 1833, to October, 1834.* 3 vols. London, 1835.
African Repository. Vols. XIII (1837), XXV-XXXIV (1849-58).
Alvord, Clarence W. (ed.). *Kaskaskia Records.* Vol. V, *ISHLC.* Springfield, 1909.
"An Act to Regulate Blacks and Mulattoes," *AI,* III (Apr., 1897), 145-147.
Annual Report of the American Anti-Slavery Society, 1857-58. New York, 1859.
Annual Report of the Colonization Society of the State of Iowa. Iowa City, 1857.
Annual Reports of the American Colonization Society. Twenty-Eighth (1845) and Thirty-Sixth (1853). Washington, D.C., 1845, 1853.
Baker, George (ed.). *The Works of William H. Seward.* 5 vols. Boston, 1884.
Barnes, Gilbert Hobbs, and Dwight L. Dumond (eds.). *Letters of Theodore Dwight Weld, Angelina Grimké Weld and Sarah Grimké, 1822-1844.* 2 vols. New York, 1934.
Basler, Roy P. (ed.). *The Collected Works of Abraham Lincoln.* 9 vols. New Brunswick, New Jersey, 1953.
Beale, Howard K. (ed.). *The Diary of Edward Bates, 1859-1866.* Vol. IV, *AHAAR* (1930). Washington, D.C., 1933.
Birkbeck, Morris. "An Appeal on the Question of a Convention," *ISHST* (1905), 147-163.
Blair, Francis P. (comp.). *Collection of Pamphlets on the Slavery Question.* N.d., n.p.

————. *The Destiny of the Races on This Continent.* Washington, D.C., 1859.

Bond, Beverley W., Jr. (ed.). "Memoirs of Benjamin Van Cleve," *QPHPSO,* XVII (Jan.-June, 1922), 1-71.

Borthwick, J. D. *Three Years in California.* London, 1857.

Browne, J. Ross. *Report of the Debates in the Convention of California, on the Formation of the State Constitution, in September and October, 1849.* Washington, D.C., 1850.

Buck, Solon J. (ed.). "Pioneer Letters of Gershom Flagg," *ISHST* (1910), 139-183.

Burnet, Jacob. *Notes on the Early Settlement of the North-Western Territory.* Cincinnati, 1847.

Burnett, Peter H. *Recollections and Opinions of an Old Pioneer.* New York, 1880.

California, State of. *Journal of the House of Representatives of the State of California,* 1850, 1852, 1857, 1858. Title and imprint vary.

————. *Journal of the Senate of the State of California,* 1850, 1852, 1858, 1860. Title and imprint vary.

————. *Laws of the State of California,* 1850, 1858. Title and imprint vary.

Carey, Charles Henry (ed.). *The Oregon Constitution and Proceedings and Debates of the Constitutional Convention of 1857.* Salem, 1926.

Carpenter, Richard V. (ed.). "The Illinois Constitutional Convention of 1818," *ISHSJ,* VI (Oct., 1913), 327-424.

Carter, Clarence Edwin (ed.). *The Territory of Indiana, 1810-1816.* Vol. VIII, *The Territorial Papers of the United States.* Washington, D.C., 1939.

Caruthers, R. L., and A. O. P. Nicholson (comps.). *A Compilation of the Statutes of Tennessee.* Nashville, 1836.

Catterall, Helen (ed.). *Judicial Cases Concerning American Slavery and the Negro.* 5 vols. Washington, D.C., 1926-37.

Caughey, John Walton (ed.). *The Jacob Y. Stover Narrative: Southwest from Salt Lake City in 1849.* San Francisco, 1937.

Cawley, Elizabeth (ed.). *The American Diaries of Richard Cobden.* Princeton, 1952.

Chase, Salmon P. (ed.). *The Statutes of Ohio and of the Northwest Territory.* 3 vols. Cincinnati, 1833.

Christy, David. *A Lecture on African Colonization, Delivered in the Hall of the House of Representatives of Ohio, January 19, 1849.* Cincinnati, 1849.

Cist, Charles. *Sketches and Statistics of Cincinnati in 1859.* Cincinnati, 1859.

Cole, Arthur C. (ed.). *The [Illinois] Constitutional Debates of 1847.* Vol. XIV, *ISHLC.* Springfield, 1919.

Colton, Walter. *Three Years in California.* New York, 1860.

Constitution of the State of California, 1849. San Francisco, 1849.

Constitution of the State of Illinois, 1818. Washington, D.C., 1818.

Constitution of the State of Illinois, 1847. Springfield, 1847.

Constitution of the State of Indiana, 1816. Washington, D.C., 1816.

Constitution of the State of Indiana, 1851. Indianapolis, 1930.

Constitution of the State of Iowa, 1857. Iowa City, 1857.

Constitution of the State of Michigan, 1850. Lansing, 1907.

Constitution of the State of Ohio, 1802. Chillicothe, 1802.

Constitution of the State of Ohio, 1851. Columbus, 1941.

"Contemporary Editorial Opinion of the 1857 Constitution," *IJH,* LV (Apr., 1957), 115-146.

Curry, George B. "Address Before the Oregon Pioneer Association," *OPAT* (1887), 34-47.

Cutler, Julia Perkins (ed.). *The Life and Times of Ephraim Cutler, Prepared from His Journals and Correspondence.* Cincinnati, 1890.

Deady, Matthew P. (comp.). *The Organic and Other General Laws of Oregon, 1845-1864.* Portland, 1866.

DeGroot, Henry. *Recollections of California Mining Life.* San Francisco, 1884.

Dorr, Harold M. (ed.). *The Michigan Constitutional Convention of 1835-1836, Debates and Proceedings.* Ann Arbor, 1940.

Dunn, Jacob P. (ed.). *Slavery Petitions and Papers.* Vol. II, *IHSP.* Indianapolis, 1895.

Edwards, Cyrus. *An Address Delivered at the State House in Vandalia, on the Subject of Forming a State Colonization Society, Auxiliary to the American Colonization Society.* Jacksonville, Illinois, 1831.

Eleventh Annual Report of the Indiana Colonization Society, 1845. Indianapolis, 1846.

Ellison, William H. (ed.). "Memoirs of Hon. William M. Gwin," *CHSQ,* XIX (1940), 1-26, 157-184, 256-277, 344-367.

Ewbank, Louis B., and Dorothy L. Riker (eds.). *The Laws of Indiana Territory, 1809-1816.* Vol. XX, *IHC.* Indianapolis, 1934.

Flint, Timothy. *Recollections of the Last Ten Years, Passed in Occasional Residences and Journeyings in the Valley of the Mississippi.* Boston, 1826.

Goodnow, Isaac T. "Personal Reminiscenses and Kansas Emigration, 1855," *KSHST,* IV (1886-90), 244-253.

Grover, LaFayette (ed.). *The Oregon Archives, Including the Journals, Governors' Messages and Public Papers of Oregon.* Salem, 1853.

Huggins, Dorothy H. (comp.). "The Annals of San Francisco," *CHSQ,* XVI (1937), 79-84, 182-184, 282-285, 336-347; XVII (1938), 81-85, 168-185.

Illinois, State of. *Journal of the House of Representatives of the State of Illinois,* 1845, 1849, 1853. Title and imprint vary.

————. *Journal of the Senate of the State of Illinois,* 1828-29, 1849, 1853. Title and imprint vary.

———. *Laws of the State of Illinois,* 1819, 1827, 1829, 1831. Title and imprint vary.

Indiana, State of. *Journal of the House of Representatives of the State of Indiana,* 1816, 1823, 1829, 1849, 1850, 1851, 1852, 1853. Title and imprint vary.

———. *Journal of the Senate of the State of Indiana,* 1816, 1849, 1850, 1852, 1853, 1858. Title and imprint vary.

———. *Laws of the State of Indiana,* 1817-18, 1825, 1828, 1831, 1847-48, 1852, 1853, 1855. Title and imprint vary.

———. *Report of the Debates and Proceedings of the Convention for the Revision of the Constitution of the State of Indiana.* 2 vols. Indianapolis, 1850-51.

———. *Reports of the Agent of the State Board of Colonization of the State of Indiana for the Years 1853, 1855, 1857, and 1859.* Indianapolis, 1853, 1855, 1857, 1859.

Iowa, State of. *The Debates of the Constitutional Convention of the State of Iowa, Assembled at Iowa City, Monday, January 19, 1857.* 2 vols. Davenport, 1857.

———. *Laws of the State of Iowa,* 1850-51, 1858. Title and imprint vary.

Iowa, Territory of. *The Statute Laws of the Territory of Iowa.* Dubuque, 1839.

Julian, George W. *Speeches on Political Questions.* New York, 1872.

Kansas Constitutional Convention: A Reprint of the Proceedings and Debates of the Convention Which Framed the Constitution of Kansas at Wyandotte in July, 1859. Topeka, 1920.

Kemble, John H. (ed.). "Andrew Wilson's Jottings on the Civil War in California," *CHSQ,* XXXII (1953), 209-224, 303-312.

Kentucky, State of. *Laws of the State of Kentucky,* 1834, 1852. Title and imprint vary.

Knower, Daniel. *The Adventures of a Forty-Niner.* Albany, New York, 1894.

Koerner, Gustave P. *Memoirs of Gustave P. Koerner, 1809-1896.* Edited by Thomas J. McCormack. 2 vols. Cedar Rapids, Iowa, 1909.

Laws and Ordinances of the State of Deseret. Salt Lake City, 1919.

"Letters from Ogle and Carrol Counties, 1838-1857," *ISHST* (1907), 247-261.

"Letters of John and Sarah Everett, 1854-1864," *KHQ,* VIII (1939), 3-35, 143-174, 279-310, 350-383.

"Letters Received by the Committee of Arrangements of the Quarter-Centennial Celebration," *KSHST,* III (1883-85), 459-469.

Lindley, Harlow (ed.). *Indiana as Seen by Early Travelers: A Collection of Reprints from Books of Travel, Letters, and Diaries Prior to 1830.* Indianapolis, 1916.

Lockley, Fred (ed.). "Reminiscences of Mrs. Frank Collins, Nee Martha Elizabeth Gilliam," *OHQ,* XVII (Sept., 1916), 358-372.

————. "Some Documentary Records of Slavery in Oregon," *OHQ*, XVII (Mar., 1916), 107-115.

Martin, John A. "Address of Gov. John A. Martin," *KSHST*, III (1883-85), 372-389.

McBride, John. "Annual Address Before the Oregon Pioneer Association," *OPAT* (1897), 31-58.

Menard, J. W. *An Address to the Free Colored People of Illinois.* N.p., 1860.

Michigan, State of. *Journal of the House of Representatives of the State of Michigan,* 1843. Detroit, 1843.

————. *Journal of the Senate of the State of Michigan,* 1845. Detroit, 1845.

————. *Laws of the State of Michigan,* 1846, 1857. Title and imprint vary.

————. *Laws of the Territory of Michigan.* 2 vols. Lansing, 1874.

————. *Report of the Proceedings and Debates in the Convention to Revise the Constitution of the State of Michigan, 1850.* Lansing, 1850.

Michigan, Territory of. *Journal of the Proceedings of the Convention to Form a Constitution for the State of Michigan.* Detroit, 1835.

[Mitchell, Alexander]. *An Address to the Inhabitants of Indiana Territory, on the Subject of Slavery, by a Citizen of Ohio.* Hamilton, Ohio, 1816.

Mitchell, James. *Answer of the Agent of the Indiana Colonization Society to the Resolution of Inquiry on the Subject of African Colonization.* Indianapolis, 1852.

————. *Letters on the Relation of the White and African Races in the United States, Showing the Necessity for the Colonization of the Latter. Addressed to Lincoln, Douglas, Bell, and Breckenridge.* Springfield, Illinois, 1860.

Morrison, Robert, and others. *Report of the Committee on the Petition of Sundry Inhabitants of the Counties of St. Clair and Randolph in the Territory Northwest of the River Ohio.* N.p., 1796.

Nebraska, Territory of. *Journal of the Council of the Territory of Nebraska,* 1855, 1859, 1860. Title and imprint vary.

————. *Journal of the House of Representatives of the Territory of Nebraska,* 1858, 1859, 1860. Title and imprint vary.

New Mexico, Territory of. *Journal of the House of Representatives of the Territory of New Mexico,* 1858-59. Santa Fe, 1859.

————. *Laws of the Territory of New Mexico,* 1856-57, 1858-59. Title and imprint vary.

Niles Weekly Register. Vols. XXX (1826), XXXVIII (1830).

Ohio, State of. *Journal of the House of Representatives of the State of Ohio,* 1840-41, 1848, 1849. Title and imprint vary.

————. *Journal of the Senate of the State of Ohio,* 1837, 1838, 1849, 1858. Title and imprint vary.

————. *Report of the Debates and Proceedings of the Convention for the Revision of the Constitution of the State of Ohio, 1850-51.* 2 vols. Columbus, 1851.

———. *Revised Statutes of the State of Ohio, 1860.* 2 vols. Cincinnati, 1860.

Ohio, Territory of. *Journal of the Constitutional Convention of Ohio, 1802.* Chillicothe, 1802.

Oregon, Territory of. *Journal of the Council of the Territory of Oregon,* 1849, 1854, 1856, 1857. Title and imprint vary.

———. *Journal of the House of Representatives of the Territory of Oregon,* 1849, 1854, 1856, 1857, 1858. Title and imprint vary.

Organization of the Free State Government in Kansas with the Inaugural Speech and Message of Governor Robinson. Washington, D.C., 1856.

"Pardon of Six Men of the Crime of Being Negroes," *ISHST* (1910), 50.

Parish, John C. (ed.). "A Project for a California Slave Colony in 1851," *HHLB*, VIII (Oct., 1935), 171-175.

Pease, Theodore Calvin (ed.). *Illinois Election Returns, 1818-1848.* Vol. XVIII, *ISHLC.* Springfield, 1923.

Perkins, Howard C. (ed.). *Northern Editorials on Secession.* 2 vols. New York, 1942.

Philanthropist, Vol. IV, No. 5 (May 27, 1820).

Philbrick, Francis S. (ed.). *The Laws of Indiana Territory, 1801-1809.* Vol. XXI, *ISHLC.* Springfield, 1930.

———. *The Laws of Illinois Territory, 1809-1818.* Vol. XXV, *ISHLC.* Springfield, 1950.

———. *Pope's Digest, 1815.* Vol. XXX, *ISHLC.* Springfield, 1940.

Provisional Laws and Joint Resolutions of the General Assembly of Jefferson Territory. Omaha, 1860.

Quaife, Milo M. (ed.). *The Convention of 1846.* Vol. XXVII, *WSHSPubs.* Madison, 1919.

Reports of Cases Argued and Determined in the Supreme Court of Judicature of the State of Indiana. Vol. V. Indianapolis, 1890.

Reports of Cases Argued and Determined in the Supreme Court of Ohio. Vol. IX. Cincinnati, 1887.

Reports of Cases Argued and Determined in the Supreme Court of the State of Illinois. Vols. II, V, VII, XXXIII. Chicago, 1877-88.

Reports of Cases Argued and Determined in the Supreme Court of the State of Wisconsin. Vol. XV. Chicago, 1879.

Rockwood, Ruth E. (ed.). "Letters of Charles Stevens," *OHQ,* XXXVII (1936), 137-159, 241-261, 334-353; XXXVIII (1937), 63-91, 165-193, 328-354.

Shambaugh, Benjamin F. (ed.). *Documentary Material Relating to the History of Iowa.* Vol. I, *ISHSC.* Iowa City, 1897.

———. *Fragments of the Debates of the Iowa Constitutional Conventions of 1844 and 1846, Along with Press Comments and Other Materials on the Constitutions of 1844 and 1846.* Iowa City, 1900.

Sherman, Allen B. (ed.). "Sherman Was There: The Recollections of Major Edwin A. Sherman," *CHSQ*, XXIII (1944), 259-281, 349-377.

Smith, O. H. *Early Indiana Trials and Sketches: Reminiscences*. Cincinnati, 1858.

Smith, William Henry (ed.). *The Life and Public Services of Arthur St. Clair, with His Correspondence and Other Papers*. 2 vols. Cincinnati, 1882.

Staples, Arthur G. (ed.). *The Letters of John Fairfield*. Lewiston, Maine, 1922.

State Constitution of Michigan, 1837. Lansing, 1907.

Strohm, Isaac. *Speeches of Thomas Corwin with a Sketch of His Life*. Dayton, Ohio, 1859.

Sturtevant, Julian M. "The Destiny of the African Race in the United States," *Continental Monthly*, III (May, 1863), 600-611.

Sturtevant, Julian M., Jr. (ed.). *Julian M. Sturtevant: An Autobiography*. New York, 1896.

Thornbrough, Gayle, and Dorothy Riker (eds.). *Journals of the General Assembly of Indiana Territory*. Vol. XXXII, *IHC*. Indianapolis, 1950.

Tocqueville, Alexis de. *Democracy in America*. Edited by Phillips Bradley. 2 vols. New York, 1945.

"Topeka Movement: Documents," *KSHSC*, XIII (1913-14), 125-249.

"Transplanting Free Negroes to Ohio from 1815-1858: Documents," *JNH*, I (July, 1916), 302-338.

Treat, Samuel, Walter Scates, and Robert Blackwell (comps.). *The Statutes of Illinois in Force, 1857*. 2 vols. Chicago, 1858.

Trollope, Frances. *Domestic Manners of the Americans*. Edited by Donald Smalley. New York, 1960.

U.S. Bureau of the Census. *Eighth Census of the United States: 1860, Population*. Washington, D.C., 1864.

————. *Fifth Census of the United States: 1830, Enumeration of Inhabitants*. Washington, D.C., 1832.

————. *Fourth Census of the United States: 1820, Enumeration of Inhabitants*. Washington, D.C., 1821.

————. *Negro Population in the United States, 1790-1915*. Washington, D.C., 1918.

————. *Seventh Census of the United States: 1850, Statistics*. Washington, D.C., 1853.

————. *Sixth Census of the United States: 1840, Enumeration of Inhabitants* (corrected). Washington, D.C., 1841.

U.S. Congress, *Annals of Congress*, 6, 7, 8, 9, 10 Congresses, 1799-1809.

————. *Congressional Globe*, 29, 30, 31, 32, 33, 34, 35, 36, 38 Congresses, 1845-61, 1863-65.

————, House of Representatives. *House Executive Document*, 29 Congress, 1 Session, I, No. 2 (ser. no. 480).

———, House of Representatives. *House Executive Document,* 31 Congress, 1 Session, No. 59 (ser. no. 577).

———, House of Representatives. *House Miscellaneous Document,* 31 Congress, 1 Session, No. 44 (ser. no. 581).

———, House of Representatives. *Report of the Special Committee Appointed to Investigate the Troubles in Kansas,* 34 Congress, 1 Session, No. 200 (ser. no. 869) (*Howard Report*).

———, Senate. *Senate Executive Document,* 28 Congress, 1 Session, I, No. 1 (ser. no. 431).

[Vaux, Roberts]. *An Impartial Appeal to the Reason, Interest and Patriotism of the People of Illinois on the Injurious Effects of Slave Labour.* N.p., 1824.

Virginia, State of. *Digest of the Laws of Virginia.* Richmond, 1841.

Wheat, Carl I. (ed.). "California's Bantam Cock: The Journal of Charles E. DeLong, 1854-1863," *CHSQ,* IX (1930), 50-80, 129-181, 243-287, 345-397.

Whig Almanac and United States Register. 1851 and 1858.

Wilder, Daniel W. *The Annals of Kansas.* Topeka, 1875.

Williams, George H. "Annual Address Before the Oregon Pioneer Association," *OPAT* (1885), 18-33.

[———]. "The 'Free-State Letter' of Judge George H. Williams (Reprinted from the Oregon Statesman of July 28, 1857)," *OHQ,* IX (Sept., 1908), 254-273.

Wisconsin, State of. *Journal of the House of Representatives of the State of Wisconsin, 1857.* Madison, 1857.

———. *Journal of the Senate of the State of Wisconsin,* 1849, 1852, 1857. Title and imprint vary.

Wisconsin, Territory of. *Journal of the Convention to Form a Constitution for the State of Wisconsin, with a Sketch of the Debates.* Madison, 1848.

———. *Journal of the Council of the Territory of Wisconsin, 1845.* Madison, 1845.

———. *Journal of the House of Representatives of the Territory of Wisconsin,* 1844, 1845. Title and imprint vary.

Wood, Daniel B. *Sixteen Months in the Gold Diggings.* New York, 1851.

Wood, Samuel. "Address of Col. Samuel Wood," *KSHST,* III (1883-85), 426-431.

Woodson, Carter G. (ed.). *The Mind of the Negro as Reflected in Letters Written During the Crisis, 1800-1860.* Washington, D.C., 1926.

Works Progress Administration. *Annals of Cleveland.* 59 vols. Cleveland, 1936-38.

SECONDARY ACCOUNTS

Adams, Franklin G. "The Capitals of Kansas," *KSHST,* VIII (1903-4), 331-352.

Alvord, Clarence W. *The Illinois Country, 1673-1818*. Vol. I, *The Centennial History of Illinois*. Springfield, 1920.

Bancroft, Hubert Howe. *History of Arizona and New Mexico, 1530-1888*. Vol. XVII, *The Works of Hubert Howe Bancroft*. San Francisco, 1889.

———. *History of California, 1848-1859*. Vol. XXIII, *The Works of Hubert Howe Bancroft*. San Francisco, 1888.

———. *History of Oregon, 1848-1888*. Vol. XXX, *The Works of Hubert Howe Bancroft*. San Francisco, 1888.

Barnes, Gilbert Hobbs. *The Antislavery Impulse, 1830-1844*. New York, 1933.

Barnhart, John D. "Sources of Southern Immigration into the Old Northwest," *MVHR*, XXII (June, 1935), 49-62.

———. "The Southern Influence in the Formation of Illinois," *ISHSJ*, XXXII (Sept., 1939), 358-378.

———. "The Southern Influence in the Formation of Indiana," *IMH*, XXXIII (Sept., 1937), 261-276.

Beasley, Delilah L. *The Negro Trail Blazers of California*. Los Angeles, 1919.

———. "Slavery in California," *JNH*, III (Jan., 1918), 33-44.

Bell, Howard H. "A Survey of the Negro Convention Movement, 1830-1861." Ph.D. dissertation, Northwestern University, 1953.

Beller, Jack. "Negro Slaves in Utah," *UHQ*, II (Oct., 1929), 122-126.

Bergmann, Leola Nelson. "The Negro in Iowa," *IJHP*, XLVI (Jan., 1948), 3-90.

Berwanger, Eugene H. "Western Prejudice and the Extension of Slavery," *CWH*, XII (Sept., 1966), 197-212.

Blackmar, Frank. *The Life of Charles Robinson*. Topeka, 1902.

Blazer, D. N. "The History of the Underground Railroad of McDonough County, Illinois," *ISHSJ*, XV (Oct., 1922), 579-591.

Brown, William H. *An Historical Sketch of the Early Movement in Illinois for the Legalization of Slavery*. Vol. IV, *Fergus Historical Series*. Chicago, 1876.

Buck, Solon Justus. *Illinois in 1818*. Springfield, 1917.

Burlingame, Merrill G. "The Contribution of Iowa to the Formation of the State Government of California in 1849," *IJHP*, XXX (Apr., 1932), 182-218.

Carey, Charles Henry. *A General History of Oregon Prior to 1861*. 2 vols. Portland, 1935.

Carter, John D. "Thomas Sim King, Vigilante Editor," *CHSQ*, XXI (Mar., 1942), 23-38.

Cavanagh, Helen Marie. "Antislavery Sentiment and Politics in the Old Northwest, 1844-1860." Ph.D. dissertation, University of Chicago, 1938.

Chaddock, Robert E. *Ohio Before 1850: A Study of the Early Influence of Pennsylvania and the Southern Populations in Ohio.* Vol. XXXI, *Columbia University Studies in History, Economics and Public Law.* New York, 1908.

Cole, Arthur C. *The Era of the Civil War, 1848-1870.* Vol. III, *The Centennial History of Illinois.* Chicago, 1919.

Cole, Cyrenus. *Iowa Through the Years.* Iowa City, 1940.

Cordley, Richard. "The Convention Epoch in Kansas History," *KSHST,* V (1891-96), 42-47.

Counties of Warren, Benton, Jasper and Newton, Indiana: Historical and Biographical. Chicago, 1883.

Craik, Elmer LeRoy. "Southern Interest in Territorial Kansas, 1854-1856," *KSHSC,* XV (1919-22), 334-450.

Craven, Avery. *The Coming of the Civil War.* 2d ed. Chicago, 1966.

Cunningham, J. O. "The Bloomington Convention of 1856 and Those Who Participated in It," *ISHST* (1905), 101-110.

Dancy, John C. "The Negro People in Michigan," *MHM,* XXIV (Spring, 1940), 221-240.

Dangerfield, George. *The Era of Good Feelings.* New York, 1952.

Davenport, T. W. "The Slavery Question in Oregon," *OHQ,* IX (1908), 189-253, 309-373.

Davidson, John Nelson. "Negro Slavery in Wisconsin," *WSHSP,* XL (1892), 82-86.

Davis, Winfield J. *History of Political Conventions in California, 1849-1892.* Sacramento, 1893.

Dillon, Merton L. "The Anti-Slavery Movement in Illinois, 1809-1844." Ph.D. dissertation, University of Michigan, 1951.

Dodd, William E. "The Fight for the Northwest, 1860," *AHR,* XVI (July, 1911), 774-788.

Douglas, Jesse S. "Origins of the Population of Oregon in 1850," *PNQ,* XLI (Apr., 1950), 95-108.

Drake, Thomas E. *Quakers and Slavery in America.* New Haven, 1950.

Duberman, Martin (ed.). *The Antislavery Vanguard: New Essays on the Abolitionists.* Princeton, 1965.

Dumond, Dwight L. *Antislavery: The Crusade for Freedom in America.* Ann Arbor, 1961.

Duniway, Clyde A. "Slavery in California After 1848," *AHAAR* (1905), I, 241-248.

Dunn, Jacob P. *Indiana: A Redemption from Slavery.* Boston, 1888.

———. *Indiana and Indianans: A History of Aboriginal and Territorial Indiana and the Century of Statehood.* 5 vols. Chicago, 1919.

Elliott, R. G. "Proceedings of the Territorial Convention Held at Big Springs on the 5th and 6th of September, 1855," *KSHST,* VIII (1903-4), 362-377.

Ellison, William H. "Constitution Making in the Land of Gold," *PHR*, XVIII (Aug., 1949), 319-330.

Eriksson, Eric M. "The Framers of the Constitution of 1857," *IJHP*, XXII (Jan., 1924), 52-88.

Fehrenbacher, Don E. *Prelude to Greatness: Lincoln in the 1850's*. New York, 1964.

Filler, Louis. *The Crusade Against Slavery, 1830-1860*. New York, 1960.

Fishel, Leslie H., Jr. "Wisconsin and Negro Suffrage," *WMH*, XLVI (Spring, 1963), 180-196.

Flower, George. *History of the English Settlement in Edwards County, Illinois, Founded in 1817 and 1818 by Morris Birkbeck and George Flower*. Chicago, 1882.

Ford, Thomas H. *A History of Illinois from Its Commencement in 1818 to 1847*. Edited by Milo M. Quaife. 2 vols. Chicago, 1945.

Franklin, John Hope. *From Slavery to Freedom: A History of American Negroes*. 2d ed. New York, 1964.

Franklin, William E., Jr., "The Political Career of Peter Hardeman Burnett." Ph.D. dissertation, Stanford University, 1954.

Gaeddert, G. Raymond. *The Birth of Kansas*. Topeka, 1940.

Ganaway, Loomis M. "New Mexico and the Sectional Controversy, 1846-1861," *NMHR*, XVIII (1943), 113-147, 205-246, 325-348.

Gates, Paul Wallace. *Fifty Million Acres: Conflict over Kansas Land Policy, 1854-1890*. Ithaca, New York, 1954.

Genovese, Eugene D. *The Political Economy of Slavery*. New York, 1965.

Going, Charles Buxton. *David Wilmot Free-Soiler: A Biography of the Great Advocate of the Wilmot Proviso*. New York, 1924.

Goodwin, Cardinal. *The Establishment of State Government in California, 1846-1850*. New York, 1914.

Graebner, Norman A. (ed.), and others. *Politics and the Crisis of 1860*. Urbana, Illinois, 1960.

Gray, William Henry. *A History of Oregon*. New York, 1870.

Gray, Wood. *The Hidden Civil War: The Story of the Copperheads*. New York, 1942.

Gridley, James N. "A Case Under an Illinois Black Law," *ISHSJ*, IV (Jan., 1912), 401-425.

Guinn, J. M. "How California Escaped State Division," *SCHSAP*, VI (1905), 223-232.

Harris, Norman Dwight. *History of Negro Servitude in Illinois, and of the Slavery Agitation in That State, 1719-1864*. Chicago, 1906.

Hart, Albert B. *Slavery and Abolition, 1831-1841*. New York, 1906.

Herriott, F. I. "The Conference in the Deutsches Haus, Chicago, May 14-15, 1860," *ISHST* (1928), 101-191.

————. "Iowa and the First Nomination of Abraham Lincoln," *AI*, VIII (1907-8), 186-220, 444-466; IX (1909), 45-64, 186-228.

Hickok, Charles. *The Negro in Ohio, 1802-1870.* Cleveland, 1896.

Hill, D. G. "The Negro as a Political and Social Issue in the Oregon Country," *JNH*, XXXIII (Apr., 1948), 130-146.

Hinsdale, B. A. *The Old Northwest.* Boston, 1888.

History of San Diego County, California with Illustrations Descriptive of Its Scenery, Farms, Residences, Public Buildings. San Francisco, 1883.

Holmes, Frederick L. "First Constitutional Convention in Wisconsin, 1846," *WSHSP*, LIII (1905), 227-251.

Hubbart, Henry Clyde. *The Older Middle West, 1840-1880: Its Social, Economic and Political Life and Sectional Tendencies Before, During and After the Civil War.* New York, 1936.

Hunter, W. H. "The Pathfinders of Jefferson County," *OAHP*, VI (1898), 95-313.

James, Harold Preston. "Lincoln's Own State in the Election of 1860." Ph.D. dissertation, University of Illinois, 1943.

Johannsen, Robert W. *Frontier Politics and the Sectional Conflict: The Pacific Northwest on the Eve of the Civil War.* Seattle, 1955.

Johansen, Dorothy O., and Charles M. Gates. *Empire of the Columbia: A History of the Pacific Northwest.* New York, 1957.

Johnson, Lulu Merle. "The Problem of Slavery in the Old Northwest, 1787-1858." Ph.D. dissertation, State University of Iowa, 1941.

Johnson, Samuel A. "The Emigrant Aid Company in the Kansas Conflict," *KHQ*, VI (Feb., 1937), 21-33.

Kettleborough, Charles. *Constitution Making in Indiana.* 2 vols. Indianapolis, 1916.

King, Ameda Ruth. "The Last Years of the Whig Party in Illinois, 1847 to 1856," *ISHST* (1925), 108-154.

Kooker, Arthur Raymond. "The Antislavery Movement in Michigan, 1796-1840." Ph.D. dissertation, University of Michigan, 1941.

Krug, Mark M. *Lyman Trumbull, Conservative Radical.* New York, 1965.

Litwack, Leon F. *North of Slavery: The Negro in the Free States, 1790-1860.* Chicago, 1961.

Lockley, Fred. "The Case of Robin Holmes vs. Nathaniel Ford," *OHQ*, XXIII (June, 1922), 111-137.

Luthin, Reinhard. *The First Lincoln Campaign.* Cambridge, Massachusetts, 1944.

————. "Indiana and Lincoln's Rise to the Presidency," *IMH*, XXXVIII (Dec., 1942), 385-405.

Lynch, William O. "The Flow of Colonists to and from Indiana," *IMH*, XI (Mar., 1915), 1-8.

————. "Popular Sovereignty and the Colonization of Kansas from 1854 to 1860," *MVHAP,* IX (1917-18), 380-392.

————. *Population Movements in Relation to the Struggle for Kansas.* Vol. XIII, *Indiana University Studies.* Bloomington, 1925.

Macy, Jesse. *The Anti-Slavery Crusade.* New Haven, 1919.

Malin, James C. *John Brown and the Legend of Fifty-Six.* Vol. XVII, *Memoirs of the American Philosophical Society.* Philadelphia, 1942.

————. "The Topeka Statehood Movement Reconsidered: Origins," *Territorial Kansas, Studies Commemorating the Centennial, University of Kansas Social Science Studies,* No. 4, Lawrence (1954), 33-69.

Mandel, Bernard. *Labor: Free and Slave.* New York, 1955.

McClure, James R. "Taking the Census and Other Incidents in 1855," *KSHST,* VIII (1903-4), 227-250.

McColley, Robert. *Slavery and Jeffersonian Virginia.* Urbana, Illinois, 1964.

McPherson, James M. *The Struggle for Equality: Abolitionists and the Negro in the Civil War and Reconstruction.* Princeton, 1964.

Mehlinger, Louis R. "The Attitude of the Free Negro Toward African Colonization," *JNH,* I (July, 1916), 276-301.

Meier, August, and Elliott Rudwick. *From Plantation to Ghetto: An Interpretive History of American Negroes.* New York, 1966.

Meyer, Leland W. *The Life and Times of Colonel Richard M. Johnson of Kentucky.* New York, 1932.

Minto, John. "Antecedents of the Oregon Pioneers and the Light These Throw on Their Motives," *OHQ,* V (Mar., 1904), 38-63.

Monaghan, Jay. *Civil War on the Western Border, 1854-1865.* Boston, 1955.

Mothershead, Harmon. "Negro Rights in the Colorado Territory," *CM,* XL (July, 1963), 212-223.

Nichols, Alice. *Bleeding Kansas.* New York, 1954.

Olbrich, Emil. *The Development of Sentiment on Negro Suffrage to 1860.* Vol. III, *Bulletin of the University of Wisconsin,* No. 477, History Series. Madison, 1912.

Patterson, Robert W. *Biographical Sketches of Some of the Early Settlers of the City of Chicago.* Vol. VI, *Fergus Historical Series.* Chicago, 1876.

————. *Early Society in Southern Illinois.* Vol. XIV, *Fergus Historical Series.* Chicago, 1881.

Paul, Rodman. *Mining Frontiers of the Far West, 1848-1880.* New York, 1963.

————. "The Origin of the Chinese Issue in California," *MVHR,* XXV (Sept., 1938), 181-196.

Pease, Theodore Calvin. *The Frontier State, 1818-1848.* Vol. II, *The Centennial History of Illinois.* Springfield, 1918.

Pelzer, Louis. "The History and Principles of the Democratic Party in Iowa, 1846-1857," *IJHP,* VI (Apr., 1908), 163-246.

————. "The Negro and Slavery in Early Iowa," *IJHP,* II (Oct., 1904), 471-484.

Pendergraft, Daryl. "Thomas Corwin and the Conservative Republican Reaction, 1858-1861," *OSAHQ,* LVII (Jan., 1948), 1-23.

Phillips, William. *The Conquest of Kansas by Missouri and Her Allies.* Boston, 1856.

Poulton, Helen. "The Attitude of Oregon Toward Slavery and Secession, 1843-1865." M.A. thesis, University of Oregon, 1946.

Powell, Etta Olive. "Southern Influences in California Politics Before 1864." M.A. thesis, University of California, Berkeley, 1925.

Quillin, Frank U. *The Color Line in Ohio: A History of Race Prejudice in a Typical Northern State.* Ann Arbor, 1913.

Ramsdell, Charles W. "The Natural Limits of Slavery Expansion," *MVHR,* XVI (Sept., 1929), 151-171.

Randall, Emilius O., and Daniel J. Ryan. *History of Ohio.* 5 vols. New York, 1912.

Robinson, Charles. *The Kansas Conflict.* New York, 1892.

————. "Topeka and Her Constitution," *KSHST,* VI (1897-1900), 291-305.

Roseboom, Eugene H. *The Civil War Era, 1850-1873.* Vol. IV, *The History of the State of Ohio.* Columbus, 1944.

Royce, Josiah. *California from the Conquest in 1846 to the Second Vigilance Committee in San Francisco.* Boston, 1886.

Savage, W. Sherman. "The Contest over Slavery Between Illinois and Missouri," *JNH,* XXVIII (July, 1943), 311-325.

————. "The Negro in the History of the Pacific Northwest," *JNH,* XIII (July, 1928), 255-264.

————. "The Negro on the Mining Frontier," *JNH,* XXX (Jan., 1945), 30-46.

Scott, H. W. "The Formation and Administration of the Provisional Government of Oregon," *OHQ,* II (June, 1901), 95-118.

Sheldon, Addison E. *Nebraska: The Land and the People.* 3 vols. Chicago, 1931.

Shunk, Edward Wesley. "Ohio in Africa," *OSAHQ,* LI (Apr., 1942), 79-88.

Silbey, Joel H. "Proslavery Sentiment in Iowa, 1838-1861," *IJH,* LV (Oct., 1957), 289-318.

Simpson, Benjamin. "The Wyandotte Constitutional Convention: A Recollection," *KSHST,* I (1881), 236-247.

Smith, Theodore Clarke. "The Free Soil Party in Wisconsin," *WSHSP,* XLII (Dec., 1894), 97-162.

————. *The Liberty and Free Soil Parties in the Northwest.* New York, 1897.

————. *Parties and Slavery, 1850-1859.* New York, 1906.

Sparks, David S. "The Birth of the Republican Party in Iowa, 1854-1856," *IJH*, LIV (Jan., 1956), 1-33.

Speer, John. *The Life of General James H. Lane*. Garden City, Kansas, 1897.

Spring, Leverett. *Kansas: The Prelude to the War for the Union*. Boston, 1885.

Stadenraus, Philip J. *The African Colonization Movement, 1816-1865*. New York, 1961.

Stephenson, Wendell Holmes. *The Political Career of General James H. Lane*. Vol. III, *KSHSP*. Topeka, 1930.

Stirton, Thomas. "Party Disruption and the Rise of the Slavery Extension Controversy, 1840-1846." Ph.D. dissertation, University of Chicago, 1957.

Taylor, Bayard. *Eldorado or the Adventures in the Path of Empire*. New York, 1861.

Thacher, Timothy Dwight. "Leavenworth Constitutional Convention," *KSHST*, III (1883-85), 5-15.

————. "The Rejected Constitutions," *KSHST*, III (1883-85), 436-448.

Thornbrough, Emma Lou. *The Negro in Indiana: A Study of a Minority*. Indianapolis, 1957.

————. "The Race Issue in Indiana Politics During the Civil War," *IMH*, XLVII (June, 1951), 165-188.

Thurman, Sue Bailey. *Pioneers of Negro Origin in California*. San Francisco, 1949.

Trefousse, Hans L. *Benjamin Franklin Wade: Radical Republican from Ohio*. New York, 1963.

————. "Ben Wade and the Negro," *OSAHQ*, LXVIII (Apr., 1959), 161-176.

Turner, Frederick Jackson. *The Frontier in American History*. New York, 1920.

Utley, Henry M., and Byron M. Cutcheon. *Michigan as a Province, Territory, and State*. 4 vols. New York, 1906.

Utter, William T. *The Frontier State, 1803-1825*. Vol. II, *The History of the State of Ohio*. Columbus, 1942.

Voegeli, Jacque. "The Northwest and the Race Issue, 1861-1862," *MVHR*, L (Sept., 1963), 235-251.

Wade, Richard C. "The Negro in Cincinnati, 1800-1830," *JNH*, XXXIX (Jan., 1954), 43-57.

Walls, Florence. "The Letters of Asahel Bush to Matthew P. Deady, 1851-1863." B.A. thesis, Reed College, 1941.

Washburne, E. B. *Sketch of Edward Coles, Second Governor of Illinois, and of the Slavery Struggle of 1823-4*. Chicago, 1882.

Weisenburger, Francis P. *The Passing of the Frontier, 1825-1850*. Vol. III, *The History of the State of Ohio*. Columbus, 1941.

Wilder, Daniel W. "The Story of Kansas," *KSHST*, VI (1897-1900), 336-342.

Wiley, Earl W. " 'Governor' John Greiner and Chase's Bid for the Presidency in 1860," *OSAHQ*, LVIII (July, 1949), 245-273.

Williams, George H. "Political History of Oregon from 1853 to 1865," *OHQ*, II (Mar., 1901), 1-35.

Williams, James. *The Life and Adventures of James Williams, a Fugitive Slave*. San Francisco, 1874.

Wilson, Charles Jay. "The Negro in Early Ohio," *OSAHQ*, XXXIX (Oct., 1930), 717-768.

Woodson, Carter G. *A Century of Negro Migration*. Washington, D.C., 1918.

————. "The Negroes of Cincinnati Prior to the Civil War," *JNH*, I (Jan., 1916), 1-23.

Woodward, Walter C. "The Rise and Early History of Political Parties in Oregon," *OHQ*, XI (Dec., 1910), 323-354; XII (1911), 33-86, 123-163, 225-263, 301-350.

Wright, Luella M. "Henry A. and George D. Perkins in the Campaign of 1860," *IJHP*, XLII (Apr., 1944), 162-191.

Index